Pastoral Care
Through Worship

Donna,

You are a delightful, wonderful friend. May you always find ways to offer Pastoral care through worship.

Faithfully yours,

Howard W. Roberts

Pastoral Care Through Worship

by

Howard W. Roberts

Smyth & Helwys Publishing, Inc.®
Macon, Georgia

ISBN 1-880837-74-9

Pastoral Care Through Worship
Howard W. Roberts

©1995
Smyth & Helwys Publishing, Inc.®
6316 Peake Road
Macon, Georgia 31210-3960
1-800-568-1248

All biblical quotations are taken from the
New Revised Standard Version (NRSV) unless otherwise indicated.

Library of Congress Cataloging-in-Publication Data

Roberts, Howard W., 1947–
    Pastoral care through worship / by Howard W. Roberts.
    vi + 213   6" x 9" (15 x 23 cm.)
    Includes bibliographical references.
    ISBN 1-880837-74-9
    1. Public worship. 2. Pastoral theology.   I. Title.
BV15.R59 1995   94-41122
264—dc20   CIP

Cover design by Stephen Hefner

Contents

Part One

A Synergy of Worship and Pastoral Care

If the life and ministry of the church were summarized in one word, the word would be relationships. We participate in worship as a part of our relationship with God and with others. We call upon the church to help us when our families are in trouble, when someone is sick, when people important to us die, when we cannot get along with the people next door, when children are born, when children leave home, and when children marry. All of these issues are involved in and come out of relationships.

The first section of this book sets the stage for the remainder of the book. Two significant functions of the church are worship and pastoral care. These are vital to our relationships with God and one another. They are not mutually exclusive functions. Rather, they are closely related and actually serve complementary functions in the life and ministry of a congregation.

Currently, there is debate as to how many people are members of congregations and how many participate in the life of a congregation each week. A wide discrepancy exists between the number of members and participants reported by poll takers and the number of members and participants reported by congregations. Even more debate and discussion arise when the issue of why people participate in worship is raised. Invariably, people participate in worship for a variety of reasons.

There seems to be an increased interest in and desire to participate in worship during times of transition in people's lives. With the variety of transitions that occur in people's lives and with these transitions occurring at varying times in their lives, there is no one time or one season of the year more than another when people find their way to worship other than the high holy days. Of course these days vary with the religion. The unexhaustive list of high holy days include Yom Kippur, Rosh Hashana, Ramadan, Christmas, and Easter. The high holy days represent in the different religious traditions the emphasis of help worshipers are invited and the ways in which God's presence is made available to people.

Beyond the high holy days, one of the reasons people wind their way to worship with a community of faith is because a particular transition in their lives has rendered them vulnerable. They desire some comfort and direction in coping with what is happening in their lives. Someone has quipped that a pastor is in the hatch, match, and dispatch ministry. In a crude way, this expresses the big three transitions where people are the most willing in some way to seek the help and hope that worship may provide for them. When people have children, when people marry, and when death invades their lives, they are most likely to seek the aid of a congregation although they may in no way verbalize their need or what they are seeking. Probably their vulnerability is urging them to seek assistance where it may be found.

Paul Tournier has given one of the most picturesque descriptions of vulnerability with his story of the trapeze artist.[1] The trapeze artist swings high above the crowd, gaining momentum to leave one bar and grab onto another. In this motion, the artist's timing is essential. The artist swings and gets her motion synchronized with the motion of the empty bar. Then, at just the right time, she lets go of one bar and reaches for the other. At the moment of transition between bars she is most vulnerable. If her timing is off, if her grasp is slippery, or if she takes her eye off the bar to which she is reaching, she falls. Are not our transitions in life a lot like this? The transition, whatever it is, is a high risk maneuver during which we feel most vulnerable to falling, failing, being rendered helpless emotionally, or being destroyed professionally, personally, or literally.

There are many transitions in life in addition to the "big three" mentioned above. These include ages and stages in our development such as adolescence and the postponed generation, mid-life and retirement, vocation and long-term illness, conversion and confession, and many points between each of these. In a sense, this entire book is about transitions and how the church gathered for worship can support and encourage people who are scattered, even shattered, by the various tran-sitions they may experience along the journey. The religious practices, customs, and meanings associated with these transitions are what Arnold van Gennep describes as "rites of passage." Different "rites" help people and groups as they are separated from one era of life, give support and challenge in the intervening time, and then bring them into full status in a new era of life.[2] The spiritual community, as Wayne Oates points out, helps people move from one stage of life to another without breaking the continuity of personhood. People are kept from being isolated and left completely alone. With the inspiration of a new relationship people are born out of an old life and ushered in to a new one.[3]

Integrating Worship

Worship does not occur in a vacuum. Perhaps the most revealing worship event recorded in the Gospels occurred on the Mount of Transfiguration (Mark 9:2-29). Peter wanted to camp out on the mountain and revel in the "good feelings" he had experienced. But worship is never something to be captured, bottled, and kept. Worship energizes, nurtures, nourishes, and comforts so that worshipers may be dynamically involved in living.

Matthew, Mark, and Luke record the transfiguration event. All of them follow the event of Jesus moving from the mountain of worship to the valley of need where an epileptic boy was in need of healing. Was this Jesus's way of teaching the disciples that what is experienced in worship is to be integrated with the rest of life, and what happens in the daily lives of people affects their need and ability to worship?

As a pastor, I can identify the circumstances that impact the lives of many people and their ability to worship. Sometimes it is an event of great joy in their lives that causes them to want to participate in worship. More often it is an event resulting in strife and struggle that drives them to church. They are hoping to find help there, hoping to hear a word from God, and hoping there will be a balm in Gilead for them.

The intent of this book is to demonstrate that what happens in worship—support, comfort, care, and challenge—impacts people's lives during the week. Corporate worship can address personal needs and open us to receive God's love, grace, and care.

The first section of the book defines both worship and pastoral care. Their interrelatedness and how they complement each other in the life of a congregation is considered. My rationale for this approach is that people are holistic. What happens in one area of life affects all other areas. Thus, whatever happens to us impacts the spiritual dimension of our lives. Conversely, whatever affects the spiritual dimension of our lives impacts the other areas of their lives.

William Willimon has expressed well the importance of worship and pastoral care, and their interrelatedness.

> Worship is a major, if recently neglected, aspect of pastoral care. Worship can be enriched by a better awareness of the pastoral dimensions of so-called priestly acts. Just as pastoral care has often neglected the corporate context, so liturgical studies have frequently mired down in historical and textual trivia, archaism, and clericalism, forgetting the pastoral, people dimension in divine worship. In turn, pastoral care can be enriched by more attention to the priestly dimensions of so-called pastoral functions.[4]

By addressing the needs of people in public worship, the church becomes more clearly identified as a place to go to celebrate and mourn, to laugh and cry, to challenge and comfort, to affirm and question. Addressing personal and pastoral needs of people through worship is not a substitute for the pastoral care of individuals. Rather, individual and corporate pastoral care are complementary. As a person is ministered to individually, she begins to feel that this community of faith is a place for her to be involved. As a congregation senses that worship is designed to guide it to draw strength from God in coping with personal struggles, the members feel more comfortable approaching a minister for individual care and guidance. Now, let us focus on the meaning of worship.

Notes

[1]Paul Tournier, *A Place For You* (New York: Harper & Row 1968) 168.

[2]Arnold van Gennep, *The Rites of Passage,* trans. Monika B. Vizedom and Gabrielle L. Caffee (Chicago: University of Chicago Press, 1961).

[3]Wayne E. Oates, *The Christian Pastor* (Philadelphia: Westminster Press, 1982) 19.

[4]William Willimon, *Worship as Pastoral Care* (Nashville: Abingdon Press, 1979) 47.

Chapter 1

Worship Is Rehearsal

Worship is a natural form of human behavior and is only possible because of our capacity for self-consciousness. People can ascribe value and worth to something outside of themselves that they consider to be of ultimate significance. Generally, worship refers to the reverence people hold for any object of ultimate worth. Worship, therefore, involves a subject-object relationship. The revered object, therefore, becomes a god. Clarence Skinner defines worship this way:

> Worship exists wherever there is tension between the individual and an object which he reverently holds to be of highest significance and value. It is the outreach of man to attain union with this object—to know it, to feel it, to experience it. Wherever there is tension between the actual and the ideal and wherever there is a reverent outreaching for the unattained—there is worship.[1]

From this definition, worship can be understood to be directed by any person to any object.

An understanding of Christian worship requires us to telescope our focus of worship. If we take seriously God as the reator, then we understand that worship will be an act of lifting ourselves to the source of life. For the Christian, God is personal; therefore, worship is communion of a person with The Person.

Because humans are created as moral and cultural beings, we cannot escape the necessity to reach upward and outward toward what is greater than ourselves. The issue involved in worship is our response to the awareness of our own finitude and our deep conviction that there is an infinite one. This stirs awe and reverence in us as we become aware that our reaching is in response to God's reaching for us. Worship, then, is the craving for reality that transcends our daily experience.

> Worship is an avenue which leads the creature out from his inveterate self-occupation to a knowledge of God, and ultimately to that union with God which is the beatitude of the soul. Worship is above all the work that mysterious "ground" of our being, that sacred hearth of personality, where the created spirit of man adheres to the increated Spirit of God.[2]

We narrow the definition of worship further by claiming the name "Christian" and identifying our worship as "Christian." But what is distinctive about Christian worship? The time of Christian worship traditionally is set for Sunday, which reveals an important aspect about our worship. Sunday is the "little Easter." The early Christians chose Sunday, the day of their re-presentation and remembrance of the resurrected Lord, as the day for worship. Worship involved the invitation to live resurrected lives.

Such remembrance of the Lord's gift of grace naturally leads to experiencing worship as appreciation and offering. It is the awed and glad spontaneous response of the spirit of people confronted by God of Christian revelation—the God of creation and redemption. The response itself is God-initiated.[3]

In addition, Christian worship is offering; we are invited to offer ourselves to God. Through our lives God possesses new entrances into the world, and through the offering of our lives to God true worship occurs. Paul's instruction to the Romans is applicable to us.

> So then, my brothers and sisters, because of God's great mercy to us I appeal to you: Offer yourselves as a living sacrifice to God, dedicated to God's service, pleasing to God. This is the true worship that you should offer.[4]

Worship itself is a gift we offer to God. Worship is easier to describe than to define. After more than forty years in the ministry, one pastor described worship this way: "If you leave church with your faith stronger, your hope brighter, your love deeper, your sympathies broadened, your heart purer, and with your will more resolute to do the will of God, then you have truly worshiped!"

Individual and Corporate Worship

Individual and corporate worship are essential; both are needed to nourish and nurture our lives. One does not replace the other. I am indebted to my colleague Tom Austin for the following observations about worship.

> As important as service to others is, as significant as Bible study is, as stimulating as group discussion is, none of those alone or together come close to replacing the worship of God.

In fact, worship is the only thing we can ever do for God. We cannot add to God or take away from God, we cannot get God to love us more or less, we cannot foster or retard the coming of God's kingdom, but we can with meaning and purpose engage in the private and public worship of God. This must be done even if it is inconvenient, or when it calls us away from doing other things.

I am concerned that we will fail to understand how impoverished our lives can become without regular, systematic and consistent public worship.[5]

Individual Worship

All of our human faculties—our minds, emotions, and wills—are involved in our worship of God. The integration of these faculties results in the biblical concept of wholeness. Jesus' words are instructive for us: "You must love the Lord your God with all your heart, and with all your soul, and with all your mind."[6]

Thinking is one of our greatest abilities. Other creatures have instincts and can be modified behaviorally, but only human beings know and know that they know. We have seen tremendous advances in many areas of life, and much advancement is the result of insight gained by people using their minds. Often the criticism leveled against the church is that it is out of touch with the times. There are numerous examples when the church has been archaic, and observation indicates that religion is the last aspect of culture to change.

One reason for the Church's irrelevant appearance is that we often "check" our minds at the entrance to the sanctuary much like we check our hats and coats. We believe we will not be needing our minds while we worship, so why bring them with us? What greater faculty do we need to contemplate the infinite, immanent, transcendent God than our minds? Clarence Skinner describes our failure to use our minds in worship: "We have become shabby hunters at spiritual bargain counters, seeking to find life's blessings at reduced prices."[7]

To love God with our minds means to worship God with our minds, to use our minds in plumbing the depths of who God is, and to expect those who lead in worship to stimulate and challenge our intellect. As Skinner said,

Worship when it is intelligently directed, gives the human mind its most worthy object. That is worship at its best; a vision which is high and holy enough to command our reverence, and an untrammelled quest after the meaning and value of the vision.[8]

To worship God calls for us to use the good minds God has given us.

Jesus' concern for people included his challenge that people love God with all their hearts. From the biblical perspective, the heart is viewed as the seat of emotions. Our emotions are to be used in our worship of God, but our purpose in worshiping is not in hopes of having "an emotional experience."

> To think and speak of worship as "experience" holds the fatal possibility that man will come to worship his experience instead of God. He can twist the meaning and diminish the fullness of Christian revelation to conform to his own desire, trying out God for size, as it were, and he can measure the reality of worship solely in terms of his subjective reaction.[9]

Without emotion, worship certainly would be cold and unmoving. People are created as emotional beings, and they are less than human to the degree that any part of their being, including emotion, is ignored or un-engaged as unredeemable. We must include our emotions as part of our worship of God, being fully aware of the temptation to become over-awed, to develop a religious fixation, and to be prone to worship with our emotions but without our minds. Both emotion and mind are to be used to worship God.

The worship of God does not occur consistently by accident. We must desire to worship and through our intent focus our minds and emotions on the "holy other" in order to worship God in "spirit and in truth." Worship involves us totally—mind, emotion, and will. William Temple gives the classical expression of this.

> Worship is the submission of all nature to God. It is the quickening of the conscience by God's holiness; the nourishment of the mind with God's truth; the purifying of the imagination with God's beauty; the opening of the heart to God's love; the surrender of the will to God's purpose—and all of this gathered up in adoration, the most selfless emotion of which our nature is capable and therefore the chief remedy for that self-centeredness which is our natural sins and the source of all actual sin.[10]

Corporate Worship ———

Our purpose in corporate worship is threefold. The primary purpose is to ① adore God. By adoring God we acknowledge that God is our maker and without God nothing was made. The first thing that occurs in worship should be something that aids worshipers in adoring God. The second ② purpose of worship is to offer thanksgiving. We give thanks to God for the abounding grace that comes to us. We easily ask, "What will I get out of worship?" when our real concern should revolve around the question, "What thanksgiving will I give to God in worship?" ③

Proclaiming the word of God is our third purpose in worship. This does not mean only to deliver a sermon, although a sermon may proclaim the Word. The purpose of each element of public worship is to turn the many-sided Word so that the worshiper may "see glimpses of truth thou has for me."[11]

To take worship seriously and to value it greatly requires preparation and planning by worship leaders and worshipers alike. The preparation involves anticipating the worship service, expecting to encounter God through worship. The planning involves the intention to be present and participate in worship with other believers who make up a community of faith.

Worship requires a combination of structure and spontaneity. The proportions of structure and spontaneity depend upon the congregation, the worship leader, and the intent of the service planned. When worship becomes so structured that it is methodical and mechanical, then worshipers lose sight of the reason for what they are doing. For those who think there is no need to prepare and plan for worship, B. B. McKinney, a famous Southern Baptist hymn writer, made the observation that Baptists may not be ritualists, but they usually are "rutualists." If congregations do not plan some order or ritual, they usually drift into a rut that they follow as slavishly as the more liturgical churches follow their liturgies.

A visitor gave his impressions of certain worship services carelessly conducted:

> People who would hiss a play which was so ill-planned that the order of the acts and scenes was of no importance or would throw into a wastebasket a novel which was so utterly without form that chapter 3 and chapter 16 are interchangeable, still pathetically go to church on Sunday morning to take part

in a disorderly medley of music, hymn singing, scripture reading, praying, and the sermon. . . . Many church services today are a quaint mixture of concert, lecture, and prayer meeting.[12]

Paul, writing to the Corinthians concerning worship, said, "Let all be done decently and in order" (1 Cor 14:10). This can be accomplished by incorporating unity, movement, and design into the worship service. Unity is primarily a thematic approach. Unity is akin to a symphony. A sequence of movements voices different states of feeling: serious and happy, serene and troubled, overwhelmed and triumphant. These states of feeling are the result of the awareness by people of God and their need to relate to God.

Public worship must also have movement. Attention is "held" by being gripped, and then released, and gripped again by something arresting. Worship is to turn the worshiper upward, inward, and outward. Rhythm in worship provides movement. The rhythm is caused by God coming to the people and the people responding to God. Worship is an event in which we are engaged and grasped by God. We respond, then are released, and then grasped again. God initiates and we respond; the entire encounter involves various movements of initiative by God and responses by us.

Design is also necessary for public worship. Design involves ways to incorporate fresh content into worship. Freshness is the key to design. Freshness may occur by rearranging the order as well as choosing new ways to express old truths. When there is freshness, there is greater possibility for movement and unity. The order of worship serves as a compass providing direction toward a destination but allowing a variety of routes for the journey.

Worship requires preparation by both leaders and worshipers, and it requires work. With our entertainment-oriented mentality, many of us tend to attend worship to see what will happen. If we understand worship to be dramatic at all, we tend to view the worship leaders as actors, God as promptor, and the congregation as the audience. I think this type of attitude prompted Walter Shurden to make the following observation.

Worship is not the entertainment of people or the recreation of the people. Worship is not the people at play. Worship is the people of God at work. . . . Too many want "welfare worship," worship doled out without effort on the part of the worshiper. We prefer passivity to activity at eleven o'clock on Sunday morning. . . . Rather than acting, we want to be acted upon; rather than praying, we want to be prayed for; rather than singing, we want to be sung to. . . . And where does all this laziness in worship lead? To spectating rather than participating![13]

The word "liturgy" identifies the various elements that make up the worship service. The English word comes from the Greek word "*leitourgia*" and means "people work." Liturgy is the work the people do in worship. Perhaps understanding worship to be the work of the people gave Søren Kierkegaard his insight into worship. Kierkegaard suggested that worship is a drama in which the persons in the congregation are the actors, the worship leaders are the prompters, and God is the audience.

Worship: Important, Imperative, and Empowering

In one sense, no two congregations are exactly the same, even though we may worship in the same place every Sunday. Presence in worship is *important*. We draw comfort, encouragement, and support from each other by joining together in worshiping God as a congregation. All of the same people are not present at the same time more than once. How we respond to being grasped by God is never exactly identical to a previous time. In this way, no worship service is a repeatable event.

If we are sincere and honest about our relationship with God, then worship is essential and *imperative* for us. Our primary reason for being present in a worship service is to worship God. We can find a variety of reasons not to be there. We may say that the people are not friendly, the choir does not sing our kind of music, the pastor's prayers are too long, the sermons do not speak to our needs, the congregation does not sing any of the old hymns, or they are always asking for money at the church.

While any or all of these statements may be true from time to time, none of them are the reasons for attending church. Our reason is to worship God. When our motive for being in church is to worship God, many of the petty complaints we have begin to fall away. When they don't fall away, the fact we have come to worship helps us find constructive ways to communicate our concerns to others. Jesus said the first commandment in our lives is to love God with our total beings. To love God totally is to worship God. Worship is the only thing that you and I can do in response to God's initiative and, ironically, it is the only

~~and I can do in response to God's initiative and, ironically, it is the only~~ thing we need to do. Yet, it is imperative that we worship God.

Each of us, I imagine, can point to times when we have felt ourselves empowered because we have been involved in the worship of God with other believers. I am not talking about a warm, emotional, and comforting feeling when what was sung or said was what you already believed. Worship is *empowering* when a person experiences the very presence of God in the service. The experience empowers a person to make a decision with which they had been struggling; to resolve a conflict that had been raging; to tackle a difficult situation; or to be overwhelmed by the love, grace, and acceptance of God. The result of joining with others in the worship of God is a renewed freedom and empowerment in the person's life.

The public worship of God is important, imperative, and empowering because it is rehearsal. The word rehearsal is of French derivation and means "to harrow again." The public worship of God is rehearsal in the sense that it churns and turns our lives in such a way that new insights take root and begin to burst forth into new growth, eventually producing fruit in our relationships with God and with one another.

Notes

[1]Clarence R. Skinner, *Worship and the Well Ordered Life* (Boston: Universalist Historical Society Meeting House Press, 1955) 66.

[2]Evelyn Underhill, *Worship* (London: James Nisbet & Co., Ltd., 1936) 339.

[3]Henry Sloane Coffin, *The Public Worship of God* (Philadelphia: Westminster Press, 1956) 16.

[4]Rom 12:1, author's translation.

[5]Thomas D. Austin, *Expressions*, Knollwood Baptist Church, Winston-Salem NC (15 April 1993).

[6]Matt 22:37, TEV.

[7]Skinner, 142.

[8]Ibid., 83.

[9]Paul Hoon, *The Integrity of Worship* (Nashville: Abingdon Press, 1971) 210.

[10]William Temple, *Readings in St. John's Gospel* (London:Macmillan & Co.,1940)68.

[11]These words are from the hymn, "Open Mine Eyes That I May See."

[12]D. Macleod, *Word and Sacrament: A Preface to Preaching and Worship* (Englewood Cliffs NJ: Prentice Hall, 1960) 119ff.

[13]*The Calendar*, Newsletter of First Baptist Church, Savannah GA (26 October 1988).

Chapter 2

Pastoral Care in the Context of Worship

It has been suggested by some and substantiated by many that if ministers attend to their relationships with members of the congregation and care for the members during times of crisis in their lives, the members will permit the ministers to say anything they want in worship services. Members are more attentive to what ministers have to say when they have connected with the congregation on an emotional and spiritual level in their times of stress and struggle. Through their care of members, ministers earn the right to be heard.

Pastors are in the public eye, at least in the eyes of the members of the congregations they serve. As a result of the issues with which they are called to minister—sometimes accidentally and casually, sometimes intentionally and deeply—ministers address the vulnerability in members of their congregations. People will approach a minister about an issue before they will go to anyone else. Often they will discuss the matter with a minister, or they will not discuss it at all. People expect their ministers to be able to help members through the stressful transitions in their lives.

In one study, 12,000 laity and clergy from forty-seven denominations were surveyed. The study revealed that the most expected characteristic of a Christian pastor was that of an "open, affirming style." This meant that the pastor, first of all, must be capable of "handling stressful situations by remaining calm under pressure while continuing to affirm persons."[1]

Wayne Oates has defined pastoral care as "the Christian pastor's combined fortification and confrontation of persons as persons in times of both emergency crisis and developmental crisis."[2] A Christian pastor is one dedicated to the care of people in the name of Christ. The Christian pastor is to comfort and confront. To comfort is to encourage, support, strengthen, and sustain. To confront means to bring people face-to-face with themselves; one another; and the issues of justice, mercy, peace, truth, integrity, and understanding.

The pastor's care of people is called for in times of crisis. A crisis is a dangerous opportunity; people often want and need assistance, guidance, comfort, and challenge in order to negotiate the crisis so the danger becomes an opportunity to grow. An emergency crisis takes a person by surprise. It is unexpected and unpredicted such as a bicycle accident that puts a young girl's life in jeopardy. A developmental crisis is a common venture that many people in the culture experience such as baptism, marriage, or retirement. These are moments of achievement, celebration, separation, and reorganization of life.

Pastoral Care and the Church

The latter half of the twentieth century has seen the development of pastoral care as a specialized ministry. Some persons have seen it as separate from the ministry of the church and, mistakingly, divorced from worship. A pastor caring for members of a congregation and working for the cure of lives in earlier times meant leading people in worship. J. H. Jungmann has noted that "for centuries, the liturgy, actively celebrated, has been the most important form of pastoral care."[3]

Historical documentation supports four functions of pastoral care: healing, sustaining, guiding, and reconciling.[4] Healing meant praying for people and anointing them with oil. At times it also involved exorcisms. Sustaining involved baptism, the administration of the eucharist, confirmation, solemnization of marriage, the administration of last rites, and other visible communal acts of support and grace. Guiding involved the teaching function and role of the pastor, which was a part of the worship service. Pastors wore robes symbolizing their connection with the university, learning, and their teaching role. Reconciling involved the mending of broken relationships between people and between people and God. Reconciliation was acted out through the rituals of confession, forgiveness, penance, and absolution.

Evidence exists that pastoral care was both corporate and individual from its earliest days. One could even point to the difficulty the early church faced regarding the care of the widows mentioned in the sixth chapter of Acts. Apparently, the issue was addressed in the public meeting of the followers of Christ. Servants were selected to care for the individual needs of the widows.

Through the centuries, the pastoral dimensions of worship have evolved. Pastors have the responsibility of caring for and building up the Christian communities entrusted to their care. The work of pastors will involve counseling one-to-one as well as group counseling. But their work also involves care for and edification of the whole community, all of which call attention to the context in which ministry occurs. Don Browning has spoken to the importance of the context.

> There is no justifiable way of speaking about the care performed by the church unless one envisions this care in the context of an inquiring and worshipping church. The fundamental ambiguity of much that is called pastoral care today is exactly its tendency to perceive itself as an activity independent of or somehow not fundamentally influenced by this context. This is especially true of much that goes by the name of "pastoral counseling."[5]

The last quarter of the twentieth century has seen more emphasis on pastoral care in the context of the local congregation. There are clinical pastoral education programs based in local churches and increased emphasis in seminaries that pastoral care and counseling be part of what the pastor—the general practitioner of ministry—does. These emphases have helped many pastors to be more sensitive to the needs of congregants and to find ways to address many of those needs through worship. Pastoral care ministries help build understanding, care, and support for people within the congregation and in turn helps build up the body of Christ.

Individual and Corporate Wholeness

Pastoral care has both a corporate and an individual dimension. As the healing, sustaining, guiding, and reconciling needs of congregants are addressed in the context of worship, members will experience the church as a place they want to go. They will discover that they are going to a place where God knows their names and where their needs are addressed.

All of this points to the single unifying goal of ministry, which is increasing human wholeness centered in God. Howard Clinebell has pointed out how person-centered preaching, worship, and pastoral counseling are interrelated and contribute to the wholeness of people.[6]

Worship can be a way of helping people renew their basic trust, resolve their guilt, experience the transcendent dimension of life, and have their spiritual hungers nourished. By being involved in pastoral care through worship, pastors can bring the wisdom of the Bible to bear on the real concerns of people.

People come together in worship to be addressed by God and to address their needs to God. The pastor is priest and prophet; the responsibility is to present God's case to the people and the people's case to God. Perhaps this is why some persons have quipped that the pastor comforts the afflicted and afflicts the comfortable.

We probably have made too much of a distinction between work and worship. Certainly there is a clear sense that whether the minister is leading a worship service or sustaining and guiding a person in the office, the same responsibilities and expectations are fulfilled. When a pastor visits a member in the hospital, talks with members in the hallway, converses by telephone, or visits in their homes, the pastor is doing the same work as baptism, communion, and a Sunday morning worship service. The minister is guiding people through narrow passages in their lives, sustaining them in difficult crises so the continuity of their personhood is not broken, and bringing healing to their hurts and reconciliation to their broken relationships. Through worship leadership and personal involvement, the minister is caring for the needs of the person in the congregation and enabling them to negotiate the transitions they are facing in their lives.

Notes

[1]Daniel O. Aleshire, "Eleven Major Areas of Ministry," in *Ministry in America,* ed. David S. Schuller, Merton P. Strommen, and Milo L. Brekke (San Francisco: Harper & Row, 1980) 31.

[2]Wayne E. Oates, *New Dimensions in Pastoral Care* (Philadelphia: Fortress Press, 1970) 3.

[3]J. H. Jungmann, S.J., *Pastoral Liturgy* (New York: Herder & Herder, 1962) 380.

[4]William A. Clebsch and Charles R. Jaeckle, *Pastoral Care in Historical Perspective* (Englewood Cliffs NJ: Prentice-Hall, 1964) 34-66.

[5]Donald S. Browning, *The Moral Context of Pastoral Care* (Philadelphia: Westminster Press, 1976) 105.

[6]Howard Clinebell, *Basic Types of Pastoral Care and Counseling* (Nashville: Abingdon Press, 1991) 38-40.

Part Two

Pastoral Care through Rituals

Through the centuries people have asked the church to help them with transitions in life. People have requested the church's help in making the rough places smooth and the crooked places straight. For several centuries the church saw the dawning of faith, the confession of sin, marriage, and death as the major transitions in life. The church sought to have something to say during significant transitions in the lives of people. The result was the development of rituals around these transitions.

Religious rituals develop because they convey meaning and value in the life of a congregation. These rituals basically address the same themes and needs each time but may involve new people and circumstances. I am suggesting that we take seriously the needs of people often expressed through repeated events in the life of the congregation. The four rituals addressed in this section are baptism, communion, wedding, and funeral. The personal and corporate issues that surface during these transitions include belonging, acceptance, confession, forgiveness, commitment, reflection, introspection, grief, and growth.

A chapter is devoted to each of these rituals. Each chapter identifies the issue or issues that the particular ritual addresses and how it ministers to the congregation through the worship experience. Each chapter concludes with a worship service illustrating how the issue or issues are addressed and how pastoral care is provided through worship.

Chapter 3

Baptism

Baptism is the outward, visible sign that people are consciously accepting God's love and grace at work in their lives. Regardless of denomination, the rite of passage into Christianity is baptism. The mode of baptism varies with each denomination from sprinkling to pouring to immersion. The timing of baptism varies from infancy to adulthood. The meaning of baptism may be interpreted as washing away original sin or as the faith response of a believer. In spite of all these differences, baptism for Christians has become the symbol and the drama to act out beginning and belonging. Baptism dramatically portrays the beginning of the faith journey of the Christian and belonging to the faith community of the church.

The reason that baptism has such a significant place in Christianity is because Jesus was baptized. Since the first century Jesus' baptism has created its own problems for the followers of Christ. Evidence of the difficulty the early followers had is demonstrated in the different ways Matthew, Mark, Luke, and John report the event. Matthew and John are the extremes. Matthew reflects the struggle many early Christians had with Jesus being baptized by John by depicting John at first refusing to baptize Jesus. On the other hand, if John's Gospel were the only record we had, we would not know that Jesus was baptized.

Reporting the baptism of Jesus indicates its importance. Obviously, the event was important to Jesus, and he probably described the event to his disciples. No doubt this underscored the value of the event for those persons who decided to compile written records of Jesus' life. In whatever manner the descriptions of this event were first formulated, the church has interpreted and reinterpreted the meaning of Jesus' baptism for twenty centuries. Exploring the context and circumstances of Jesus' baptism provides the foundation for the practice of baptism today. The exploration in the beginning of this chapter provides the underpinning for the worship service included at the end of the chapter.

Baptism by John the Baptist

Attempting to understand Jesus' baptism calls for examination of the significance of the baptism of John the Baptist. All four Gospel writers record John baptizing while only Matthew, Mark, and Luke record that John baptized Jesus. None of the Gospel writers give us any information about the preparation of John the Baptist for his prophetic ministry. They tell us nothing about his education, experience, or decision to preach and baptize. About the only facts we have are that his parents, Zechariah and Elizabeth, were old when he was born, his mother and Jesus' mother were cousins, and that John was six months older than Jesus. Other information about John can be pieced together from data unearthed in archaeological digs and discovered from sources that describe events in Palestine during the first half of the first century A.D.

Each Gospel writer portrays John as thundering out of the wilderness, stopping at the stony banks of the Jordan River to baptize those who would repent. John the Baptist was a straight man. John wore a camel hair jacket with a leather belt, drank no wine, ate bugs and wild honey, and stayed in the desert as a recluse. Often he has been portrayed as an anger filled man bellowing his message in a fashion that both intrigued and frightened his audience. Even his contemporary religious leaders said John was demon possessed.

We have often read John's life and his preaching with too much venom. From too many pulpits the only tone for the call to repentance, the change of direction in life, is anger. The tone of John's message was one of urgency but not necessarily one of anger or hatred. His voice was like that of Isaiah, a lonely one because he was the only one at the time calling for radical change. The roar of John's message was not so much in its volume and tone as it was in its urgency.

I suspect that whatever was the content of John's sermons, they were delivered with a tone of hope that listeners could and would change for the better. John's lifestyle—his attire, diet, and spoken word—was part of his message. In Hebrew thought, word and deed were inseparable. To speak was to act, and to act was to speak. Thus, Luke wrote that John preached a baptism of repentance.

The Greek word, *baptizō*, means to immerse. Josephus used the word to mean "to dye." The New Testament uses *baptizō* only in the literal sense "to dip in" (Luke 16:24; John 13:26) and "to dye" (Rev 19:13).

Baptize is used only in the cultic sense, infrequently of Jewish washings and otherwise in the technical sense "to baptize." This usage suggests that baptism was considered to be something new and strange.[1]

By the first century A.D., Judaism was made up of three factions: Pharisees, Saduccees, and Essenes. The Essenes' theological position was that they should withdraw from the world. They had a passion for cleanliness and were convinced that the only way to live and achieve spiritual cleanliness was to withdraw totally from the world and the influences of anyone other than their own Essenes.

The Essenes may have taken John the Baptist in when his parents died, or John became influenced by them fairly early in his life. Certainly it is possible that he associated with and was influenced by the Essenes. Evidence is clear that if John associated with the Essenes, he also broke from them because it was only for themselves that they were preparing the way of the Lord in the wilderness. John came out of the wilderness preaching a baptism of repentance. John may have been a straight and narrow man, but he was not as rigid or as isolationistic as the Essenes were.

There does seem to be more than a coincidental connection between the demand of the Qumran community for holiness and the ethical demand of John. Both understood their demands to be internal ones, and the close connection of the two demands is expressed in the Manual of Discipline of the Qumran community. "No one is to go into the water in order to attain the purity of holy men. For men cannot be purified except they repent their evil."[2]

John Baptized Jesus

John's manner and message struck a responsive chord in the lives of people, and they flocked to the Jordan River to be baptized by him. Jesus was a part of the crowd that heard John preach, and he stepped forward asking John to baptize him. According to Matthew, John refused. Why? Had he and Jesus met previously? That is probable, at least at some of the festivals in Jerusalem, but it is doubtful that they knew each other intimately. Jesus had been in Nazareth, apparently learning a carpenter's trade, and John had been in the desert robbing bees and eating bugs. Was John aware of some of Jesus' insights and inquisitiveness that began in the temple but had been nurtured and cultivated throughout the intervening eighteen years? Was John so in awe of Jesus that he could not bring himself to baptize him?

Many persons would argue that John recognized Jesus as the messiah or that he already knew Jesus was the messiah before Jesus requested baptism. A major problem with this foreknowledge position is that later Matthew records (11:1-6) that John the Baptist sent some of his disciples to Jesus to ask him if he were the Coming One or should they look for another. If John were certain at baptism who Jesus was, why was he uncertain after being imprisoned? Jesus did not fit the messianic mold that people cast for him, including John the Baptist. Apparently John and his disciples had some doubts about Jesus. To say that John the Baptist recognized Jesus as the messiah at baptism is not substantiated by Matthew later in recounting the visit John's disciples paid to Jesus.

John sounded a clear call for people to repent, for them to autograph their repentance by baptism, and John gladly baptized them. Exactly why John was stunned by Jesus' request for baptism is speculation because only Matthew records John's resistance. No interpretation of his resistance is given other than to identify John's feelings that he should be baptized by Jesus.

Jesus heard in John's word the clear call by which Israel could and must change the course. He sensed a new age was ushering in for his people and for the world, and John was sounding forth the call to people in a way that it had not been sounded for generations. Jesus saw the new age coming and sensed his desire and need to be part of that age. He stepped forth to be baptized, signaling a beginning.

Reasons for Jesus' Baptism

The unanswered question is why Jesus was baptized by John. The problem has been intensified by the claim of the church that Jesus, who was sinless, asked to be baptized by John, whose baptism was a sign of repentance from sin. Several possible answers have been offered through the centuries. Each of the following suggestions has some truth and needs not be antagonistic to the others.

(1) Jesus was baptized to identify with human beings. This answer is helpful to some but raises at least two difficulties. It suggests that the baptism had no authentic significance to Jesus personally and begs the

question of identification. No other event in the Gospels has Jesus going through the motions of an event. By being born a human being and growing emotionally, physically, and spiritually, Jesus had identified with human beings.

(2) Jesus was baptized to please his mother and family, as is indicated in the Gospel according to the Hebrews. There are other examples of family pressures on Jesus, and this one may have been among them. What personal authenticity did his baptism have if he were doing it either to please his family or to get them to cease pressuring him?

(3) Jesus had heard of the work of John the Baptist and the moral awakening that it was producing. He may have wanted to join his own comradeship and efforts with John.

(4) Perhaps the expectation of John's message aroused urgency in Jesus. The urgency was a signal that the search for direction and mission he had anticipated was ready to begin.

(5) Jesus never thought of himself in isolation. Thus he identified himself completely with his nation's needs. Vicariously he would be baptized into its need for repentance and with Israel and for Israel he expressed the urgency of commitment to the kingdom of God.

(6) Jesus' baptism is referred to by many as the fulfillment of prophecy (Isa 11:2). Certainly in examining Jesus' life after his resurrection, it was easy for his followers to say that the spirit of the Lord was upon him. Nothing in Isaiah's prophecy suggests baptism as a sign of this. Jesus himself clearly stated that what occurred internally rather than externally demonstrated the presence of God.

(7) Since Jesus grew as a human being and faced life as a human being, it seems appropriate that his awareness of himself, who he was and who he hoped to be, was gradual developments that came through deepening awareness during his years in Nazareth. Is it not possible that in hearing the preaching of John the Baptist that Jesus heard the word of God that struck a responsive chord in his life? Perhaps then he recognized that the opposite of repentance was to stay the course. He heard in John's word the clear call by which Israel could and must change the course. He sensed a new age was ushering in for his people and for the world and John was sounding forth the call to people in a way that it had not been sounded for generations. Jesus saw the new age coming and sensed his desire and need to be part of that age. He stepped forth to be

baptized, signaling a beginning. In that sense Jesus redefined the form—baptism—as he later pointed out that when forms, old wineskins, had lost their usefulness and flexibility to carry the substance, new wine, the old wineskins should be thrown away and new wineskins should be used.

Interpreting Baptism

Regardless of how one deals with the difficulty caused by Jesus being baptized by John, the church clearly has seen Jesus' baptism as his inauguration, commissioning, and ordination to ministry. In this regard Jesus' baptism was a beginning.

Baptism was an outward, visible sign of Jesus' commitment to ministry. The synoptic Gospels have a similar sequence of events: the preaching of John the Baptist, the baptism of Jesus, Jesus' sojourn in the wilderness, the calling of disciples, and the expansion of ministry. The Synoptic writers intentionally portray the ministry of Jesus as beginning at his baptism.

Not only did John's baptism of Jesus inaugurate Jesus' ministry, but it also revealed its unexpected nature. John presented his baptism as a washing from sin. Jesus interpreted it as repentance and self-denial that led all the way to Golgotha. John invited people to be clean. Jesus called people to die. Jesus used the word baptism to refer to his own impending death (Mark 10:38).

Jesus' baptism was also a time of blessing, acceptance, approval, and assurance. Mark and Luke suggest that the communication of the blessing was between God and Jesus; "You are my beloved son in you I am well pleased" (Author's translation Mark 1:11 and Luke 3:21). Matthew has the voice announcing "This is my beloved son with whom I am well pleased" (Matt 3:17), which seems to be his attempt to reconcile John's baptism of Jesus by suggesting that the blessing was for all who were present to hear. What the writers record is that God affirmed and approved of Jesus before he ever did anything. Jesus' baptism signaled that he belonged to God.

Baptism marks the dividing line between the old and the new. Baptism signals the beginning of faith commitment to God just as Jesus' baptism signaled the beginning of his faith commitment to ministry. Baptism confirms that people recognize God's love, acceptance, and approval of them before they ever do anything. It really does signify the end of the search to belong. Baptism is the rite of belonging.

John Smyth was concerned that persons who were committing themselves to a faith journey respond to this decision through baptism. In 1609 he called for believer's baptism. He was convicted that people needed to make conscious decisions for themselves about starting the faith journey rather than have someone make the decision for them. The concept of believer's baptism is that a person is baptized as a result of a growing, evolving faith and a desire to commit one's life faithfully to God. It is affirming that one belongs to God by beginning the faith journey.

For three centuries nearly all the people baptized in Baptist congregations were adults. During this century and especially during the last half of this century, however, the age of baptism has become younger and younger. Many Baptist congregations are baptizing preschoolers, some of them as young as three years of age. No doubt part of the reason for younger and younger candidates is the emphasis by some that persons are not acceptable or approved unless they are baptized. This emphasis touches the need, especially of young children, to belong. They do not want to be left out, and so they request to be baptized. Baptism is the right of belonging and beginnng. By being baptized people acknowledge they belong to God and are beginning a lifelong journey.

What follows is the order of worship for a service in which everything flows out of baptism. The service begins with a call to worship related to baptism and leads into the baptismal liturgy. All parts of this service contribute to the interpretation of baptism.

Beginning and Belonging
A Service of Christian Worship

We Are Invited to Be People of Faith

The Chiming of the Hour
The Prelude   "I Am Thine O Lord"   I Am Thine
The Responsive Call to Worship

Pastor: Come, let us worship God and celebrate the dawning of faith in our
          midst.
People: **As eagerly as Jesus strode toward the Jordan River, we come to**
          worship God and celebrate the dawning of faith in our midst.
Pastor: Jesus was baptized in the Jordan River, lived abundantly, loving the
          world for God's sake.
People: **Let us journey through life as disciples of Christ loving the world**
          abundantly for God's sake.
Pastor: We do not journey alone. Joining us on the journey today are fellow
          pilgrims _____ and_____. They are here to autograph their
          faith journey by being baptized. What do you want them to know?
People: **They are not alone. We are traveling with them. We love them and**
          care for them as our own. They are part of our family of faith.
          Their needs and concerns will be ours. As they acknowledge they are
          receiving God's grace, so are we.
Pastor: Come, let us worship God and celebrate the dawning of faith in our
          midst.

To Autograph the Beginning of Our Faith with Baptism

The Baptismal Liturgy
Pastor: _____ , do you come to be baptized as a sign of commitment to Jesus Christ
          as the Lord of your life?
_____: **I do.**
Pastor: Do you also come to be baptized as a sign of your commitment to serve Christ
          through the church?
_____: **I do.**
Pastor: Will you, members of this community of faith, pronounce the baptismal
          blessing?
People: **We baptize you, our sister/brother, _____ in the name of God our**
          creator, Jesus our redeemer, and the spirit of God our sustainer. Amen.
          (The liturgy is repeated for additional persons)

*Hymn   "We Know That Christ Is Raised"   Stanford

The Welcome
The Old Testament Lesson   Genesis 1:1-5
The Concerns of the People
The Pastoral Prayer

To Celebrate Belonging to the Body of Christ with Baptism

*Hymn   "Lord, When You Came to Jordan"   Genevan
The New Testament Lesson   Mark 1:1-11
The Choral Worship   Caithness
        "Christ, When for Us You Were Baptized"

The Sermon   "The Rite of Beginning and Belonging"

If you have been baptized, I would like for you to revisit that event today. I invite you to remember that experience. Call to mind the meaning that event had then and how you have reinterpreted its meaning through the years. When were you baptized? Why were you baptized? How were you baptized?

If you have never been baptized, I would like for you to think about why you would want to be baptized. What meaning would being baptized have for you?

I recall the day I was baptized. I remember thinking after the worship service that this was really a big event. The clue was that my grandparents had gotten up extra early that morning to milk the cows and do their other daily farm chores and then driven for three hours to be in church at 11 o'clock when I was baptized.

Out of the setting of your thinking personally about baptism, I want to explore baptism as a rite of beginning and a rite of belonging. I will do this by examining briefly Jesus' baptism and then explore the meaning, timing, and mode of baptism.

Baptism is the religious rite of beginning. Baptism has many other meanings. Throughout our lives we are interpreting and reinterpreting baptism. Every person who has been baptized has reinterpreted the meaning. Each of us would say some things about the meaning of baptism now that we did not think about or say at the time we were baptized. And no wonder! We are dealing with an important religious ritual that has meaning and mystery wrapped in it. Regardless of how much meaning we comprehend baptism to have, there is mystery that we are unable to explain or interpret.

Belonging is a significant spiritual and emotional dimension in our lives. On at least one occasion, and probably many others, we have felt we did not belong. Belong is a small word but carries a big message. Wrapped up in belonging is acceptance, approval, being a part of a group, fitting in, confirming I am not a social outcast. The word means longing to be and clearly suggests that our longing to be is tied to relationships. Belonging confirms that we are relational beings by nature and need. We want to belong and we struggle with what we can do that will make us acceptable, approved, able to belong.

An important message is conveyed in the biblical accounts of Jesus' baptism. God approved of and accepted Jesus before he ever did anything. The same is true for us. We are people created in the image of God, and before we ever do anything and after we have done all kinds of things, God loves, approves, accepts, and blesses us. We long for God, often failing or unable to realize that we already belong to God.

Baptism has come to represent the beginning of a faith journey and belonging to the body of Christ. After all, what does one have to do to join the church? There are no achievement tests, popularity polls, or dues. Initiation into the church is by the rite of baptism, the single most powerful symbol of faith. It is a symbol of rebirth, the recognition that we make conscious decisions of commitment to be disciples of Christ. The ancients saw baptism as representing death, as a communicant was lowered into the water (symbolic of the grave) in order to be reborn and resurrected to new life as the communicant emerged out of the water.

The movie, *Tender Mercies*, produced several years ago, is about a rough-edged former country music singer named Max who is just about at the end of his hope: broke and out of work, on the bottle, twice divorced, estranged from his only daughter, no friends left. He is bumming across north Texas when, by chance, he is thrown upon the mercy of a young Vietnam widow with an adorable eight-year-old son named Sonny. In time, Max marries Sonny's mother, quits abusing alcohol and carousing, becomes a regular family man and good father to his adopted son. He even starts attending the little country Baptist church where Sonny's mother sings in the choir. When Sonny decides to be baptized, Max follows suit. After the service, the three are riding home in the pickup when Sonny says, "Well, Max we did it." "Yep," says Max, "we did it." Only Sonny won't let it loose: "They said I'd be different after I was baptized." Then peering into the rear view mirror, he continues, "I sure don't look any different . . . and you don't look any different, Max. I don't feel any different . . . do you feel any different, Max?" Max answers, "Nope, I don't feel any different," adding after a pause, "at least not yet."

It is the "not yet" that is a clue to a deeper understanding of the symbol of baptism. The test of the teaching of the church is to build on our baptism, helping each other grow into a wider understanding of who we are, where our loyalties lie, and how it all fits together. Baptism is a rite of beginning and a rite of belonging.

Baptism as a rite of beginning was a well-known practice in the pagan world as the door through which people entered many of the mystery religions. There are early examples of sacral water ceremonies in Babylon, Persia, and India. The Ganges and Euphrates Rivers came to have a significance to Eastern religions comparable with that of the Jordan to Judaism and Christianity. The common root for these customs is impossible to unearth.

The process for a proselyte, one not born a Jew, to enter Judaism included baptism. There were three necessary elements involved for a non-Jew to enter Judaism: circumcision, baptism, and a sacrifice. The baptism was to be conducted in the presence of three witnesses. The candidates' nails and hair were cut, and all of his clothing was removed. He was immersed in water so that his body was totally covered. When he was raised out of the water, the essence of the law was read to him, he was warned of dangers and persecutions, he confessed his sins to the fathers of his baptism. All of this was a means of acting out a total break with the past and was based on the many washings of the Jewish law for purification.[3]

The history of baptism for followers of Christ can be traced back to John the Baptist. Whether or not John the Baptist knew about sacral water ceremonies and baptisms in other religions is unknown. It is probable that some who heard him preach were familiar with these practices.

John the Baptist came out of the wilderness preaching a baptism of repentance. Although baptism was not new, there were some characteristics about John's message that made his message and his baptism distinctive. One major distinctive of John's preaching was his call to repentance. Periodically a voice summoned Israel to repentance and it was believed by many that if the nation would repent for one day, the redeemer would arrive. To this point John had been preaching what had been preached before but with the renewed zeal, tone, and drama of a prophet. However, when John tied baptism to repentance and called for Jews to be baptized "to show that you have repented" (Matt 3:11a), he interjected a completely new and disturbing concept into the religious climate. From John's perspective, everybody, Jews included, desperately needed the cleansing that God alone could give. John confronted the Pharisees and Sadducees warning them that family names and pedigree exempted no one from accountability to God.

John's manner and message struck a responsive chord in the lives of people, and they flocked to the Jordan River to be baptized by him. One day Jesus was a part of the crowd that heard John preach and he stepped forward asking John to baptize him. All of the synoptic Gospels tell of Jesus' baptism by John, but John's Gospel doesn't even hint about Jesus' baptism. The more time that passed after Jesus' life, the more interested Jesus' followers became in events of his life.

His baptism was one of the events in which people in the early church had significant interest.

John's preaching sounded a clear call for people to repent, for them to autograph their repentance by baptism, and John gladly baptized them. Exactly why John was stunned by Jesus' request for baptism is speculation because the Synoptic writers only record John's resistance. They do not interpret his resistance other than to identify John's feelings that he should be baptized by Jesus.

Apparently Jesus heard in John's message a clear and certain call for people to establish their relationship as the people of God. He acknowledged John's baptism as an appropriate sign of that covenant relationship. His statement, "It is fitting for us to fulfill all righteousness," may refer to John and himself or to others and himself who desired to be baptized by John.

Jesus' baptism was also a time of blessing, acceptance, approval, and assurance. Mark suggests that the communication of the blessing was between God and Jesus; "You are my beloved son in you I am well pleased" (author's translation Mark 1:11). The Gospel writers clearly state that God affirmed and approved of Jesus before he ever did anything.

Since Jesus grew as a human being and faced life as a human being, his awareness of himself, who he was and who he hoped to be, were gradual developments that came through deepening awareness during his years in Nazareth. Hearing the preaching of John the Baptist, Jesus heard the word of God that struck a responsive chord in his life. Then, he recognized that the opposite of repentance was to stay the course. He heard in John's word the clear call by which Israel could and must change the course. He sensed a new age was ushering in for his people and for the world, and John was sounding forth the call to people in a way that had not been sounded for generations. Jesus saw the new age coming and sensed his desire and need to be part of that age. He stepped forth to be baptized, signaling a beginning. In that sense Jesus redefined the form—baptism—as he later pointed out that when forms, old wineskins, had lost their usefulness and flexibility to carry the substance, new wine, the old wineskins should be thrown away and new wineskins should be used.

John's baptism of Jesus inaugurated Jesus' ministry and revealed its unexpected nature. John presented his baptism as a washing from sin. Jesus interpreted it as repentance and self-denial leading all the way to Golgotha. From the biblical information available, we can conclude that Jesus' baptism signaled his commitment of faith in his relationship with God, which was a consummation of the covenant relationship. In this regard Jesus' baptism was a beginning. It was not an ending nor was it an end in itself. His baptism pointed in the direction in which Jesus was marching. He was setting sail on a course of life. It was a course that turned out to be very difficult and disturbing but a course on which he was willing to remain in spite of the many offers he was given to live differently. Jesus' baptism was an outward expression of his inner commitment. John invited people to be clean. Jesus called people to die. Jesus used the word baptism to refer to his own impending death (Mark 10:38). He redefined the form and suggested that baptism is not as much water that washes as it is the flood that drowns.

Various New Testament writers use a rich variety of meanings for baptism: forgiveness, rebirth, cleansing, death, resurrection, refreshment, adoption, light. For the early believers, baptism was patterned on the death and resurrection of Christ (Acts 2:38, Rom 6:3-4, Gal 3:27, 1 Cor 12:13). Because Jesus was baptized, baptism became important as the early church was forming. The church clearly has seen Jesus' baptism as his inauguration, commissioning, and ordination to ministry.

In the biblical record of the early church, baptism means that the one being baptized is dying to the old life in sin and rising to a new life in Christ. Baptism signals a reshaping and redirecting of one's thinking because of the impact that the awareness of God's presence has had on the individual's life. Baptism is an act of commitment and promise in which the old life is buried and the believer is raised to a new life—new in direction, purpose, and objective. Baptism is an outward, visible sign of the inward, invisible grace of God at work in a person's life.

The words attributed to Goethe are apropos: "The highest cannot be spoken; it can only be acted." Thus, baptism is a drama, a reenactment outwardly of the change that has begun inwardly. Baptism serves as a seal of the promise of God's love, care, and presence. There is no recorded instance in the New Testament of the baptism of any persons other than new converts. Baptism has become a symbolic way of saying, "I am ready to grow. I willingly entrust myself to God's creative power to grow me beyond where I am." Thus baptism has become the signal of the dawning of a person's faith in God which completes the covenant relationship. Baptism became the rite that marked the conscious beginning of a person's faith relationship with God. It has been said that baptism is not the end of the road but the end of a search for one.

Baptism marks the dividing line between the old and the new. It is a signal that people are beginning their faith commitment to God just as Jesus' baptism signaled the beginning of his faith commitment to ministry. A person does not know at the beginning of a journey all that is in store on the way. Jesus did not know all that would unfold during his ministry. He had no idea that his disciples would have such a difficult time learning or that religious leaders would be so resistant to change.

Three Features of Baptism: The meaning, timing, and mode were significant features of Jesus' baptism. These three features are also significant of our baptism. By far the most important of these three features is the meaning that baptism has for the individual. In order for baptism to have meaning for the individual, baptism must have meaning for the congregation. When baptism has meaning for the congregation, then the congregation seeks to educate those within its fellowship about the meaning of baptism. The meaning of baptism for Jesus was that it was an outward expression of his inner commitment. At a time when he was ready to say which direction his life was moving, what lifestyle he was going to adopt for his own, he asked to be baptized.

In New Testament records of the church in the latter half of the first century, baptism was for new converts, new disciples of Christ. It was a dramatization of the cleansing that a person experienced through the grace of God and the commitment that the person was making to live life as a disciple of Christ. There is no indication in the New Testament that the apostles or any of the first 120 disciples of Jesus were baptized. Apparently, Jesus did not baptize anyone. However, by the time of Paul's conversion, baptism had become a common practice among the followers of the Way as a signal of the directional change that a person's life was taking.

The interpretation given to baptism was that it signaled a reshaping and a redirecting of a person's life because of the impact that the awareness of God's presence had upon the individual's life. Baptism came to be patterned on the death, burial, and resurrection of Christ. Paul descriptively identified baptism into Christ also as baptism into the body of Christ, the church, the whole church, the church universal. We often misinterpret this to mean that baptism is necessary for membership in or an initiation rite into the local congregation. Our misinterpretation is the result of having too narrow a focus or vision of the church's mission. Too easily we see it as this building and this group of people. The church has no geographical boundaries and no racial lines. Membership in the church, the body of Christ, comes from all over this world and from all over any other worlds that may exist.

Closely related to the meaning of baptism is the timing. New Testament baptism always marked the beginning of the Christian life and entry into the Christian community. It was at conversion (Acts 9:18; 16:15; 22:15-16) when people "believed" (Mark 16:16; Acts 8:36-39; 16:31-33) or when they "received his word" (Acts 2:41) that baptism occurred. In the New Testament, baptism represented the move from unfaith to faith. It marked the dividing line between the old and the new. Any time that baptism is practiced or required for some other reason, such as for membership in a local congregation, it is a baptism that has no basis in the New Testament.

The one being baptized is saying, "My faith has just begun to unfold," rather than, "My faith is full-grown." It was John Smyth in 1609 who recovered the concept of believer's baptism. Believer's baptism means that a person acting on the faith in God that has developed in him, desires to be baptized to mark the beginning of the Christian journey and entry into the Christian community.

The third feature of baptism is the mode or method. How a person is baptized is the issue with which the mode of baptism deals. Little argument can be supported from the biblical material that baptism as identified in the New Testament was done in any manner other than by immersion. This is the best symbol of death, burial, and resurrection. It is a double symbol, representing Christ and representing what is happening in the life of the person who is moving from unfaith to faith. Thus, congregations do well to urge and encourage new converts to the way of Christ to be immersed unless there is some providential reason why they cannot be. Then, it is appropriate to offer some other mode or method of baptism rather than to have no baptism at all.

An additional issue is raised regarding how a person is baptized when a congregation practices one method and someone wants to unite with that congregation who has been baptized by another method. Requiring a specific mode of baptism for membership in a specific congregation makes the mode of baptism a requirement for belonging to a particular congregation rather than a rite of belonging to the body of Christ. If people are satisfied with the meaning, timing, and mode of their baptism, then let the congregation welcome them gladly. If they are not satisfied, then, let them request baptism; and let the congregation celebrate with them in their choice of a new meaning, a new time, and a new mode of baptism.

Several years after the resurrection of Christ, it became increasingly important to those early disciples of his to examine and trace his life so that they could learn from his life as a model for theirs. The baptism of Jesus was important in the accounts of Jesus' life and ministry of Matthew, Mark, and Luke.

Baptism has continued to be an important practice of the church from its early days. It was well established at least by the time of Paul's conversion. It seemed to have gotten its impetus at Pentecost when the apostles used it to represent the coming of the spirit or the presence of God upon those who heard them preach and responded positively.

Many congregations developed in Asia Minor and Europe in addition to the congregation in Jerusalem in the first century of the common era, but there was only one church, the body of Christ. Today there is only one church. There are many congregations that have all kinds of names, but there is only one church. In this one church there is one baptism which is a rite of beginning and a rite of belonging.

If you have been baptized, I hope you will continue to revisit that event. When were you baptized? Why were you baptized? How were you baptized? Remember that experience. Call to mind the meaning that event had then and how you have reinterpreted its meaning through this years.

If you have never been baptized, think about it. Think about why you would want to be baptized? What meaning would being baptized have for you?

The meaning, timing, and method were three important features of baptism for the church in those early days. These three features of baptism continue to be important for the church in these later days. Thus, there is value and learning for us by revisiting and reexamining baptism, the rite of beginning and belonging.

To Respond with Faith to Each New Invitation from God

*The Hymn of Discipleship[4]   St. Clement
        "With Grateful Hearts Our Faith Professing"
*The Offertory Sentences

God has come to our aid with the gifts of hope, love, peace, and joy. God has been generous to us. Let us now be generous with our gifts. May our tithes and offerings be given with grateful lives, and may these gifts be used to share God's generous gifts with others.

The Offertory   "Take My Life, and Let It Be"   Hendron
The Receiving of Tithes and Offerings
The Doxology
The Presentation of New Members
*The Benediction

And now, may God the creator continue the creative work begun in you, may God the redeemer continue redeeming and recreating you, and may God the sustainer sustain you throughout this week in work, in relationships, and in leisure. May we go now, assured that faith has begun in us and that we belong to God and to this community of faith, part of the family of God. Amen.

*The Choral Response   "The Bond of Love"   Skillings
The Organ Postlude   "Jesu, Joy of Our Desiring"   Bach
*Congregation standing

Notes

[1] Albrecht Oepke, "*Baptizo*," *Theological Dictionary of the New Testament*, Gerhard Kittel and Gerhard Friedrich, eds., 10 vols. (Grand Rapids MI: Eerdmans)1: 530.

[2] William Barclay, *The Mind of Jesus* (New York: Harper & Bros., 1960) 22.

[3] Ibid. 19.

[4] Hymns may be found in *Hymns, Psalms, and Spiritual Songs* (Louisville: Westminster/John Knox Press, 1990).

Chapter 4

Communion

Forty years ago in Monticello, Kentucky, a huge home-cooked meal after church on Sunday was common fare. Sunday was a relaxed day. Nothing was scheduled for Sunday afternoon. The family gathered for the meal. We usually ate around 2:00 P.M., and the remainder of the afternoon was free time. This was in the home where I was reared.

Twenty-five years ago in Burlington, Kentucky, a huge home-cooked meal after church on Sunday was common fare. This was the family into which I married. The extended family was invited to share in the meal. After the meal family members sat around, visited with each other, and played games. Sunday afternoon was a free time. The meal and the afternoon activities served as a way for family members to remain connected with each other.

This meal bonding prompted the matriarch of the family to express her feelings in poetic fashion, "Sitting around The Table after Everybody's Through."

You've had a delicious dinner
And everybody's quite content
And ready for some fellowship
Just sit there—won't cost a cent.

The best time for simply visiting
Sharing ideas on subjects tall
Is sitting around the table
When finished with the haul.

Yes, sitting around the table
After everybody's through
Is a very simple pleasure
That every one should do.

The closeness that you feel
To those with whom you've shared
Your food and conversation
It cannot be compared.

So next time you share a meal
With friends and loved ones too
Just sit around the table
After everybody's through.[1]

Much has changed during the last generation, but the value of people eating together remains important. Meals shared may not be limited to nuclear or extended family members, but meals are often shared in many places. Some of these meals are in churches, some in homes, but many of them are in fast food restaurants where several people join together after worship service to eat.

What seems to be happening is a continuation of a practice that has thousands of years of history. There may really be some truth to the opinion that people who eat together stay together. Biblical material suggests that the simple act of eating together is a significant means of familial unity. As William Willimon observes:

> Something sacred happens to people who have shared food and drink. Across all cultures and faiths, the act of eating together is a universal sign of unity and love. Jesus knew this. One need only recall the progression of meals in the Gospels in which he ate with saints and sinners to be reminded of the centrality of table fellowship and the symbolic power of sharing food and drink.[2]

Eating a meal together is often a liberating experience. People open their lives to each other around a table in a way they never seem to do at other times and places. Deliverance was the theme of the exodus meal eaten by the Israelites, and the same theme is central in holy communion.

Corinthian Lessons on Communion

When the entire focus of the meal is on the food substance, its meaning and those gathered to share it are abused. This was the problem in the Corinthian church as the economically elite were able to arrive early, and therefore, eat and drink all the food and wine. Nothing was left for the poorer members who did not have the luxury of leaving work early. Since the food was considered "heavenly manna," the popular view was the more one ate the holier one was. Many of the Corinthians had transferred the magic of the mystery religions to the early church. They understood the bread and wine alone to be sacramental. What was important to them was what was on the table. They were completely oblivious to who was at the table.

The Gospels clearly portray Jesus at meals emphasizing who was at the table and what was on the table. The Gospels indicate that if the weight falls more toward one, it is that of relationships—who is at the table. Around the table the disciples discovered most clearly who Jesus was (Luke 24:28-35). In this sense, relationships became sacramental. A sacrament, using John Baillie's definition, is the outward, visible sign of the inward, invisible grace of God at work in people's lives. The bread and wine were common food and drink that people shared. The meal was shared with people who were bound in relationship to each other. They were bound because the relationship was already established or they became bound because the relationship was in the process of being established.

The Corinthians forgot this important truth, and it became a source of major trouble in the congregation. As Conzelmann suggests, the problem with the Corinthians was that the focus of communion for them was upon some magical food rather than upon Christ and their brothers and sisters around the table who were being saved, called, and gifted to form a community of faith, the body of Christ in the world.[3]

Several elements are necessary for community formation. The community of faith has both vertical and horizonal dimensions. There must be a way of meeting if community is to be formed. Acceptance of each other and a sense of belonging are necessary. There is a need for understanding, shared common ground, confession—acknowledgement of having sabotaged community, forgiveness, and reconciliation.

In writing to the Corinthian Christians Paul spoke to the vertical dimension of community formation. He clearly stated that through communion the risen Christ forms community. Erik Erikson in his seminal work on ages and stages of human development, has demonstrated the importance of rituals, of relationships during infancy. If children are deprived of these rituals they may have difficulty forming and maintaining relationships later in life. Rituals for meeting, affirming, and supporting one another are essential for us to be in relationship with others.

Pastoral Dimensions of Communion

Communion is a ritual for meeting. In the context of worship, communion helps us rehearse our relationships. Through communion we act out the way life is to be lived in the world. Then we leave worship having shared in communion and go out into the world to put into practice what we rehearsed. We do some things better, but are complete failures at other things. Thus, we return to worship to rehearse again the way we are to live.

We see and sense a tremendous amount of brokenness in the world. The estrangement of relationships is an extremely wrenching agony, and there is great need for reconciliation. In the context of worship, communion communicates the reconciliation that people need and is available. William Hulme has noted:

> The Lord's Supper is a sacrament of reconciliation. As such it is a healing antidote for guilt and estrangement; however, the sacrament has suffered from the distortions of individualistic piety. . . . The trend was either toward assurance of personal forgiveness and intimacy with God or toward the individual reception of sanctifying grace. These are no longer predominant emphases. In their stead is the corporate significance. . . . It is not the individual believer who receives from the Lord but the fellowship of believers, who receive also from each other.[4]

The ritual of communion also helps us grow and change. Participation in communion enables people to catch a glimpse of God's world view. The Psalmist wrote that God's ways are not our ways and God's thoughts are not our thoughts. Part of our task and need is to permit God's ways to become our ways and to seek to think God's thoughts as our thoughts. Communion helps us embrace God's thoughts and ways. We discover through communion that this really is one world with one God and all of us are brothers and sisters in God's family. Communion enables us to pretend, to act like brothers and sisters rather than strangers. In the process of pretending and acting we discover that we really are family, brothers and sisters; that faith is thicker than water; and that the love of God continues to be poured out for everybody—male and female, old and young, gifted and differently abled, Jew, Arab, Samaritan, Hispanic, Asian, African, European, North American, Central American, South American, African-American, European-American, and

Native American. Through communion we discover the truth expressed in the hymn

> In Christ there is no east or west,
> in him no south or north,
> but one great fellowship of love
> throughout the whole wide earth.

What follows is the order of worship for a service in which Communion is central. All parts of this service either point to communion or draw from it.

Reconciliation through Communion
A Service of Christian Worship

The Chiming of the Hour
The Lighting of the Altar Candles

The Service of Preparation

The Organ Prelude   "Immortal Love, Forever Full"   Arr. Pethel
The Choral Call To Worship   Patricia Owens
    "The Lord Is My Strength and My Shield"

The Invocation (in unison)
    O God, prepare our lives. Prepare our minds to think your thoughts. Prepare our eyes to see your vision. Prepare our ears to hear your instruction. Prepare our hearts to love you and each other. Prepare our hands to reach out to our brothers and sisters. Prepare our feet to walk compassionately with others. O God, prepare our lives.

The Service of Confession

The Scripture of Confession   Psalm 32
The Hymn of Confession   "Dear Lord and Father of Mankind"   Rest
The Meditation

The Need for Confession: Confession in the context of the church has not been the strong suit of many of us. Yet, Jesus suggested in the model prayer that confession was a daily need of ours along with food and deliverance from evil.

    The need for confession of sin is indicated clearly throughout the Bible. The thirty-second psalm expresses the importance and value of confession. Confession and forgiveness seem to be complementary of each other. Various scriptures talk about both simultaneously. The Psalmist begins with a discussion of the blissful state or the happiness he has experienced as a result of the forgiveness of his sins that has come from God. He follows this discussion with a graphic portrayal of what life was like for him when he did not confess his sins— which was when he sought to handle, cope, and deal with his sins by himself.

Confession is best done in the presence of another human being because we need the tangibleness of another person there. In this sense we can be priests to each other. Who serves as your priest? Your priest does not have to be an ordained minister. Your priest may be anyone in whom you can and do confide your innermost struggles, your misconduct, and your sins.

Being sorry for our sins is never enough. Confession involves seeing the consequences of a sin and desiring to be freed of the guilt of sin so as to live more constructively. Confession calls for integrity and integration. Confession calls for action, identifying, calling by name what the sin is and giving oneself to God for God to deal with.

Confession of our sins to God causes us to acknowledge that we are completely at God's mercy. It is such honesty to God, however, that causes a catharsis for us as we name our sins to God. This catharsis brings us relief from our emotional agony and enables us to turn loose of our sins and turn them over to God who then is able, willing, and eager to forgive us because our relationship to God is important and essential to God as well as to us.

(in unison) Because we have sinned, we have broken our relationship with God and with one another. Let us now privately name our sins to God because first and foremost our sins are against God and only God can deal properly with our sins.

The Silent Confession

The Responsive Confession
Minister: Now let us confess our sins collectively to God. Against whom have we sinned?
People: We have sinned against God and each other.
Minister: What sins do we confess?
People: We confess that we have sinned against God by going at life our way. We have attempted to create God in our image.
Minister: What do you want God to do?
People: O God, hear our prayers of confession. Have mercy on us. Forgive us for our sin of idolatry.
Minister: Are there other sins to confess?
People: Yes. We have been dishonest in our relationships. We have been hypocritical in our faith. We have heard gossip, enjoyed it, embellished it, and passed it on.

Minister: What do you want God to do?

People: O God, hear our prayers of confession. Have mercy on us. Forgive us for our sins of dishonesty, hypocrisy, and lying.

All: **Amen.**

The Words of Assurance

"There is no condemnation now for those who live in union with Christ Jesus. For the law of the Spirit, which brings us life in union with Christ, has set us free from the law of sin and death" (Rom 8:1-2). "If any person be in Christ, he is a new being" (2 Cor 5:17). Friends, believe the Good News. We are forgiven of our sins and cleansed of all unrighteousness.

The Service of Communion

The Call to Communion "What Is on the Table and Who Is at the Table?"

Communion has the same root as common and communicate. Communion contains the common elements of bread and wine—daily, basic staple food items of Jesus' day. There is meaning and mystery in communion. The meaning and mystery of Communion makes us a bit uncomfortable with communion. Let me share what I mean.

Have you thought about the meaning and mystery of what is on the table and who is at the table? The history of communion is traced to the last passover Jesus shared with his disciples. He had made arrangements with the owner of a house for him and his disciples to share the meal there. It was a meal of liberation. The Hebrews were familiar with their history, the bitterness of bondage and slavery, and the liberating action of God in guiding their ancestors from slavery to freedom. God became known as the liberating God who always seeks to free people from what enslaves and captivates them.

Jesus and his disciples gathered for a meal of roasted lamb, bitter herbs, unleavened bread, and wine—a meal eaten against the backdrop of deliverance. In this context Jesus took the common, daily staple food items of bread and wine and turned them into carriers of the love and grace of God. The act of eating together is a universal sign of unity and love that spans all cultures and faiths. Jesus took the basic items of a meal and translated them into elements of a covenant relationship that delivers people from bondage. Jesus broke the bread. To break bread together meant then and still means today sharing a meal together. Jesus broke the bread to signify the unity of all the disciples in sharing the meal and the covenant.

Jesus said the bread meant his body, referring to the life he had lived and given to reveal God's love for all people. He invited his disciples to make a covenant with him to live and give their lives to reveal the love of God for all people. To make a covenant as translated from the Hebrew language means to cut a covenant. In Jewish antiquity, an ox would be killed, hung up, cut in two, and the ones making a covenant walked between the two sides of the animal stating that if they broke the covenant they expected to happen to them what had happened to the ox. That made a covenant serious business.

Wine was also on the table at Jesus' last meal with his disciples. Referring to the wine, Jesus said that it represented his blood. In Hebrew thought the life of any animal or person was in the blood. It is in our thinking as well. If the flow of blood to a part of the body is blocked for very long, that part of the body dies. Jesus voluntarily lived and gave his life in love for others, demonstrating the depth of God's love for all people. Jesus invited his disciples to drink from the same cup he was drinking. By doing that they were making a covenant with Jesus to pour out their lives in love for others communicating God's love for all people.

When we come to this table and receive from the table what is on the table, we are cutting a covenant with God, promising to be God's representatives in the world and to love the world for God's sake. We are acknowledging that we are both recipients of God's deliverance and messengers of that deliverance. As we come to receive what is on the table, we also benefit from realizing who is at the table. Considering who was at the table at Jesus' last meal will be insightful about who is welcome at the table today. They were ordinary people who made an extraordinary mixture.

Matthew was a tax collector. Many looked on him as a man who sold himself into the hands of the country's authorities for personal gain. Jesus was condemned by the religious leaders for eating with tax collectors. After Matthew became a disciple, Jesus was with him often, and there is no indication that Matthew gave up his tax collecting. Maybe Jesus' daily contact with Matthew caused the religious leaders to condemn him.

Simon was a Zealot. The Zealots were a fourth party in Judaism. They stood firmly for liberty and were prepared to face any kind of death for their country. They would undergo pain and were prepared to go to the length of secret murder and assassination in order to rid their country of foreign rule. Had Simon met Matthew anywhere other than in the company of Jesus, he would have considered him a traitor and killed him.[5]

Peter, Andrew, James, and John were two sets of fisherman brothers. Fishing was hard, strenuous work done by common laborers. Peter was eager to please and on more than one occasion overextended himself by promising more than he was willing to deliver. Andrew seemed to be the kind of person who was willing to take second place and remained in the background. James and John had short fuses and were nicknamed "sons of thunder."

Thomas was at the table. He was the one who consistently had questions about what was happening and why. He later refused to believe anything about the resurrection that was based on second-hand information.

As John tells events, Philip was one of the first disciples called. He introduced Nathanael to Jesus and assisted in feeding the 5,000. He had five daughters and later became an evangelist according to tradition.

Bartholomew or Nathanael, James the son of Alpheus, and Thaddaeus also were at the table but we know almost nothing about these three. Then, there was Judas who became identified as the betrayer. He was treasurer of the group, called by Jesus to be a disciple. He had potential and there is no clear, ascertainable reason why he betrayed Jesus. Up to the very end Jesus reached out to Judas and kept the door open for change.

Do you recognize yourself in any of these disciples who were at the table? When we consider who was at the table the first time and who is at the table today, is the list really that different? Oh, the names have changed, but are not many of us unknowns, people in the background, ones who have jumped at the chance to call ourselves disciples of Christ and just as quickly jumped at opportunities to deny and betray the very one we claim to follow and emulate in our lives?

Clearly, through Jesus' attitude and action at the table during the last meal with his disciples, he demonstrated that at this table everybody is welcome. While that sounds nice to most of us, we really don't come to the table with that attitude. Our private attitudes may be: "What is he doing here?" or "The nerve of some people to show up here and now," or "After the way she acted, I can't believe she would take communion."

There are tables where everybody isn't welcome. In the 1960s there were lunch counters where blacks were prohibited to eat. There are still tables where blacks, Hispanics, Arabs, Iranians, Jews, Germans, Africans, Japanese, or Russians are not welcome. But not at God's table. All are welcome here.

You may choose to have a dinner party in your home. As the host or hostess you are free to invite whomever you wish. You may choose to exclude whomever you desire. It is your home, your table, and you are free to include or exclude anybody. But that is not permissible at this table because this is not your table, or my table, or our table. Not one of us is the host or hostess at this table. This is God's table. God is the host. All are invited here. The decision is yours and mine as to whether we will come to this table. There is meaning in this table. There is meaning in communion. The meaning is wrapped up in what is on the table and who is at the table.

There is also mystery in communion. Sharing what is on the table with who is at the table may lead to communion with Christ if we experience what it is like to tremble in the presence of the table. The Israelites knew what it was to tremble at the foot of the holy mountain where they experienced the presence of God. The book of Exodus (19:16-19) records that just before Moses led the people in a processional to the mountain where they would hear the voice of God and experience the mystery who was God, they—and the mountain itself—trembled.

This experience left a lasting mark on the Hebrews' experience of God. Their reverence for the name of God, the deep sense of the holy, the wonder of God's majesty and mystery, entered the spiritual bloodstream of the Israelites when they trembled on the verge of experiencing God at the foot of the sacred mountain.[6]

It is at the table that the presence of God in Christ may become real for us. But often we tremble in fear rather than awe and move away from the mystery who is here. There is nothing magical about this table, but there is great mystery as Paul wrote to the Colossians. The mystery that has been hidden through the ages is now uncovered, disclosed, revealed, and the secret is this: Christ is in you that you might share the glory of God.

The mystery at this table is that Christ takes form inside of you—the real presence of Jesus—with you and in you. The mysterious but real and immediate presence of God at Mount Sinai was fleshed out in Jesus the Christ, and now the mystery who is in Christ is in you.

Why shouldn't we tremble as we come to the table? The bread we put in our mouths and the cup we hold in our hands are signs of the real presence of Christ with us. And when we swallow, these somehow become holy; and each of us is a holier vessel for having swallowed.[7]

We come now to the table to share in communion. There is meaning and mystery at this table because of what is on the table and who is at the table. We take a bread crumb and a swallow of juice. They represent the love of God demonstrated in Christ and poured out for all people. All are welcome at this table and all who take these common elements into their bodies are inviting Christ to be formed in them and to touch every cell of their lives as this bread and wine will go to every cell of their bodies. What meaning! What mystery! Come, share the meaning. Come, share the mystery.

The Invitation to the Table

All children of God and disciples of Christ are welcome at this table. This is God's table and God invites all of us to partake of what is on the table. Come, all of you, to the table.

Receiving the Bread

Minister: Will you speak the words of instruction?
People: Jesus said, "Take, eat, this is my body."

Receiving the Wine
Minister: Will you speak the words of instruction?
People: Jesus said, "Drink, all of you."

The Silence of Reflection
(Reflect on what has happened to you at this table today.)

(This community of faith is open to all. Persons wishing to make a decision about their personal faith or desiring to become a candidate for membership in this congregation are invited to come forward during the hymn to be introduced and welcomed to the congregation)

Hymn "In Christ There Is No East or West" McKee

Minister: God has been gracious and generous to us.
People: And we are grateful to God for giving us all that we are and hope to be.
Minister: How do you want to express your gratitude to God and provide support for the community of faith that begins here and spreads throughout the world?
People: We want to bring our tithes and offerings symbols of presenting ourselves and all that we manage to God.
Minister: Then let us bring our tithes and offerings with great joy and gratitude.

The Offertory "Carillon on 'Christ Is the World's True Light' " Haan
Receiving the Tithes and Offerings
The Doxology

The Benediction
Now, may the God who has heard our confessions, forgiven our sins, invited and accepted all of us at the table, and bound us in love into a community of faith go with us now. May we remain connected through love and grace to God and each other now and forevermore. Amen.

The Congregational Response "The Bond of Love" SKILLINGS
The Organ Postlude "One World, One Lord, One Witness" Reynolds

Notes

[1]Dorotha Cason Griesser, "My Thoughts in Verse," vol. IV (Unpublished poetry, 3 February 1990).
[2]William Willimon, *Worship as Pastoral Care* (Nashville: Abingdon Press, 1979) 166-67.

[3]Hans Conzelmann, *An Outline of the Theology of the New Testament*, trans. John Bowden (New York: Harper, 1969) 52-53.

[4]William Hulme, *Pastoral Care Comes of Age* (Nashville: Abingdon Press, 1970) 85.

[5]Stated by William Barclay in his commentary on Matthew.

[6]Steve Hyde, "Facing Our Fear Of . . . Communion," First Baptist Church of Silver Spring MD (6 November 1988).

[7]Ibid.

Chapter 5

The Wedding Ceremony

Marriage is one of the significant transitions in life recognized by culture and church alike. Marriage involves a conscious decision by two people who have had separate goals and directions to commit themselves to live life in the same direction with similar goals. Marriage involves a change from being basically concerned about oneself to including consideration of another person in nearly every choice and decision that is made. Dependency, interdependency, commitment, life-long goals and objectives, vulnerability, and sharing are some of the issues that marriage raises.

Grief is the emotional reaction that many people have to the issues at work in the lives of people involved in a wedding. Anyone who has ever married will tell you there is grief related to a wedding. Any parent who has had a child who married also will tell you there is grief at a wedding. Some of the grief is the result of conflict and strife the family had buried, but the tension comes to the surface under the pressure of the marriage crisis. Parents come to celebrate the marriage feast of their children and discover emotions welling up inside and sometimes spilling over their cheeks as tears of joy. Maybe they are joyful tears, but they also reveal the pain of change and loss.

Invariably someone cries during a wedding. Most often it is the parents of the groom and bride, and usually it is when their children enter the sanctuary during the processional. The parents are experiencing the loss with every choice people make in life. Their children have chosen to marry. While their children will always be their children, the relationship is altered forever. The child's spouse will be the confidant, the friend, the one on whom to rely. The parents' place in the child's life decreases as the spouse's place increases.

A husband and wife leave their fathers and mothers and cleave to each other. Usually the clearer and healthier the leaving, the stronger and better the cleaving. It is helpful to acknowledge this transition during the wedding service by calling attention to the importance of parents and grandparents in the lives of the groom and bride. This could entail involving family members in parts of the service such as scripture readings or prayers. Another way is to invite the family to verbalize support during the service.

Siblings persons who are marrying discover their lives changing. There is an additional person with whom to relate who has not been present all that long. The sibling who has been around, is not around as much any more. Every member of the family must deal with a change.

Jokes are made about the groom or bride being nervous. I have yet to meet an unnervous bride or groom. Why should they not be uneasy? They are venturing into a relationship and commitment in which they have no way of knowing what will happen. One man, after forty years of marriage, said that on his wedding day he had no idea that the "better" could be so good and the "worse" could be so bad. Regardless of how well they know each other, the bride and groom are leaving the familiar surroundings of the routine to which they have grown accustomed and venturing into a relationship and daily interaction with each other.

In 1969 I stood in the front of a sanctuary and looked down the aisle at a beautiful bride. For two years we had talked, planned, and antic-ipated the day. It was what we both wanted. Then I felt a flood of fear pour over me. I felt my face blend with my white shirt. My legs felt like water. I was scared, and I was scared that I was scared. What was happening to me? I was taking an irreversible action. No longer was marriage a dream or a subject for conversation. It was about to be a reality. Life would be different from that point, but exactly how different was unknown. Persons who marry have some of these feelings as well as many other hopes and fears and bring these feelings to the wedding ceremony.

The Wedding as Worship

Calling a wedding a ceremony may be problematic. It probably contri-butes to the idea that a wedding is a production, a show, a chance for a family to display most of its idiocentricies at one time. While it is pos-sible for the wedding ceremony to be a worship experience, it requires the best efforts of all involved to make it happen.

One never knows when agreeing to conduct a wedding what may be expected or requested. Will you be asked to conduct the ceremony while floating over the community in a blimp? Will the couple request an outdoor wedding in a garden or near a lake that is a beautiful setting to them? Of course most weddings take place in the sanctuary or chapel of a church. The church is the usual place where the congregation gathers for worship. However, the idea of the wedding ceremony being a type of worship service seldom enters the minds of those planning this particular wedding.

Why do people want to get married in the church? Their reasons vary, but nearly everyone who wants a "church wedding" says that it means God will be a part of their wedding or that somehow God will bless their marriage. Often I am struck by how close magic and religion seem to be in people's expressions. Some couples seem to be suggest that by having their wedding ceremony in a church somehow, through osmosis, God is infused into their marriage. Other couples want their wedding to occur in the church because their faith development is important to them. God has been significant in their lives, and they anticipate a continued faith development that involves God in their marriage. They want their wedding ceremony to occur in the place where they worship because they see their wedding as a special type of worship service.

Several things can be done that will contribute to a wedding ceremony being a worship service. It is especially helpful for a congregation to develop guidelines and policy for weddings that are conducted in the sanctuary or chapel. These guidelines can include the following suggestions: (1) the style of music; (2) types of decorations; (3) what furniture may be moved and who is to move it; (4) fees are involved and when these are to be paid; and (5) restrictions regarding the musicians and ministers. (Are visiting ministers welcome to conduct weddings? Is the minister of the church where the wedding is held expected to have a part in the ceremony?)

Included in the wedding policy of a congregation can be the expectation that the couple be involved in premarital counseling with a minister or counselor. If at all possible, this is best done with the minister who will conduct the ceremony. The first of these sessions can be approximately three months prior to the ceremony. This is a time when the minister and couple can discuss the meaning and significance of the ceremony as a special type of worship service. When most couples come to me for premarital counseling, they do not want to acknowledge many, if any, struggles or difficulties in their relationships.

The approach that works best for me is to have five sessions with a couple. The first two are scheduled prior to the wedding—the first one three months prior to the wedding and the second one about one month before the wedding. Often the assignment for the second session is for the prospective bride and groom individually or together to write their own vows. These may or may not be used in the service. Asking them to write their own vows, however, helps them take this part of the service more seriously as well as helping this part of the service to have more meaning to them. The third session is scheduled a week before the wedding in order to go over the details of the service. The fourth session is usually scheduled one month after the wedding, and the fifth session occurs three months after the service.

This format is most workable for couples who are members of the congregation and will remain in the area after their marriage. Even those who will live in another place have been willing to make arrangements to return for the last two sessions. In a couple of cases, where logistics were extremely difficult, the couple and I have corresponded with each other. I find couples appreciate being taken seriously and appreciate someone who is genuinely interested in their relationship.

If a wedding director is used, the minister must communicate directly with that person. The director can be very helpful if the director's role is one of helper and if he/she understands that this is a worship service. However, if the director sees the wedding as a production, everyone involved may sense they are mere performers in the director's production.

A bulletin or printed program is a helpful tool for a wedding. It helps communicate that this is a worship service with purpose and design. The printed program also provides a place to communicate with the congregation that pictures are not to be taken during the ceremony. Pictures taken during the ceremony, by a professional photographer or members of the congregation, are disturbing and distracting. They draw attention to the photographers and away from the service. Permitting photographs during the processional and recessional and reenacting segments of the service afterward provide ample opportunity for people to capture the event on film, actually resulting in better pictures.

A wedding service marks a significant transition in the lives of the people who are marrying and in the lives of their families. Currently, it is more the norm that at least one of the families represented will be a blended family. Dealing with stepparents can be an emotionally wrenching experience for the marrying couple. I have had circumstances where it was necessary that the bride's mother and dad not sit on the same pew because of the animosity that continued even though they were divorced and both had remarried. I also have had situations where there was tension, but the parents recognized the importance of this event for their children and put their personal feelings aside. There have been blended family situations where everyone was amicable and supportive.

Commitment is the theme that runs throughout the wedding service. Commitment is an issue of equanimity and equality. Often it is said that the day of the wedding is the "bride's day." I submit that it is also the "groom's day," and more importantly it is the groom and bride's day of publicly committing their lives to each other in marriage. I discuss with a couple the importance of communicating equality in the relationship throughout the service. I encourage the groom and groomsmen to enter down the same aisle and in the same manner, order, and style as the bride and bridesmaids. It is appropriate for the groom to be escorted by his parents and the bride by her parents. (This is often done at Jewish weddings.) The groom and bride having equal commitment, involvement, and responsibility in the relationship is best symbolized when both come down the same aisle.

In the order of worship for a wedding service that follows, you will see commitment expressed by the various elements of the service. I have also sought to touch on the grief that may be felt, the issue of interdependency, and the significance of this celebration taking place as a gift of worship to God.

A Worship Service Celebrating the Marriage of
_____ and _____

Saturday, June 18, 1994
Five O'Clock
Auburn First Baptist Church
Auburn, Alabama

Prelude to Worship

Organ Meditation
    "God Gave to Us This Glorious Day"   Walther
    "Allegro"   Handel
    "Pastorale in F Major"   Bach
Chiming of the Hour
The Processional**
    "Trumpet Voluntary"   Purcell
    "Bridal Chorus"   Wagner

Service of Praise

The Spoken Call to Worship
    Come, let us worship God and celebrate the marriage of _____ and _____. Come, let us give thanks and praise to God for the gift of life we see and know in the forms of _____ and _____. Come, let us celebrate with joy their desire to unite in marriage. Come, let us worship God and offer our support to _____ and _____. Come, let us express our love for God and our love for _____ and _____ through this time of worship. Come, let us pray for _____ and _____ in their journey together. Come, let us worship God and celebrate the marriage of _____ and _____.

The Invocation
    God, may we delight in you as you delight in _____ and _____. Fill our hearts with your joy for them. Stir our minds to think your thoughts of love. Open our arms to hold _____ and _____ in our lives. Guide our words and thoughts as gifts of gratitude to you for _____ and _____. May your peace and presence we experience here be only a twinkle of the peace and presence we receive throughout our lives. Amen.

The Hymn   "Joyful, Joyful, We Adore Thee"   Beethoven

Service of Marriage

Address to the Congregation

Family and friends, _____ and _____ have invited us here to celebrate and participate with them in their wedding. We have been invited to participate because we are important people in their lives. They want our love, support, and encouragement. They want us to share our joy with them as they share their joy with us. Thus, we are not spectators here, watching what is happening. We are participants actively involved in their lives, offering our care and celebration to them.

Marriage is one of the most exhilarating, enriching, exciting, aggravating, agonizing, frustrating relationships in which two people can be involved. Marriage enables two people to know each other in ways they have never been known before. Marriage makes people vulnerable like they have never been. Marriage makes possible a depth of sharing, understanding, and communication that two people may never have known existed. Marriage can deepen love and commitment so that two people really live and function as one.

For these and many other reasons, marriage is a serious and celebrative endeavor. People need to approach marriage carefully, thoughtfully, reflectively, and prayerfully. As _____ and _____ have shared with me about their relationship, they come here today excited and serious, happy and reflective. They come here to promise in the presence of God and in our presence their love for each other in a way that does not count the cost of loving and caring for one another.

Responsive Reading of 1 Corinthians 13

Minister: If I speak in the tongues of people and of angels, but have not love, I am a noisy gong or a clanging cymbal.

People: And if I have prophetic powers, and understand all mysteries and all knowledge and if I have all faith, so as to remove mountains, but have not love, I am nothing.

Minister: If I give away all I have, and if I deliver my body to be burned, but have not love, I gain nothing.

People: Love is patient and kind; love is not jealous or boastful; it is not arrogant or rude. Love does not insist on its own way; it is not irritable or resentful; it does not rejoice at wrong, but rejoices in the right.

Minister: Love bears all things, believes all things, hopes all things, endures all things.

People: Love never ends; as for prophecies, they will pass away; as for tongues, they will cease; as for knowledge, it will pass away.

Minister: For our knowledge is imperfect, and our prophecy is imperfect; but when the perfect comes, the imperfect will pass away.

People: When I was a child, I spoke like a child, I thought like a child, I reasoned like a child; when I became more mature, I gave up childish ways.

Minister: For now we see in a mirror dimly, but then face to face. Now I know in part; then I shall understand fully, even as I have been fully understood.

People: So faith, hope, love abide, these three; but the greatest of these is love.

Psalm 90

The Declaration of Intention and Support

Minister: (Groom), this is a very important, significant day in your life. You have come to this place of worship to commit yourself in marriage to _____. Do you come today promising to love and care for, honor and respect _____ so long as you both shall live?

(Groom): I do.

Minister: (Bride), this is a very important, significant day in your life. You have come to this place of worship to commit yourself in marriage to _____. Do you come today promising to love and care for, honor and respect _____ as long as you both shall live?

(Bride): I do.

Minister: Who is here in support of (Groom) being married to _____?

The Groom's Family: We are!

Minister: Who is here in support of (Bride) being married to _____?

The Bride's Family: We are!

The Exchange of Vows

Marriage vows are promises. They are statements of what you are going to do. Then, you either do them or you don't. There is a sense in which you would be wise to renew your vows daily because the chances are strong that you will not keep all of these vows completely every day. The marriage vows verbalize commitment. Perhaps the most important aspect of your relationship is your commitment to each other. There will be many opportunities and invitations to break your marriage vows. What will enable you to scale the peaks and struggle through the pits of your relationship will be your commitment to each other.

Perhaps the clearest biblical expression of commitment is found in the Book of Ruth. Although the statements that Ruth made had nothing to do with marriage, her words are powerful expressions of commitment. The husbands of Naomi and Ruth have died. They are living in Moab, Ruth's homeland, but Naomi has decided to return to Israel, her homeland. Naomi insists that Ruth remain in Moab because life will be better for her there. Ruth refuses and her words express strongly her commitment to Naomi. "Wherever you go, I will go. Where you live, I will live. Your people will be my people. Your God will be my God. And where you die, that is where I will die too" (Ruth 1:16-17). That is commitment.

_____ and _____, you have shared with me your desire to be committed to each other in marriage. Together we have written vows that express your intentions and commitment to each other. Will you please face each other and join hands. (Groom), will you express your commitment to _____?

I, (Groom), commit myself to you, (Bride), to be your husband from this day forward. I invite you to be my wife. I know there will be exhilarating and exhausting times. There may be times when we will be rich beyond measure and other times when poverty may overtake us. We may experience unbelievable times of bliss and other times of struggle and conflict. We are in good health. Let's enjoy it. There may be times when illness and disease dominate our lives. Although we cannot know all that will happen to us in life, I know this: I am committing my life to you in

marriage. I promise to be a caring and faithful husband. I promise to help you be yourself, to encourage you to grow, to comfort you when you are sad and to celebrate with you when you are happy. I promise myself to you so long as we both shall live.

(Bride), will you express your commitment to _____?

I, (Bride), commit myself to you, (Groom), to be your wife from this day forward. I invite you to be my husband. I know there will be exhilarating and exhausting times. There may be times when we will be rich beyond measure and other times when poverty may overtake us. We may experience unbelievable times of bliss and other times of struggle and conflict. We are in good health. Let's enjoy it. There may be times when illness and disease dominate our lives. Although we cannot know all that will happen to us in life, I know this: I am committing my life to you in marriage. I promise to be a caring and faithful wife. I promise to help you be yourself, to encourage you to grow, to comfort you when you are sad and to celebrate with you when you are happy. I promise myself to you so long as we both shall live.

The Exchange of Rings

For centuries rings have been used to seal important agreements and documents. Signet rings served as the official signature of kings. In order for a law officially to become enacted in a country, a document worded the way the king wanted the law stated was developed. When it was just as the king wanted it, he stamped his signet ring in a splotch of wax at the end of the document. That was his official signature and made the wording in the document legal and binding.

The marriage vows that you, _____ and _____, stated serve as a verbal document of your commitment in marriage. The rings you are giving and receiving today serve as your signatures to your marriage vows. Wherever you go, whether together or apart, when anyone sees the ring each of you wears, that person will know that you are committed to another in marriage.

_____ and _____, you have shared a lot about yourselves with me. You are convinced of your love for each other. You have given witness to me of your love for each other. However, you have been unable to identify the exact moment that your love began for each other. You can only testify that it did begin and that your love is growing deeper and stronger as you share more and more of yourselves with each other. The rings you are exchanging are circular. They have no beginning and no ending. May they symbolize your love for each other. Just as you cannot identify its beginning, may your love for each other have no ending. May your rings represent your growing, unending love for each other.

The rings are made of gold, the purest of metals. The gold ore is mined from the earth. Then, it is placed in a fiery furnace. The heat from the fire burns away the impurities and leaves only the pure gold. Fortunately, I have had some people to love me. Their love has burned away some of the impurities in my life. May your love for God and your love for each other burn away your impurities and continue to purify your relationship.

The wedding rings you wear are your signatures. They autograph your commitment to each other in marriage.

Minister: (Groom), place this ring on the third finger of (Bride) left hand. Do you give this ring as an expression of your love and commitment to _____ in marriage?

Groom: I do.

Minister: (Bride), will you wear this ring as an expression of your love and commitment to (Groom) in marriage?

Bride: I will.

Minister: (Bride), place this ring on the third finger of (Groom) left hand. Do you give this ring as an expression of your love and commitment to _____ in marriage?

Bride: I do.

Minister: (Groom), will you wear this ring as an expression of your love and commitment to (Bride) in marriage?

Groom: I will.

The Unity Candle

_____ and _____ are grateful for the love and support their families have given them through the years. Their parents have nurtured and nourished them from infancy through childhood and adolescence and into adulthood. They have guided them through being totally dependent on their parents for everything into being interdependent on their parents and others and dependent on God for guidance and direction in their living. Prior to the ceremony today, _____ and _____ parents lit candles representing their families. Today marks the beginning of a new family as _____ and _____ embark on their marriage together. Today symbolizes that _____ and _____ are leaving their fathers and mothers and being united together as husband and wife. At this time, _____ and _____ will take the candles their parents lit and light the unity candle signifying the union of their lives together in marriage and the beginning of a new family.

Holy Communion

_____ and _____ recognize they are part of a much larger family, the family of God. They are committed to loving God with all their hearts, minds, and souls and to loving others as they love themselves. They are grateful to God for the gift of life God has given to each of them and for the gift of each other's life to be shared in marriage. They are also grateful for the constant presence of God in their lives. Nothing represents the continual presence of God and God's love, grace, and mercy like the elements of communion. Now, _____ and _____ will receive communion.

_____ and _____, as you receive and eat this bread, you are acknowledging the love and care God has for you. As your body takes this bread to every cell of your body, may God's love and grace touch every dimension of your lives.

As you receive and drink this wine, you are acknowledging the breadth and depth of God's love, how far God will go to demonstrate love for you even to the point of pouring out life in love. As your body takes this wine to every part of your body, may you willingly and lovingly pour out your lives in love for God and for others.

The Prayer of Dedication

Thank you, God, that _____ and _____ invited us to celebrate this important day with them. Their nervousness and ours indicate something of the significance and seriousness of marriage. God, we are grateful for the gift of life beautifully wrapped as _____ and _____. We are grateful for the people they are and the people they are becoming. Thank you for their love for you and their love for each other. They want to give themselves to each other, but they cannot without some struggle. They are saying good-bye to life they have known and hello to life together that is unknown. They are excited and uneasy. Calm them with your presence and encouragement.

May they always be open to grow. May they be closed to hatred and bitterness. May they be comforted in times of agony and distress, and may they seek to comfort others. May their commitment and love grow deeper and stronger each day. May we, their family and friends, offer them our love, support, and care throughout the journey. May their youthful fascination grow toward mature charm. As time and trials leave traces upon their faces, may they keep holding hands in the dark, keep reaching for each other, and keep tuning their love.

O God, may your love that will not let us go enrich _____ and _____ and give them help and hope every day of their lives. We offer our prayer with the attitude and intention with which Jesus our Lord prayed.

The Choral Prayer   "The Lord's Prayer"   Malotte

The Declaration

_____ and _____, you have shared a lot about yourselves with me. You have come to this place of worship and in the presence of God, family, and friends you have declared you love and commitment to each other. You have stated your intentions and promises to each other and autographed those promises by giving and receiving rings. You have signified the beginning of your life together as a family by lighting the unity candle. You have represented your commitment to the family of God by receiving communion. Together we have prayed for your journey together. By the power granted to me by almighty God, I pronounce you husband and wife. What God has sought to join together, may none of us do anything that would tear this relationship apart. You may seal your affection and commitment with a kiss.

The Presentation

I present to you _____ and _____.

The Recessional   "Wedding March"   Mendelssohn

**The groomsmen and groom enter down the center aisle then, the bridesmaids and the bride likewise. Or, the groomsmen and bridesmaids enter as couples down the aisle. Then, the groom enters, followed by the bride. Let the processional depict equality and mutuality.*

Chapter 6

The Funeral Service

One of the major ironies in life is that people who want nothing to do with the church—do not want to be involved in a congregation, do not want people from a congregation inviting them to church—request a minister to conduct the funeral service of a family member who dies. Why is this? Certainly death is the ultimate transition. Death renders people vulnerable in ways they may never have experienced previously. Our lives also hold a lot of magic and superstition: Many subconsciously feel they had better cover all the bases. By having a minister conduct the funeral, they hope in some way it will help the person who has died. Just in case the family was wrong about the importance and place of the church in their lives, they request a minister.

The reasons for not having anything to do with the church are numerous and varied. There may have been a time and set of circumstances in the past in which the family experienced the rejection of the church. In recent years, some congregations have rejected anyone who had AIDS. The rejection has been expressed through statements and stances on lifestyles and through judgments about the activities of people. For other people, there may have been a time when they felt the need of the church's help and support but did not receive it. The hurt of that experience continued to fester and keep them away from the ministry of the church. Others simply do not believe in anything the church stands for. Their family members, however, especially in dealing with death, reach out to the church for help.

Regardless of the situation, the funeral service provides a unique opportunity to offer care, understanding, support, and acceptance to people who are caught in the midst of grief. Out of care and support given during this time may come the opening to provide further care and understanding to the family members at a later time as they continue to journey through the valley of the shadow of death.

Ministry of Death Education

A congregation can provide a significant ministry to its members and the people who live in the community prior to the funeral service by periodically having seminars and related events on grief, helping people face and plan for death, guidance about health care for the terminally ill, organ and body donations, estate planning and wills, and memorial and funeral services.

It is helpful and comforting when people discover that many of the feelings they are experiencing are similar to what has happened to others. A seminar on the grief process can be valuable. Set a time and place and advertize it for anyone who has ever lost a job or has experienced the end of a relationship, a divorce, or the death of a friend or relative. While the intensity of feelings vary with these "loss" events, the dynamics and process of dealing with the loss and readjusting to life are quite similar. Awareness of the stages of this process can be valuable in worship, pastoral care, and involvement with individuals and groups. The grief process involves a back and forth movement from one stage to another. The six stages of the process I have identified are shock, numbness, fantasy, depression, stabbing pain, and readjustment. Find a person who is competent and comfortable in leading discussion and sharing about this process. People in this group also can become ministers to others as they experience losses.

Another valuable ministry a congregation can provide is a seminar to deal with and plan for death and a memorial or funeral service. As strange as it may seem, we learn to live by preparing to die. Jesus spoke to this through his statement that those who seek to save their lives lose them and those who lose their lives save them. A seminar of several weekly sessions can be helpful. A person from the medical profession—a physician, nurse, or both—can discuss and respond to questions. The most helpful people often are those who work with a hospice organization. They are most familiar with the issues, concerns, and questions. A lawyer can inform people about wills, living wills, durable power of attorney, organ and body donations, and other matters related to death that have legal ramifications. A funeral director can inform people about the procedures involved when a death occurs, how the circumstances and place of death may determine what needs to be done, what preparation of the body is required, and the costs of the various services.

An added ministry of some congregations is providing a meal for the family at the church after the service. This is especially valuable in our mobile society when many family members live away from the place where the deceased person lived. This meal provides a time and opportunity of bonding and strengthening for the family.

Preparing for the Service

The time and place of a funeral or memorial service contribute to the service being an opportunity for pastoral care to be delivered through worship. The term "funeral" refers to the service conducted when someone has died and the body of the deceased person is present at the service. The term "memorial service" usually is used to identify a service when the body of the deceased person is not present. This may be because the deceased person's body was donated to benefit medical science, the body was transported to another place for burial but a service was wanted and needed in the area where the person last lived, or the deceased was cremated.

Families have recently begun requesting private burials for their deceased members, followed by memorial services at the church. This has proven to be a meaningful order. One of the practical dimensions is that it provides ample time in a comfortable place for friends to express their support and encouragement to family members. I have observed the family members to be more relaxed and in tune with those who are interacting with them.

The best place for the funeral or memorial service is in the church sanctuary or chapel. This is a place designated for people to gather for worship on a regular basis. In most situations, the minister asked to conduct the service is the pastor of a member of the family and the church used will be familiar to that family member. When the service is at the church, the minister is more clearly in charge of how the service is conducted. When the service is at a funeral home, the funeral director tends to dictate how the service is conducted. In spite of the efforts of many funeral homes to have their own chapels, aesthetically they seldom contribute to a sense and setting of worship. Because the only function of these chapels is funerals, this place has no connection for family and friends other than the death of an important person in their lives. Being in the place does not bring memories of celebration, hope, and support, or a sense that through this place people have been guided in other transitions in their lives.

The purpose of a funeral or memorial service is twofold: to worship and to mourn. Mourning in worship has an ancient heritage as many of the psalms suggest. The lamenting mentioned in the psalms often was the response of the people for the sins they had committed, but there also is evidence of the congregation mourning losses.

The funeral or memorial service is a special type of worship service. It is specialized both in its purpose and content. The purpose is more strictly focused than other worship services; worshipers focus their attention upon God, who will support and sustain them through the cold loneliness and painful emptiness that accompanies the death of an important person.

The content of the funeral service consists of scripture, music, and information about the deceased person's life. Gratitude is expressed to God for the gift of this person's life and to assure the worshipers of God's care, support, and guidance throughout the journey of their grief. The better the minister knows the person who died, the more personal the funeral or memorial service can be. The use of brief antidotes or bits of humor from the person's life is helpful. When the minister knows the person, then, it is possible to design a service that is an expression of what the person was like. These personal touches are comforting and supportive to those grieving and are ways of communicating that the person who died was an important, significant person. It is appropriate for the casket to be closed prior to the beginning of the service. This contributes to a more focused service by all who are present.

The manner in which a funeral service is conducted models for those participating ways of dealing with death and dying. It is appropriate not only to talk about the person's life but also about when and how he or she died. This should not be done in a way that exploits people's emotions or plays on them, but in a helpful, straightforward manner that helps the congregation deal directly with this person's death.

An example of a funeral service follows. The scripture, music, prayers, and funeral meditation are selected to help people worship God during an emotionally difficult time, express gratitude for the gift of the person's life, and assure the congregation of God's abiding love and presence.

Funeral Service for _____
A Service of Christian Worship

The Chiming of the Hour

We Gather as People of Sorrow Acquainted with Grief

*The Procession   "God of Grace and God of Glory"   Hughes

The Spoken Call to Worship
   Come, let us worship God and mourn the death of _____. Come, let us worship God and give thanks for the gift of life we have known and seen in the form of _____. Come, let us worship God and say good-bye to _____. Come, let us worship God and mourn the death of _____.

The Invocation
   O God, make your presence known to us today. Guide our lives with your hope. Fill our emptiness with your love. Warm our loneliness with your grace. Comfort our hurt with your peace. Soothe our sorrow with your help. Give us the hope and help, the love and grace we need for the facing of this hour. O God, make your presence known to us today. Amen.

We Seek Guidance and Comfort

*Hymn   "Guide Me, O Thou Great Jehovah"   Williams

The Scriptures
   Apparently, many of the writers of scripture had experiences similar to ours. That is why some passages of scripture have become so significant to us. They express exactly how we are feeling and what we are experiencing. I have selected several passages from the Psalms and the New Testament that I trust will offer us comfort, help, and hope today. (Read Ps 121:1-2; 6:6-7; 18:1-3; 6:23; Isa 40:31; Rom 8:31, 35, 37-39; Rev 21:1-4.)

We Need Help and Hope

The Choral Worship "A Mighty Fortress Is Our God"   Luther

The Funeral Meditation   "Nothing Can Separate Us from God's Love"

We are gathered here to worship God and to mourn the death of _____. All of our mourning will not be done here. All of it will not be done today. It took us a long time to develop the relationships we had with ____. It will take us a long time to say goodbye to him and to grieve his death. _____ was related to all of us in some capacity. He was a husband, a father, a father-in-law, a grandfather, a brother, a brother-in-law, an uncle, a colleague, a church member, a fellow member of the Exchange Club, a coin collector, and a friend. The grief we feel, experience, and express is in proportion to the depth and intimacy of our relationship with him.

Death is an unwelcomed, unwanted, uninvited intruder into our lives. No matter how prepared we are for death, no matter how much thinking, planning, and anticipating we do, we are never completely ready for death. As well as anyone I know, _____ got himself ready to face death, but neither he nor any of us were completely prepared for that moment when he breathed and then he didn't breathe any more. We just cannot be completely prepared for the unknown, even when we know it is inevitable.

_____ and I developed a caring and trusting friendship over the last sixteen years. It is as his friend and yours that I share with you on this difficult and painful day in our lives. The first time I met ____, as I recall, was prior to a Sunday morning worship service as he was ambling into his pew right back there. On many Sunday mornings I saw him amble in and engage one of the ushers in brief conversation. There would be laughter, and ____ would move on toward his pew. On his way he would tap someone on the shoulder who was already seated or speak to someone coming from a Sunday school class. There would be laughter, and he would move on to his pew. I call it "his pew" because that was where he sat every time he was in church.

_____ gave me many gifts through the years. He carried me to lunch at Cary Hilliard's more times than I can remember. He did my taxes one year, and he charged me so much that I have used that year's form as a model every year since. He was an avid Georgia fan and enjoyed harassing me about the Kentucky Wildcats. He gave me a ticket to the NCAA basketball championship at the Omni in Atlanta, provided I would drive and take two teenagers with me. He wrote letters of recommendation to several pastor search committees. I'm not sure what all he said about me in those letters, but I'm still at Broadview Baptist Church where I've been for fourteen years. But most of all, ____ gave me himself. He let me know who he was, how he felt, what he thought.

It was from "his pew" that he worshiped God in this place. It was from that pew that he entered into dialogue with the sermon. Later he would have a comment about how the sermon applied to him. And he would chide me a bit when a sermon missed the mark by asking me, "Do you know how many bricks are in this section of the wall? Well, there are 7 rows across and 32 down, and that is 224 bricks. I counted them during the sermon." Or he would say, "Do you know how many slots there are in the wall around the baptistry?" Anyone who knows _____ experienced his sense of humor. The ability to laugh and to laugh at oneself is learned early in life, as a young child. _____ learned early and learned well, and his humor served him and us well through the years. His humor also revealed that he did not take himself too seriously, and that helped him cope with the pain and debilitation that arthritis caused. He could have said, "Nobody knows the troubles I've seen," but he didn't. He threw very few pity parties for himself. He was at times hard on himself and angry at himself for not having more patience. He jokingly said to me on more than one occasion, "I've given up patience for Lent."

_____ served on the worship committee at Memorial. This committee helped me formulate, design, implement, and evaluate a doctoral project called "A Lenten Celebration of Memorial Baptist Church." Through that project, _____ became very interested in the Lenten season as a time of serious introspection for followers of Christ. On Ash Wednesday, the beginning of Lent, in 1978, the first Lenten season after we moved to Washington, D.C., I got a call from _____. Thus began a tradition. He called me every Ash Wednesday until this year. I jokingly would answer the phone and say, "If it's _____, it must be Ash Wednesday." This year _____ was in the hospital on Ash Wednesday. I called him and he said, "If it's Howard Roberts, it must be Ash Wednesday."

Ironically, when I arrived at my office on Tuesday of this week (the day _____ died), there was a letter from _____. He had written me last Monday to tell me, "Generally, I feel much better." He also wrote to send me a copy of the Stations of the Cross service he attended recently. He said, "It has some very meaningful passages." He didn't mark which ones were meaningful to him, but as I read it I noted some what I think he would have marked. The words of a prayer that said, "Strengthen us in our baptismal resolutions by which we renounced sin and Satan, so that through the passion of this life's sufferings we might rise to a new life of joyful service free of all selfishness." And this one, "Almighty and ever-loving God, we feel your love and understanding in the consolation and support we receive from one another." One more, "Lord Jesus Christ, stripped of everything, You stood exposed to the jeers and contempt of the people whom you loved. Clothe us with genuine love of others, so that nothing we suffer may ever fill our hearts with hatred or bitterness."

I think this last request must have been _____ prayer. In all the illness, disease, surgeries, and disability that _____ experienced, I never sensed that life became bitter for him. Frankly, that is quite remarkable!

_____ sense of humor and his honesty with God kept him from becoming bitter. He was willing to let God have it at times and tell God what he thought about the way life was going for him. _____ had enough faith in God to know that he could tell God anything, and he knew God would accept anything he had to say. So, _____ poured our his anger, frustration, aggravation, and feelings of unfairness onto God. _____ knew and believed the promise Jesus made, speaking for God, when he said, "I will never leave you or forget about you."

Because _____ received and believed that promise, he remained faithful to God throughout his journey. Indeed, _____ could say what Paul wrote to Timothy, "I have fought a good fight, I have finished the race, I have kept the faith." Except often _____ didn't keep the faith. He gave the faith away which, paradoxically, is the only way to keep the faith.

The passage read from Isaiah this afternoon was one of _____ favorite because it speaks about life as he experienced it. The promise that Isaiah records says that those who trust in God will find their strength renewed; they will mount up with wings like eagles; they will run and not grow weary; they will walk and not faint. Often all that _____ wanted or needed was to have his strength renewed. On more than one occasion when I called to see how _____ was doing, he would respond, "Well, I'm not running any races." Actually, that's true of most of us most of the time, isn't it? It certainly is true for us today.

Frankly, there were just a few times in _____ life when he felt like he was flying like the eagles. There were a few other times when it seemed he could run and not wear out. But for most of his life, about all he could do was walk and not faint. This understanding of God's strengthening presence contributed to the poem "Footprints" having so much meaning to _____.[1]

In the midst of our grief we need help and hope. God seeks to meet both of these needs. The most important promise in all of scripture is the promise God makes to never leave us or forget about us. If ever we need to experience the truth of that promise, it is today. If ever we can cash in on that truth, it is today. God often comes to us through the love and care that others express to us. Their presence and support become the carriers of God's grace and mercy for us. If ever we need to be enveloped by God's love and grace through loved ones, it is, indeed, today.

When death invades our lives, a natural response is to feel alone, separated, abandoned. We are separated from _____. Our ability to relate and interact with him ended suddenly on Tuesday. But we have not been separated from God because nothing can separate us from God's love. Regardless of how we feel and what we are experiencing, there is absolutely nothing that can place us beyond the reach of God's love and care for us. God sustained _____ throughout his life and all that he experienced. God will do the same for us. May we put our trust in God and have our strength renewed. We, too, will be able to walk and not faint. That is enough, because right now that is what we need.

I stand before you as ____ friend and your friend to offer you my love, my care, my support, and my prayers on your behalf. But I also stand before you as a messenger from God to tell you what you already know. God loves you and cares for you. God will journey with you through the valley of the shadow of ____ death. And there is absolutely nothing that can or will separate you from the love of God. ____ believed that and lived that. May we believe it and live it too.

*The Hymn   "O God, Our Help in Ages Past"   Croft

We Depart Uplifted by God's Peace

*The Benediction

Now, may the hope of God go before you. May the mercy of God follow behind you. May the grace of God undergird you. May the love of God surround. May you journey in peace. Amen.

*The Recession   "Hallelujah" from *Messiah*   Handel

Notes

[1]Daniel Willis, "Footprints in the Sand." This version is by Cristy Lane in "One Day at a Time."

Part Three

Relationships

By nature and need humans are relational beings. Our lives are nurtured and nourished through our relationships. They are also hurt and harmed through relationships. We are created capable of and in need of relationships with God and fellow humans beings. The configurations of relationships are multiple and varied. In this section I examine several kinds of relationships through the life cycle to help us discover and explore ways the church through worship can provide pastoral care for people in their relationships.

Whether you do a cursory reading of the Gospels or delve into them in depth, they are fairly clear in portraying that relationships were primary to Jesus. Therein lies a clue for us about our lives and where our focus needs to be in order for life to have meaning and value for us. For us to have close encounters of the healthy kind, we must commit time and energy to our relationships.

Jesus was concerned about primary relationships—relationships between brothers and sisters, between spouses, among family and friends (Matt 5:21-26). Why did Jesus start there? Maybe some of those relationships were in a mess. Maybe some of the primary relationships today are in a mess. I know people who have tremendous charisma in public life, but their private lives are in shambles. I know there are people involved in projects and tasks of cosmic proportions, but their personal relationships are empty shells. Often, we do not know those who live near us. We do not develop any kind of relationship with them. We begin to harbor fear and anger against them. Was this what Jesus was talking about? Does what Jesus said twenty centuries ago have application now as we move toward the twenty-first century?

Why did Jesus start with primary relationships? Maybe when there is something fundamentally wrong in the basic relationships, nothing else can be quite right. Maybe if we do not take care of these primary matters, we cannot, will not take care of secondary matters.

Jesus said that relationships are primary. Jesus was forever addressing himself to the motives for people's actions. He was concerned about how the process began. He knew there was an intricate correlation between roots and fruits in people's lives. Jesus' words regarding anger expressed a radical protest toward the person who allows his/her anger to fester and eventually poison the relationship with another human being. Jesus said that if people nurse their anger, they feed it, and cause it to grow larger and become destructive.

Through the next several chapters I want us to explore together some of the relationships in which we are involved. We will examine some of the characteristics and qualities that are essential for these relationships to have value and meaning for us. We will explore ways the church can emphasize and help us celebrate these qualities. As we explore these qualities and characteristics through worship, we will see how reconciliation, a major dimension of pastoral care, can and needs to be addressed through worship. The worship services designed in each chapter of this section relate to dimensions of the theme, "Worshiping the God who calls us into relationship." This theme ties this section together and could be used in a congregation as a theme for a series of worship services focusing on relationships.

Chapter 7

Married Relationships

Marriage is a relationship for which there are the highest expectations and the least preparation. I submit this is one of the many factors contributing to the large number of marriages that end in divorce. Factors that have an impact on marriages include lifestyle, culture, family background, employment, economy, children, conflict, and communication.

The church can provide a tremendous ministry to people who are married. This ministry can involve pre-marital counseling, marriage growth groups, and classes to deal with marriage issues. Many marriages do not work, and churches need to find ways to support those coping with separation and divorce. Another ministry of the church is offering guidance and support to people who are married by acknowledging that it is natural for couples to have difficulties and struggles in their marriages. Through this acknowledgement the church can provide guidance to help couples make their marriages better.

The most public way a congregation can do this is through worship. As the congregation gathers to worship, participants have an opportunity to experience what the church has to offer related to their needs. The following worship service illustrates one way that a congregation through worship can offer pastoral care to people in their married relationships.

Worshiping the God Who Calls Us into Relationship
A Service of Christian Worship

We Gather to Worship

The Chiming of the Hour
The Prelude   "I Love Thee"   Arr. Dennis Allen
                              Handbell Choir

The Responsive Call to Worship
Pastor: We come to worship God
People: And to seek help for our lives.
Pastor: We are invited to be in relationship with God and with one another.
People: Some of our relationships are in trouble.
Pastor: Then, let us seek help from God for our relationships.

People: **We come to worship God and to seek help for our relationships.**
Pastor: Come, let us worship God and receive the help we need. Amen.

We Celebrate Healthy Marriages

*The Hymn   "O Spirit of the Living God"   Llanfyllin
*Invocation
     O God, inspire our lives to relate to you through worship. Instruct our minds to think of others as you think. Enlarge our hearts to love others as you love. Open our arms to embrace the world for your sake. Open our hands to give as you give. Guide our feet to walk gently in your world. O God, inspire our lives to relate to you through worship.

The Old Testament Lesson   Genesis 2:18-24
*Hymn   "Christian Hearts, in Love United"   Cassell
The New Testament Lesson   Ephesians 5:21-33

We Seek Help for Hurting Marriages

The Pastoral Prayer
     O God, we thank you for creating us to be able to relate to you and to others. Some of the greatest joys we have experienced have come through our relationships. We confess to you that we have not always been faithful to you and others in our relationships. We have been selfish, deceptive, dishonest, and hurtful. Please hear our confessions, forgive us our sins, and cleanse our lives.
     Many of us are married. Our marriages are significant, valuable relationships. We are grateful for spouses who love and care for us and who seek to support us on various levels of our lives. Some of us are in marriages that are in trouble. As spouses we are having difficulty communicating and understanding each other. We seem to be in different worlds. We need help to bridge that gulf that has developed between us. Some of us have been married, but the marriage did not work for many reasons. We know the pain of broken relationships. We know the hurt of unresolved conflict. We know the agony of wanting this struggle behind us, but too often the unresolved feelings get churned up again. God, please help us to admit our need for help and to seek the best help possible for our emotional and spiritual well-being.
     God, whatever relationships we are in, help us to learn better how to love you and to love others. Instruct us in ways to have close encounters with you and others that will enrich our lives and enable us to be better disciples of Christ. We offer our prayer with the desire to pray and live our lives as Jesus prayed and lived his. Amen.

The Choral Worship   Lyndell Leatherman
            "Gracious Spirit, Dwell with Me"

The Sermon   "Marriage Mates"

Over a quarter of a century ago I walked into a church sanctuary to do what I had wanted to do for a long time: marry Peggy Griesser. Just as I arrived at my place in front of the congregation, I felt a nervousness in my stomach and my knees like I had never known! Why? What was happening to me? This was a major event. This was a life-changing event! I would never again be as I had been, single, only myself to think about and consider. I wanted to marry Peggy, but I was scared.

For more than twenty-five years Peggy and I have been on the peaks and in the pits of marriage together. Part of the reason we have been on the peaks is because Peggy is such a joy to live with, and part of the reason is because I'm a delightful person to be around. Part of the reason we have been in the pits together is because Peggy is so hard to live with, and part of the reason is because I'm such a pain to live with.

Nobody told us that marriage would be easy. Also, nobody told us marriage would be as difficult as it has been and require the intense amount of hard work that is necessary to keep a relationship alive and well. In the movie *Yentel* a reference is made to marriage and the struggles that are part of it by this statement: "This is not in any book."

What I have discovered about our marriage I have also observed in other marriages, some that were healthy and well and some that were in great difficulty. In marriages that last and in which the spouses grow and relate healthily, spouses discover that they relate to each other as playmates, stalemates, and soulmates. Negotiating the transitions from playmates to stalemates to soulmates often is a difficult, stormy journey.

Often when I meet with a couple to begin planning with them for their wedding, they are relating as Mr. and Mrs. Nice Fianceé. Many couples are united in wedlock in a rosy fog of optimism. Blinded to the shortcomings, each sees only the other's good points. But as the excitement of the new marriage wears off, sometime during the first year and more often during the first six months, they drift to the opposite extreme and view these same traits as faults. Someone has called this "reverse reasoning," giving the following examples: "She married him because he was 'strong and masculine'; she divorced him because he was a very 'dominating male.' He married her because she was so 'fragile and petite'; he divorced her because she was so 'weak and helpless.' She chose him because 'he knew how to provide a good living'; she left him because 'all he thought about was the business.' He married her because she was 'steady and sensible'; he divorced her because she was 'boring and dull.' "

You probably heard about the newlyweds. On their honeymoon, the groom took his bride by the hand and said, "Now that we're married, dear, I hope you won't mind if I mention a few little defects that I've noticed about you." "Not at all," the bride replied with a deceptive sweetness. "It was those little defects that kept me from getting a better husband."

All of this is to say that marriage is in, but many people do not know what they are in for when they marry. Marriage is a joyful, exciting, invigorating, aggravating, frustrating, challenging relationship.

Playmates: Early in the relationship, and usually for at least the first few months of marriage, a couple is in the playmate stage. They are excited to be in each other's presence. They delight in the newness of the relationship. The hassle and tension of wedding planning is behind them. The aggravation and pressure of dealing with their families' expectations is behind them, so they think. Just wait until the first major holiday! But for now they can just enjoy each other. They delight in getting to know each other better. They have fun being playful and silly. They delight in being sexual and sensual with each other. They also may have a tendency to treat each other as objects rather than as persons. However, for awhile, each enjoys being the object of so much of another person's attention that no objection is raised about the way they are treating and relating to each other. After all, having little or no experience in marriage and certainly no education and training in marriage, the couple concludes, this must be the way marriage is supposed to be.

Sometime during the first twelve months of marriage, all this playfulness hits the skids. It comes with the first major conflict, argument, or fight. Regardless of what you call it, it is a head-on confrontation that causes both spouses to say to themselves and eventually to each other, "I didn't know marriage was going to be like this. I never expected to feel so angry at someone that I thought I loved so deeply." More marriages end during the first year than any other year of marriage. The unusual couple is able to keep the playful, sexual, sensual dimension alive. More often the tension which comes with the disagreements and conflicts becomes entwined in the playful dimensions. An argument over an issue too easily drifts into personal attacks. Having been so heroic in the first months of marriage not to say anything about the little things that irritated each about the other, eventually, the pressure causes one spouse to blurt out an unrequested assessment of the other. Before either realizes what has happened, both have unloaded months of stored feelings that have begun to sour. These feelings often have become sickening colors inside the spouses. They are yellow with jealousy, green with envy, red with anger.

Often children have more insight into life and relationships than any of us recognize. A pastor was visiting the fourth-grade Sunday school class to talk about marriage as part of the lesson. He asked the class, "What does God say about marriage?" Immediately, one boy replied, "Father, forgive them, for they know not what they do." That is true. Most of the people who get married do not know what they are doing or what is going to be required of them in and through the relationship.

Stalemates: After the explosion, there is emotional debris all over the marriage. The couple are like two boxers who have gone to their respective corners of the ring. They stalk each other, and their communication is at a standstill. They have entered the stalemate stage. The playmate stage will never be the same. There was an innocence during that stage of the relationship that will never be again. This doesn't mean the playfulness cannot return, but it will be different, and it can be better, but the relationship now is forever altered. Only couples seriously committed to each other and to working on their relationship regain the more playful dimensions of their relationship.

It happened in the city of Detroit, Michigan. After applying for a marriage license, a man failed to reappear at the county clerk's office until eleven years later to claim the important document. When asked why he and his fiancee had waited so long to get married, he explained, "We had a few disagreements about details."

Few people who enter marriage are willing to admit that anger will be a part of their relationship. Even those who are willing half-heartedly to acknowledge that there may be some anger sometime in their relationship do not anticipate the intensity with which the volcano of emotion erupts in marriage. A major part of the struggle is how can people have such strong, negative feelings toward the ones with whom they relate daily in the most intimate way. How can they go on relating? Often they don't. They come to a stalemate. Their anger gets frozen; or it continues in a slow boil eventually burning both of them; or it builds up pressure and spews out inappropriately and destructively at home, work, and onto friends.

Part of the stalemate stage is that one or both spouses decide to keep their distance from each other and continue in their relationship. The issue or subject that was the source of their major disagreement becomes off limits. The pain was so surprising or so intense or both that they decide not to deal with that issue again. Most often this decision is not talked about openly. If it were, there probably wouldn't be a stalemate. Rather, the decision is made subconsciously; or if it is a conscious decision, it is made non verbally. A pattern is beginning to be established by this couple as to how they are going to deal with disagreements, conflict, and anger. Their pattern is going to lead to more distance, and their relationship will become stale. If the relationship remains stale too long, it dries up and dies.

J. Allen Petersen commented, "I do not know whether or not your marriage was made in heaven, but I do know that all the maintenance work is done on earth." Some of the hardest, most intense work anybody ever does is the working through a marriage stalemate. It requires a deep, abiding commitment to the relationship. When I talk with a couple who are planning to marry, I asked them, "Why do you want to get married?" Invariably, they answer, "Because we love each other." And I respond, "But why do you want to get married?"

My point is that Peggy and I have already celebrated our silver wedding anniversary, and we are still married because of our commitment to each other. There have been times, especially when we have been in the pits of a stalemate, when we did not love each other—that is, we didn't feel romantic warmth toward each other. No two emotions can occupy the same person at the same time. I cannot feel love and anger for Peggy at the same time. Those feelings may chase each other through my life. But I do have a deep, abiding commitment to Peggy for better or for worse. As one man said after forty years of marriage, "When we got married forty years ago, I didn't know the better could be so good and the worse could be so bad." *There* is a man who had worked through some stalemates with his wife.

Three components are essential for a couple to work through the stalemate stage of marriage in order to be soulmates and have a growing, enriching, and enlivening relationship. The man and woman must leave their parents. They must cleave to each other. And their commitment is lifelong. Undergirding all of these components is the vital principle of mutual submission.

We bristle at the word submit. We interpret submit to mean giving in, kowtowing, chaffing, and abiding by the will and desire of another person that is in conflict with mine. When Paul writes, "Wives, submit yourselves to your husbands," we hear nothing new or insightful. When the Bible was written, women were seen as subservient to their husbands. Many have continued the chain-of-command view that women are to be in chains and men are to be in command. This can be supported only by ripping verse 22 out of its context and paying no attention to what precedes and follows it.

The surprise is in verse 25 when husbands are instructed to love their wives. Until then, love had not been considered an ingredient in marriage. Occasionally, through the years some husbands may have developed love for their wives, but no one previously had considered love to be necessary or important. Paul must have thought that men needed more instruction in marriage than women because he has a lot more to say about husbands loving their wives than about wives submitting themselves to their husbands. Husbands are to love their wives as Christ loved the church. They are to give themselves in complete, sacrificial, selfless love to their wives. Paul said nothing about wives loving their husbands. Does this mean they were not to love them?

Notice that all of this follows the statement, "Submit yourselves to one another because of your reverence for Christ" (v. 21). Mutual submission is the guiding principle. This is not submission of a lowly woman lorded over by a powerful man. Too many have used this scripture to justify husbands' exploitation of their wives. That is offensive and sinful. The emphasis here is mutual submission. Husbands and wives are to be submissive to each other and to love each other and give themselves to and for one another as Christ gave himself for the church.

Soulmates: Living the principle of mutual loving submission is a process of growth in relationship. The process has three ingredients: The couple must leave their parents, join themselves to each other to become one, and commit themselves to a life-long journey together. Failure to mix any one of these ingredients into the marriage results in failure of the relationship to develop mutual loving submission.

The verse about leaving parents that Paul quotes does not say that a woman must leave her father and mother. Perhaps the reason is because it was understood that she would leave her parents. In the biblical culture, marriages were arranged, usually by fathers, and wives left their parents' homes and joined their husbands' clans. The instruction to husbands to leave their mothers and fathers was a word of healthy advice and a suggestion for husbands to do what the wives were doing: leave their parents.

The two, husband and wife, are to become one. This cannot occur without accomplishing the first. Cleaving follows leaving. The two becoming one is an involved process of sharing, giving, receiving, caring, and loving. Husband and wife complement each other and become one as they mutually submit themselves to each other.

To leave and to cleave calls for life-long commitment and results in spouses becoming soulmates. A soulmate is someone who is constantly on the same wave length as you. A soulmate is one who innately understands your struggles and celebrations, who will confront and challenge you, confident the bond of friendship not only will survive the stress of the challenge but also will be strengthened as a result. Understanding this must have been what encouraged Montaigne to write,

> We need very strong ears to hear ourselves judged frankly; and because there are few who can endure frank criticism without being stung by it, those who venture to criticize us perform a remarkable act of friendship; for to undertake to wound and offend a man for his own good is to have a healthy love for him.[1]

Couples remain with each other for better or for worse because they are committed to their relationship. Their marriage is enriched and enlivened when they respect each other. A man had been married to the same woman for over forty years. They had many differences in their personalities and strong differences in their religious and political philosophies, but their marriage obviously was a good one. He was asked what was their secret. He replied, "Alma and I have always had a healthy respect for each other." Mutual submission leads to mutual respect and vice versa.

We often have emphasized the marriage ingredient "til death do us part" but neglected leaving and cleaving. The principle of mutual submission in marriage calls for a healthy emphasis on all three ingredients. A marriage is in trouble when one ingredient is omitted, and if the couple does not include all three ingredients, the marriage will die or may never have been born. Mutual submission in marriage calls for leaving, cleaving, and committing.

Here is a recipe that will help mates become soulmates. Each day spouses should serve each other a slice of happiness cake prepared according to the following recipe:

> 4 cups of love, 3 cups of understanding, 4 tablespoons of thoughtfulness, add 3 teaspoons of helpfulness. Sift these together thoroughly, add appropriate amounts of work and play, season with security and mutual planning, and then place in a well-greased pan with a sense of humor. When the cake is done, top it with a thick coating of true spiritually and serve on a platter of friendliness garnished with smiles.

Robert Fulghum, a minister, has observed,

> I always tell couples to pay more attention to what has gone on in their talking time before the big day. . . . When couples come to me for a second marriage, they have always spent most of their time and energy on that talking time and are a lot less concerned about the big day than they were the first time. They know that companionship in the kitchen around suppertime is vastly more important than the color of the bridesmaids' dresses. They know that good company and friendship count for more than good looks. And they know that marrying a frog is fine if you really like the frog a whole lot and don't expect princely transformations. (It's also what you know if the first marriage worked and you are about five years into it and plan to stay.) It's not as romantic the second time, but it's not without love. The love tends to be richer, deeper, wiser this time.[2]

Marrying for lust, or money, or social status, or even love is usually trouble. The point is that marriage is a maze into which we wander—a maze that is best got through with a great companion—like a toad that sings while he washes dishes, for example, or a beautiful woman who makes a toad feel like a prince when she holds his hand. That's the kind of fairy tale you can believe in.[3]

For over twenty-five years Peggy and I have been on the peaks and in the pits of marriage together. I don't think our experience of the joys and struggles of marriage are that different than yours. It may be our nature to reflect a bit more about marriage than some spouses, but perhaps the reflection helps identify some ways spouses can improve their relationships. Every marriage seems to function in at least three stages: playmates, stalemates, and soulmates. A couple doesn't move through one stage into another never to return. I am suggesting these three stages as a way to identify what is happening in your marriage and what you can do to make your marriage better.

The Invitation to Discipleship
*The Hymn of Commitment   Morecambe
        "Spirit of God, Descend upon My Heart"

*The Offertory Sentences
    Out of the bounty and generosity of God we have richly received gifts of friendship, love and care. Now, let us bring our tithes and offerings, generously giving in proportion as we have received.

The Offertory   "I Am Resolved"   Arr. Bill Littleton
Receiving the Tithes and Offerings
The Presentation of New Members

We Depart to Improve Our Marriages

*The Benediction
    Now, may the God who created us for relationships guide us in our relating to God and to one another as we go from this place. May our lives be enriched by close encounters of the loving kind. Amen.

The Organ Postlude
*Congregation Standing

Notes

[1]Mortimer J. Adler and Charles Van Doren, eds. Quoted from *Essays*, III, 13, "Of Experience," in *Great Treasury of Western Thought* (New York: R. R. Bowker, Co., 1977) 240.
    [2]Robert Fulghum, *It Was on Fire When I Lay down on It* (New York: Villard Books, 1989) 147.
    [3]Ibid., 151.

Chapter 8

The Parenting Challenge

One of the most important jobs in the world for which people are the least prepared is parenting. We seem to think if people have the genes and the hormones necessary to birth a child, they have all they need to be parents. A congregation, through worship, can communicate both the importance of the parenting task, the value of children, and the necessity that the church be a safe haven for children where they will be loved, nurtured, and nourished.

The needs of parents of a newborn or of an adopted child are legion. All of them cannot be addressed in one worship service or even in a series of worship services. A worship service, however, focusing on the significance of the arrival of a child, the beginning of the parenting process, and the offering of support, encouragement, and resources of the congregation to the parents and the child convey to all involved that the church can be a significant place. This approach helps model for parishioners healthy care and sensitivity to the needs of children and their parents. Just as Jesus urged his disciples to permit the children to come to him, so we can encourage parents to bring their children to the church where the joys and struggles of life can be faced and shared with the faith community.

The arrival of a child is a major intersection in life for a family, whether that be a single-parent family or a two-parent family with siblings already present. People feel vulnerable at this intersection in their lives. Which way do they go? What do they need to do? How can they provide the best for their new child? What does the child need? How can they possibly have the energy necessary to cope with the demands this new person makes on them?

The intersection of the arrival of a child is a major crisis in life. In one Chinese dialect, two characters are used to form the word crisis. One character means danger, and the other means opportunity. A crisis is a dangerous opportunity. They may not have used the words, but all parents have had the frightening feeling that the birth or adoption of a child was a dangerous opportunity. A crisis also is anything that causes a person, a family, or a group of people to alter their regular, normal schedule and routine of life. If anybody can force people to alter their normal routine, the arrival of a child into a family constellation can do it. An infant can do it more quickly and with greater insistence than anyone I know.

Infants come into the world asking trust and security questions. As the church is able to help parents develop security and trust in their relationships, these basic questions will be answered positively by infants as they seek and search: (1) When I'm hungry will I be fed? (2) When I'm soiled and dirty, will I be cleaned and changed? (3) When I'm frightened will I be held and comforted, or will I be abandoned?

Parents need the support of knowing that it is natural to have a variety of feelings and attitudes about being responsible for an infant. Anticipating and preparing for the birth of a child, giving birth, and adjusting to the presence of an infant is an exhilarating, joyful, exciting, difficult, draining, straining, exasperating experience. The church through worship can help new parents negotiate this intersection by offering support and encouragement to them as they deal with the myriad of feelings that arise prior to, during, and soon after the birth of a child.

There is a long history of the community of faith supporting people in their parenting journey. The history is just as long of people seeing worship as an important way to express gratitude for the gift of new life and to dedicate themselves to the task of providing the nourishment and nurture that children need for their growth and development.

Biblical Illustrations of Parenting

An excellent illustration of parenting in scripture is found in Luke's account of the first days of Jesus' life. Apparent in the second chapter of Luke is the importance of the Jewish faith community to Joseph and Mary as they journey through the intersection of the birth of Jesus. Behind the approach of Joseph and Mary were the instructions, ceremonies, and traditions of the Hebrew people. Most of those ceremonies and instructions are recorded in Leviticus.

In the early development of the church January 1 came to represent the day that Jesus was circumcised and officially given his name. Luke wrote, "A week later, when the time came for the baby to be circumcised, he was named Jesus," (Luke 2: 21 TEV). By the New Testament time, the circumcision of a male child and the giving of his name were both done on the eighth day of his life. At least by the time John the Baptist and Jesus were born, it had become customary to name the male children on the eighth day at the time of their circumcision. Counting December 25 as the first day, then January 1 came to be celebrated in the early church as the day when Jesus was circumcised and officially given his name.

In addition to circumcision, two other religious rites were part of the guidelines and instruction of Judaism to which Joseph and Mary sought to be faithful as parents of a newborn child. These were the rite of purification and the rite of the firstborn. Long before the birth of Jesus, these two rites had become blended into one or at least had come to be performed at the same time. These rites did not have to be performed in the temple, but it was an appropriate place for them to occur. Since Jesus was born in Bethlehem, his circumcision and naming probably took place there.

Luke specifically stated, however, that the rites of purification and the firstborn took place in the temple in Jerusalem. In practically every age and culture, childbirth has been filled with mystery and wonder. Knowing all of the facts and details about conception, pregnancy, and birth has not diminished the mystery and wonder of childbirth in our generation.

Childbirth has carried mystery and meaning, wonder and woe, awe and fear for people through the generations of humankind. In Israel and other ancient lands, childbirth was marked with special ceremonies, denoting it as a time when the presence of God was closely felt. The birth of a child was an occasion for rejoicing as well as a particular time for fear and anxiety.

Joseph and Mary went to the temple at the appointed time for the ceremony of purification. An offering of a turtledove or a pigeon was given as an expression of thanks to God for the safe journey made through childbirth and the return to the regular routine of life (Leviticus 12: 1-8).

The third Hebrew tradition that Joseph and Mary kept was the rite of the first-born son. Early in Israel's existence there developed a custom of offering the first born animals as sacrifices to God. Later the first born animals were given as offerings to God and then to the priests as part of their livelihood. Dedicating or consecrating the firstborn to God grew out of the idea that God claimed ownership of everything, and the firstborn symbolized all that followed.

The Service of Worship

The following service serves as the biblical background and theological underpinnings of a worship service that celebrates the birth of a child. The service is designed with input from the parents of the child (children) who are dedicating themselves to rear the child (children), with the support of the church. The litany of dedication, for example, can be written with the assistance of the parents so that much of the wording is theirs. This adds to the meaning of the service for the family (families) involved as well as for the congregation.

The infant(s) is presented to the congregation during the worship service, and the parents express their commitment to participate actively in the life of the church with their child (children). A service like this can be conducted each time there is a newborn in the congregation. It can be conducted at a special time in which the congregation is invited to participate with the family in this important worship experience, or at the usual time the congregation worships, or a service like this can be conducted once or twice each year as the regular worship service for the congregation.

All families with newborns can participate in developing the litany of commitment and in standing before the congregation to present their children to God and the congregation and to dedicate themselves to be actively involved in partnership with the congregation in the rearing of their children.

Celebrating the Gift of a Child
A Service of Christian Worship

The Organ Prelude
The Chiming of the Hour

Guide Children to Discover Their Direction in Life

The Responsive Call to Worship
Pastor: We have gathered to worship God today as is our custom each week.

People: **We are delighted to gather as a family of faith to worship God together.**

Pastor: As a family of faith we offer our support and care to one another, especially during important intersections and changes that occur in people's lives.

People: **One major intersection is the birth of a child.**

Pastor: As a part of our worship focus we are celebrating with (parents) in the birth 6 _____. As we worship together today, let us celebrate with (parents) on the birth of _____. Let us join them in giving thanks to God for the gift of _____ to them.

People: **And let us offer our prayers for them and our care and support to them in their journey.**

Pastor: We have gathered to worship God today.

People: **We are delighted to worship as a family of faith and through our worship of God to offer support and love for parents and children as they grow in faith together.**

*The Hymn   "O God in Heaven, Whose Loving Plan"   St. Petersburg
*The Invocation
The Welcome

And as They Grow Older

*The Hymn   "O God, Who to a Loyal Home"   Xavier
The Old Testament Lesson   1 Samuel 1:21-28
The Solo   "Because He Lives"   Gaither
The New Testament Lesson   Luke 2:21-38
The Pastoral Prayer

They Will Know the Path that Is for Them

The Anthem   "Gracious Spirit, Dwell with Me"   K. Lee Scott

The Sermon   "Birth: Life's First Intersection"

The Gospel stories begin with a baby, the baby Jesus who is a sign of God's grace and presence. Not just the baby Jesus, but every baby is a sign of God with us in the flesh. One of the great blessings of life is to be the parent of a child. One of the great burdens of life is to be the parent of a child. Perhaps no blessing has greater burden than the gift of a child. Soon after the birth or the adoption of a child is an excellent time for the parents and congregation to give thanks to God for the gift of a child and to ask God's guidance and strength in providing nurture and care for the child.

We are joining with (parents) to celebrate the gift of _____ to their lives and to ours. This service is our way of supporting (parents) in the vocation of parenthood and our way as a congregation to commit ourselves not only to support and care for _____ but also our commitment to provide nurture, support, and encouragement to (parents) as parents.

One of the first tasks that parents of newborn infants have is to name the child. In our culture if parents don't have a name by the second day, the hospital staff gets nervous. Parents had better not even think of leaving the hospital with their baby unnamed. What if parents told the staff they were not going to name their child until s/he was eight days old? Panic!

Well, this is exactly what Joseph and Mary did. Of course there was no attending obstetrician or nurse standing around the stable telling them they couldn't leave until they gave that boy a name. Besides it was part of their religious custom to have a son circumcised and give him his name on the eighth day. Normally, circumcision and naming of a child occurred in the home because the mother was considered ceremonially unclean and could not participate in any activities at the place of worship. Reading some of the religious rules recorded in Leviticus jolt us and raise questions about their meaning and purpose. The Old Testament lesson from Leviticus tells us that the ancient Jews had a widespread preference for sons and regarded girls as inferior.

Throughout human history childbirth has been filled with mystery and wonder. Even though we know and understand so much about pregnancy and birth today—we are able to know the sexual identification of an infant before it is born, and can determine its approximate weight—childbirth still contains mystery and wonder. The mystery and wonder are the result of the arrival of new life and the result of mother and infant being at great risk at the time of the birth of a child. In the ancient world, and in many parts of the world, including Washington, D.C., the infant mortality rate is extremely high. The ancients realized that the mother and child should be properly protected. The ceremony of circumcision and naming were partly for the protection of the mother and child.

The naming of the child also was a means of giving thanks to God for the gift of life. Joseph and Mary wanted to link Jesus' life with all the rich inheritance of Israel. Every religious rite and ceremony originally was an effort to express a spiritual purpose. As long as rites and ceremonies do that, there is value in continuing them.

When Joseph and Mary came to that significant moment of giving their infant a name, they chose a name that carried with it meaning. Most names have meanings that have been derived from people who have had those names and given meaning to them. Often names are words chosen from one language and transliterated into another to convey an idea or express an attitude. A prophet like Hosea gave his children some horrible names to make a point. The name, Jesus, conveyed meaning. It comes from the Hebrew Joshua which comes from a more ancient word Yehoshua which means Yahweh is salvation. Jesus was a very popular name in the first century just as there are popular names today that run in cycles. Josephus, Jewish historian, found at least nineteen people in the first century who were named Jesus. Jesus Barrabbas is an example in the New Testament. The popularity of the name may reflect the rising tide of expectation among the Jews following the Maccabean revolt.

To distinguish the Jesus we are most familiar with from others, the New Testament writers refer to him as Jesus of Nazareth, Jesus, Son of David, the Galilean, the Nazarene, or the prophet. As Christianity spread and included more and more Gentiles, the Greek-speaking Gentile church preferred titles with theological connotations. Christ, which means messiah, anointed one, became a popular name. Jesus became identified as Christ Jesus or Jesus Christ.

As the followers of Christ shifted from Judaism to the sect that eventually became known as Christians, they developed some of their own unique rites and ceremonies. Baptism was one of those, and early in Christendom infants were baptized. Most of Christendom baptizes infants today, and there is a very good thing about that. There is no confusion about who gets the credit. The baby won't remember what went on. No one will attempt to discuss what the experience meant to the infant. But it is a dramatic way of saying that salvation is something God does. The tradition of baptizing believers has at least two temptations. One is for those being baptized who may conclude that they are in the water in response to a choice they were wise enough to make. The other temptation is for the rest of us who may secretly entertain the notion that if our witness and evangelism had not been so effective, the person might not be standing there, waist deep in water. We can easily forget that faith is a gift, and it comes from God.

Not long after Jesus was named, his parents took him to the temple for the first time. He was forty days old. By this time in Judaism apparently the two ceremonies of purification and redemption of the first-born had been united. The Jews placed great emphasis on the blood of a person or an animal. Life resided in the blood for the Jews. From that emphasis has come the identification that something is the life-blood of an organization. Of course the blood supply in our bodies is essential as the transportation system for nutriments, oxygen, carbon dioxide, and disease fighters. A person is seriously ill who has a blood disease or disorder, regardless of what it is.

The loss of blood in Judaism was considered a loss of life. The mystery of life was related to blood because blood was lost during childbirth. Usually the loss of blood accompanied the death of an animal and often accompanied the death of a person. Because of this a woman was considered unclean for forty days after the birth of a son, and eighty days after the birth of a daughter. When she went to the temple for the rite of purification, she was to offer a lamb and a pigeon or two pigeons if she could not afford a lamb. These offerings served as tangible expressions of the awareness that in childbirth the life-giving forces and the life taking-forces are especially present. These gifts were expressions of thanksgiving for the gift of life.

The rite of the redemption of the first-born was a religious ceremony acknowledging that the first-born and in essence all things, belonged to God. The offering given was to acknowledge this and in a sense to ask God's permission to have the first-born, rather than to sacrifice the first-born as Israel's neighbors often did or completely surrender the first-born to God as Hannah did with Samuel.

Luke tells us about these three ceremonies in which the infant Jesus participated. All three were ways for his parents to acknowledge and act out their convictions that a child is a gift from God. The Stoics believed that a child was loaned to parents by God. Kahlil Gibran has expressed a similar idea.[1]

While Joseph, Mary, and Jesus were in the temple, Simeon came into the temple. Simeon is described as a righteous and devout man who lived in Jerusalem at this time.

There was no Jew who did not regard his kinsmen as chosen people. The Jews of the biblical centuries believed they would some day become masters of the world and lords of nations. There were various views about how this would occur. Some believed that a great champion would descend. Others were convinced that another king of David's line would rise and all the old glories would be revived. Some thought God would intervene in the world by supernatural means. There were those who were certain that by military might God would force his reign upon the world. In contrast to all of these views, there were a few people in the country known as the Quiet in the Land. These people had no dreams of violence, nor of power, nor of armies with banners; they believed in a life of prayer and quiet watchfulness until God would come. Simeon was one of these waiting for the day when God would comfort his people.

Simeon lived on the premise that he would see the anointed one of God. He was an old man, and life was running out for him. He was in the temple when the moment finally came. One look at the baby through his cataract lenses was all it took. When he caught sight of the infant in the temple, Simeon's confidence gave way to celebration. When Simeon saw Mary and Joseph's baby, he rushed over and asked if he could hold him. Before they could respond, Simeon had Jesus in his arms.

Simeon added his own words of celebration and gratitude to this gift of life that God had given.

Now, Lord, you have kept your promise, and you may let your servant go in peace. With my own eyes I have seen your salvation, which you have prepared in the presence of all peoples: a light to reveal your will to the Gentiles and bring glory to your people Israel.

All of the hope and confidence Simeon had held for years, he projected onto this tiny infant. Simeon, who had lived on his hope in God, believed that in this new generation represented in the infant Jesus, the hope to which he had clung would become a reality for all people. There had been people before Simeon who had similar feelings and who had tied their hopes to other infants, but their hopes had not come to fruition. Because Simeon's hopes came to pass, his words were remembered, told, retold, and eventually written down and passed on from generation to generation.

Although there is great personal meaning in Simeon's blessing, the universal application must not be obscured. We want to leave Jesus' birth story as a child's story. We prefer to be sentimental about the birth of Jesus. There isn't much threatening or challenging about an infant just to look at him or hold him. But consider relating to and dealing with that infant every day. Such experience is challenging and threatening. We want to stop the story of Jesus' birth with "The shepherds went back, singing praises to God for all they had heard and seen; it had been just as the angel had told them." That is the beginning, not the ending, of the story. Simeon will not let us stop there. Birth is the beginning, not the ending of parenting responsibility. This is much of the reason why the gift of a child is both blessing and burden.

Luke combined for us the celebration of the gift of life coming in the form of an infant, the gratitude that his parents expressed for this gift through the rites and ceremonies of their covenant community, and the waiting of an old man anticipating the greatness of a child. No doubt Simeon's words were remembered and their significance highlighted by the followers of Christ as they grieved his death and recalled events in his life. Perhaps it was Mary who told Luke about Simeon. Then Luke with his skill and perceptiveness artfully wove together the personal meaning and universal application of Simeon's experience and response. Pervasive in Simeon's confidence, celebration, and concern is his supportive role as servant of hope.

All of this and much more is wrapped up in a name, the name Jesus, which means God is salvation or God is deliverer. To call his name is to acknowledge that both life and salvation are gifts. They are gifts from God offered to you and me. We are free to receive or reject these gifts; and whatever our responses are, our lives will be forever altered by either our reception or our rejection of God's gifts of life and deliverance.

The last words of Simeon's thanksgiving are noteworthy: "A light to reveal your will to the Gentiles and bring glory to your people, Israel." The treasures

God gave to Israel were meant as a gift for all people. The glory of Israel was to be in making all its life a light to lighten the Gentiles. The treasure God gives to every parent, the gift of a child, is a gift of life meant for all people. Thus, Gibran's insight is on target. Children are not the property of their parents. They are gifts to be received. As they are received, thanksgiving for them is to be offered to God, and then the process of parenting begins—which is a process of giving the gift, the child, away. It is a process not of holding on, but one of letting go. Negotiating life's first intersection, the arrival of a child, is the first of many negotiations that parents must accomplish. Indeed, it is a dynamic process of learning when to hold on and when to let go in order to teach a child the direction in which the child should go. We parents and guardians and extended family members need the support and care of the church, the family of faith, to provide the help and hope we need for the care and feeding of the children who are gifts of life given to us for us to love and nurture out of dependence on us into dependence on God.

Let us pray. O God, help those of us who are parents to be sensitive to the needs of our children. Grant us the gift of discernment that we may be able to determine the ways our children should go, and guide us to help them go in those directions. Guide us as a congregation in partnership with you to be a resource to parents and children alike, helping them in their relationships, in their nurturing, and in their faith development. Amen.

The Invitation to Respond

Our worship of God often calls for various responses from us. Some of these responses are private while others are public. Parents may want to reflect on ways you may be able to help your children grow in the ways they should go. Others may respond to God's invitation to be resources and supporters of parents and their children. Still others may want to share a public faith declaration with us. Please allow the text and the music of our hymn of commitment to guide you in your reflection and your responses.

*The Hymn of Commitment   Webb
              "To Worship, Work, and Witness"

The Offertory Sentences

May the gifts we bring today reflect the gifts we have received from God. May our gifts be generous. May they be given with gratitude. May they be used to share with others the love of God which has been shared with us.

The Offertory   "O Love That Will Not Let Me Go"   St. Margaret
The Receiving of Tithes and Offerings
The Doxology

The Presentation of Tithes and Offerings
The Procession of Parents with Infant

The Introduction and Presentation of (child's name).

Nearly three thousand years ago, Hannah went to Shiloh to worship. She took her young son with her and dedicated him to God, leaving him with the prophet Eli who was to rear him and teach him the ways of God. Nearly two thousand years ago, Joseph and Mary made their way to the temple to present Jesus to the Lord and to dedicate him to God.

We are continuing that ancient tradition today as we present _____ to God. We also are continuing the ancient knowledge that the parenting challenge is more than a father and a mother can meet. The extended family and the community of faith have through the centuries offered themselves to parents to assist in nurturing and nourishing children.

I can tell you from experience that being a parent is one of the most exhilarating and exciting, frustrating and agonizing things a person can ever do. This child dedication service is a way for us as a congregation to assure (parents) that we are with them offering our love and care and support in the important and vital enterprise of rearing their children.

The Service of Infant Dedication

The Dedication of Parents

Pastor: (Parents), you have been blessed with the gift of a child. Do you promise to provide for his/her needs of food, shelter, and clothing?

Parents: We do.

Pastor: Do you promise to love, nurture, and care for _____? Do you promise to guide him/her to grow out of dependence on you and into dependence on God?

Parents: We do.

Pastor: Do you promise to involve _____ in the life of the church, introduce him/her to the family of faith, support and guide him/her in his/her faith development?

Parents: We do.

The Presentation of (child's Name).
(Pastor takes the infant in his/her arms and talks directly the child.)

Pastor: _____, you are indeed a fortunate boy/girl. Your parents love you. Your grandmother loves you. We love you. We, the church, are your extended larger family of faith. We welcome you into our lives. (The pastor holds the infant high above his/her head so the congregation can see and says the following.) Behold! A new child of God, (child's full name).

The Presentation of Certificate and Bible
(Parents with infants stand and face the congregation)

The Congregational Support

Pastor: (parents) have promised to be caring, loving parents to their son/daughter. But they cannot do it alone. They do not have the resources and energy necessary for their parenting tasks. What will you offer them?

People: **We will pray for them and their son/daughter. We offer them our love and support, our understanding and friendship.**

Pastor: We are delighted to begin knowing _____. S/he is a special child of God. What do you want her/him to know?

People: **We already are loving her/him. We welcome her/him to God's world and to this family of faith. We promise her/him that this will be a safe sanctuary where s/he always will be welcome to question, to learn, to worship, and to examine God's world. We promise to listen to her/his needs and to encourage her/him in the ways s/he should go.**

All: May (parents), (child), and we grow together in the love and care of God. May we be family and celebrate that all of us are part of the family of God.

*The Benediction

Now, may the love of God that births us, the peace of God that shapes us, and the grace of God that reforms us go with us now from this place to all the places we go and bring us together again for worship and celebration. Amen.

The Organ Postlude

A worship service designed and conducted similar to the one above can provide support and encouragement to the parents who currently are dealing with the initial impact of the parenting challenge. A service like this also can enhance the importance of the ministry of the congregation with parents who are at other stages of the parenting spectrum. It will underscore to worshipers that the church is a place to experience and offer support, encouragement, and nurture for life's journey, including the tasks both of parenting and of growing.

Note

[1]Kahlil Gibran, *The Prophet* (New York: Alfred A. Knopf, 1971) 18-19.

Chapter 9

Children and the Church

From its inception, the church has recognized that children are some of the most vulnerable people anywhere. Growing out of its Jewish roots, the church sought to care for children as Judaism had done. The first controversial issue with which the early followers of Christ were faced was the care and feeding of widows and children.

Historically, the church also has recognized the growth and development of children to be a vital part of its ministry. Throughout his ministry Jesus gave places to people who had no place. Children were one of those groups, and the Gospel writers pointed out the reprimand Jesus gave his disciples when they were prohibiting children from being with him.

Children are interested in church and how the church functions. They often have questions about what takes place in the worship service and why. Congregations can address the issues and needs of children in several ways. Parenting classes are valuable and contribute to improved understanding of children. Educational events for people who work with children are essential. The better informed a congregation is about the ages and stages of emotional, physical, and faith development of children, the better the care and nurture of children will be.

Significant in the philosophy of the church and children is the place of children in the church and the inclusion of children as contributors to the ministry of the church. Many congregations have a children's period as part of the worship service. This helps children feel included and encourages an expectation that they will receive something from the worship service. Older children, ages nine to eleven, can be encouraged to design and lead a vespers service once or twice a year. Children are creative and energetic. With helpful adult guidance and education, they will do an excellent job.

Another way of inviting children to minister and to minister to them is to design a worship service that speaks to issues related to their lives. The children can share in leading the service by reading scripture, leading prayers, and serving as offering bearers. An older children's choir can be the choir for this service. Working with the children in the planning and leading of a worship service educates children about church and worship as well as communicating to them they are important, significant people in the life of the congregation.

The following worship service is an example of this approach. This service communicates intergenerationally the importance of children to the church and in the church.

Letting the Child in Us Come to God
A Service of Christian Worship

The Chiming of the Hour
The Prelude   "Holy Manna"   More

Jesus Said to His Disciples

The Call to Worship
Leader: Come, let's worship God with excitement and enthusiasm.
Adults: There is trouble all around. We have friends who are dying. Our jobs are burdens. Why should we be excited?
Children:We can get excited because there are people who care about us. We get excited because God loves us. We get excited because Jesus wanted children around him.
Leader: Why did Jesus want children around him?
Adults: Maybe because he got tired of people like us with long faces draining his energy.
Children:Maybe because children were honest and free to say or ask anything.
Leader: Those sound like good reasons to worship God with excitement and enthusiasm.
All: That sounds good to us. Let's do it.

*Hymn   "Joyful, Joyful, We Adore Thee"   Hymn to Joy
*Invocation
The Welcome
The Old Testament Lesson   Isaiah 65:17-25
*Hymn   "Children of the   Tryggare Kan/Ingen Vara
                              Heavenly Father"

"Let the Children Come to Me"

The New Testament Lesson   Mark 10:13-16
The Pastoral Prayer and Litany for Children

The Litany   "O God of All Children"[1]

The Presentation of Bibles to First Graders

And Do Not Stop Them

The Choral Worship   David and Madeline Bridges
                "We Sing a Song of a Friend"
                Older Children's Choir

The Sermon   "Let The Children Come To Me"

We live in a troubled world. I do not belong to the Doomsdayers Club who say the world is worse than it's ever been, getting worse by the minute, and that God can't take much more before—out of anger and frustration—God will destroy the world. Sometimes we wish life were that clear and simple, but it isn't. There are dimensions of life that are unbelievably better than they have ever been. The gifts and knowledge of people in medical science have made it possible for the quantity and quality of life to be better than many of us ever imagined.

With the advancement of knowledge and technological development have come many problems. The misuse and abuse of freedom have resulted in harm and hurt coming to people. The segment of society being damaged the most seems to be the children. The maltreatment and destruction of children is evident in our nation and the world. This morning when we woke up, 100,000 children woke up homeless in this country. Every 32 seconds, about the length of time it took us to pray the litany for children, a baby is born into poverty in this country. Every 14 minutes, while we listen to about two-thirds of the sermon, a baby dies in the United States. Every 64 seconds, while we sing about two verses of a hymn, a baby is born to a teenage mother. And every 13 hours, before we go back to sleep each night, a preschooler is murdered in our country.[2]

The third weekend in October has been designated by the Children's Defense Fund as The National Observance of Children's Sabbaths. The purpose of this designation is to encourage congregations of all faiths to raise awareness, renew commitment, and stimulate long-term efforts to meet the needs of the most defenseless people in the world: children. The problems facing children are of such a magnitude that it will take all of our persistent, faithful voices and hands, working with and for children, to ensure that we leave no child behind and to enable each to develop to her or his God-given potential.

Not only are we to be concerned about children in our community but children everywhere. Our concern begins to be real here. As Reinhold Neibhur once said, "Nothing is ever real until it's local." What does it mean for us as a congregation to say we love children? If we share Isaiah's vision of a time and a world in which "no more shall there be . . . an infant that lives but a few days, or an old person who does not live out a lifetime," how must we respond? Isaiah's vision was of a new creation in which people in partnership with God make the vision a reality. One of the delightful, remarkable things Jesus said was, "Let the children come to me" (Mark 10:14). This brief command speaks volumes to us about Jesus' attitude toward children. The statement also is instructive about the attitude we are to have toward children.

Attitude: Jesus gave a place to children. It was so characteristic of Jesus to give places to people who had no place. He was tender and sensitive to those who were shut out and excluded by the customs of culture. We shutter at the news of a mother smothering her infant because he would not stop crying. We are enraged when we hear of a father beating a young child to death because the child would not do as he was told. I hope we shutter. I hope we are enraged at the maltreatment of the most defenseless members of the human family. We shutter and are enraged not only because children are defenseless but also because we who have children have known times when they so frustrated us that we knew we were capable of doing them serious harm. If that is true for us, then all the more reason do we need to work on our attitude toward children.

In the Greek and Roman cultures, the killing of children was accepted practice. Female children were considered expendable, and they often were killed. The Jewish culture had a much higher regard for children than did the Greek and Roman cultures, but definite discrepancies existed between female and male children.

As was true in other dimensions of life, however, so it was with children, Jesus raised the place of children and the consciousness of people about how they related to children to a higher level than existed. The list of people excluded and outcast in the first century is a long one: women, sinners, tax collectors, the poor, the sick, the handicapped, Gentiles, and children. As Jesus had done for all who were considered and treated as outcasts, he did for children. He gave a place to those who had no place.

Mark writes that some people brought children to Jesus. I think it is safe to assume these were parents. Certainly, these were people who knew and cared for the children they were bringing. These were not total strangers going about the village gathering up all the children they could find and taking them to Jesus.

They were taking the children to Jesus because they wanted him to lay his hands on them and pray for them.

Most parents want what is best for their children. If there is something that can be done that will help their children do well in life, most parents are eager to take the action. This is at least part of the motivating attitude of the people bringing children to Jesus.

But also, the word was out about what kind of person Jesus was. His warm, sensitive spirit and his gentle sense of humor had made him someone that people wanted to be around. His acceptance of those who had been rejected because of vocation, location, avocation, and situation made him popular. Jesus was a different kind of rabbi. And the difference was positive. The people wanted Jesus to lay his hands on their children not only because they wanted him to touch them but also because of what was conveyed by that action.

Laying on of hands has a long, rich history. Laying on of hands came to symbolize passing on blessing. Abraham laid his hands on Isaac, and this act confirmed his approval of Isaac and his appointment of him to carry on the family tradition. We are familiar with the story of Esau and Jacob and the extent that Jacob went to get the blessing of his father. Thus began a custom that has had meaning and value for centuries.

Indeed, the highest cannot be spoken. It can only be acted. The laying on of hands came to be the acting out of the blessing not only of parents to children but the acting out of the blessing, approval, acceptance of God. After all, ultimately, it is God's blessing that we desire and seek. To know that God accepts and approves of us grants us amazing internal power and authority, a strong sense of well-being and self-esteem.

Parents brought their children to Jesus because they wanted him to love them and care for them and because they wanted the assurance of God's acceptance and approval of their children. Are we that different from our first century counterparts? Are there any parents here who do not want the assurance of God's love, acceptance, and approval of their children? Isn't this part of what goes on in the lives of parents as they present their infant in a parent dedication service? In a strong, double-barrelled statement, "Let the children come to me, and do not stop them," Jesus not only conveyed his attitude about children, he also expressed affirmations of children. Jesus wanted there to be no mistake in his disciples's minds about the place he was giving to children.

Affirmations: What Jesus affirmed about children, we also can affirm. By word and deed Jesus affirmed the worth and value of children, respect for children, and he affirmed certain rights that every child has. Jesus' statements to his disciples and his actions toward the children convey the value and importance of children.

They have value and importance because they are children of God, created in the image of God. They are people of worth.

I am amazed at how many throw-away children there are in the world. Many children who run away do so because they feel they are being thrown away. Before they can actually be physically rejected, many children choose to run away and have a bit more control over the rejection process. Children are people of worth. Let us join Christ in affirming the worth and value of children by welcoming children into our lives.

Jesus respected children. That is evident by the fact he took them seriously. He took them seriously by giving time, interest, and attention to children. Children deserve our respect. Children and young people are respected when they are included in the decision-making that affects their lives. I'm continually amazed at what better ideas children and young people have about things that affect them. When we respect children and young people, we include them in the decision making and expect them to be accountable for their decisions and actions as they have every right to expect us to be accountable for ours.

Children will have no regard or respect for people who have no regard or respect for them. Indeed, one of the causes of much of the disrespect and disregard for people that we observe in our culture today can be traced to the early, formative years of people's lives. There we discover there was little concern or care demonstrated toward them. They were not respected or regarded as people of value.

It's an old story, but one worth repeating. Brooks Adams was taught to keep a journal by his father, Charles Francis Adams, the U.S. ambassador to Great Britain in Lincoln's administration. When Brooks was eight years-old, he recorded in his journal, "Went fishing with my father. The most glorious day of my life." Throughout the next forty years of his life, he never forgot that day. He made repeated reference to it in his writings. "That day influenced the entirety of my life," he later said. Brooks' father was a busy and important man. After his death, Brooks was going through his father's things and stumbled across his father's journals. He looked up the day and discovered these words, "Went fishing with Brooks. A day wasted."

Of course, it was not a waste. Even though he failed to recognize it, it was perhaps the best spent day of his life. Children spell "love" from their parents and other significant people in their lives as T-I-M-E. Jesus knew that, and he ordered his disciples to let the children come to him. We can affirm the value and importance of children by the time and undivided attention we give them.

Our respect for children also is conveyed through our enjoyment of children. Do you enjoy children? Do you like being around children? Do you enjoy having children around you? Do you know why? Do you think children are to be seen and not heard? Or do you think children are being most productive when the noise level is near overload for you? You can't fake your attitude toward children and young people. They know if you like them.

Through Jesus' words and actions he affirmed the rights of children. He affirmed the rights of children to love, care, attention, security, food, clothing, shelter, good health, and education. As a rabbi, by taking the children into his arms and blessing them, he was affirming all of these rights and was modeling for his disciples that they also were to affirm these rights.

Actions: Our attitudes and affirmations are confirmed by our actions. There are several actions we can take that communicate our love for children and young people. We can be involved with and interact with them on an individual basis. When was the last time you had a conversation with a child or a young person when you listened to that person and interacted with what the person said rather than pumping your own agenda?

Of course many of you have been involved with children and youth through your work with them in Sunday school, music, or youth activities. Others of you are educators and work with children and youth each day at school. I, for one, appreciate your commitment and involvement because of your love and care for children and young people.

Our genuine attitude toward children and young people comes through in our actions. We cannot affirm an attitude we don't have, and the clearest affirmation of an attitude is expressed through action.

It is fairly clear in Mark's Gospel what the attitude of the disciples was toward the children. As people attempted to bring children to Jesus, the disciples scolded them and apparently were turning them away. I suppose the disciples were saying something like, "He doesn't have time to kiss every baby in town." "He can't be bothered with a bunch of kids." "The man has a hectic schedule as it is. He can't be spending a lot of time and energy with children." "Give the man a break."

The action of the disciples tells us a lot about them, and what it tells us makes us uncomfortable. We don't convey our discomfort. Actually, we cover it by expressing our contempt for the disciples. How could they be so foolish as to turn away little children!

We turn children away with our actions toward them. Children may not always be able to put their feelings into words, but they certainly can read our feelings in our faces and respond to them. If they see unusual anger or disgust on our faces, they keep their distance from us. If they read joy, openness, and acceptance in our faces, they are drawn to us.

Some of us treat children with contempt. We convey we want to have nothing to do with them and really would prefer they were nowhere near us. If they are going to be in our vicinity, we want them to keep quiet and leave us alone. George McDonald used to say that no person could be a disciple of Christ if children were afraid to play near that person's door. Perhaps a good way to evaluate our discipleship is to ask three children what they think of us, how they feel about us, do they like being around us? Maybe that's too intimidating and embarrassing! Maybe that is asking for more honesty than we are willing to receive!

One of the mistakes the disciples made was they saw themselves as the guardians of Jesus' dignity and time. They sought to protect him from those who would crowd in on him. They thought they were doing him a favor. But they were so wide of the mark of Jesus' view and purpose of his life. The disciples often were obtuse to what Jesus was saying and seeking to accomplish. In Mark's account of this event he says that Jesus was indignant with his disciples. That is a strong word and the only time it is used to describe Jesus. The disciples' impatience with children is in open contrast to Jesus' openness to them. One of the first actions we can take is to be involved with and interact with children and young people.

A second thing we can do is to pray for children and young people. Growing up is fun and exciting. It is also a difficult, struggling, and aggravating time. We need to broaden our concern for children and young people beyond our own families or our own congregation. As our prayers grow more inclusive, we will discover our attitudes and actions being more inclusive. We can pray a prayer for children.[3]

The third action you can take is to be an advocate for children. Children need people who will support and encourage them, speak up and work in their behalf, and call them to accountability when that is necessary.

The problems facing children, young people, and their families in our nation are not ones that we in the religious community can or should solve by ourselves. But they are indeed crises on which Christians and all people of faith cannot turn our backs. We in the religious community have a long tradition of directly serving children and families in need, so people of faith know better than most the depth and breadth of child-suffering in our nation. Out of this experience people of faith also recognize that our compassionate service to children, young people and their families in need must be coupled with passionate work for justice, if we are to rescue children from the brutal effects of our current national child neglect.

The problems are not in some far-off place like Washington, D.C. or even Atlanta, although the problems are there. The problems are right here in Alabama. Did you know that Alabama has the lowest percentage of adults who have completed high school in the nation. Each school day an additional seventy students drop out of school in Alabama. And with the dropouts come early preg-nancies: Almost one-third of all babies born in Alabama are born to unmarried mothers. About one-fourth of Alabama households have incomes less than $10,000; the state's per capita income is not keeping pace with the national average. These poverty factors coupled with a changing economy are contributing to a decline in Alabamians' standard of living.

The A+ Research Foundation has developed fourteen principles on which to base reform in education. I commend all of these principles to you. They provide tangible ways for us to affirm the worth, value, and respect of children. They provide ample opportunities for us to take action in behalf of children. Let me just mention three that I think every member of this congregation can and should work for.

(1) We know far more than we practice about how to succeed with all students.

(2) Each student needs an advocate—one who stands up for the student when it is necessary and insists that the student meet his or her responsibility when that is required. The parent is the advocate of choice, but when a parent is not available, you and I can be advocates for those students.

(3) Eliminate health and social barriers to learning. Hungry, abused, homeless, and significantly insecure children are not going to achieve at high levels. The issues of health and well-being are central education issues. Whether you have children or not, whether your children are in public schools or not, you can be an advocate for children in our community and in our state. You can put your love for children to work by supporting education that benefits children, and working to eliminate the barriers to education, and working for the basic rights of all children.

Jesus did it, and he called his followers to do it when he said, "Let the children come to me." Jesus' attitude gave a place to children. He made space for children to be loved, accepted, and blessed. Jesus affirmed children. He affirmed their worth and value as people created in the image of God. Jesus respected children and affirmed the rights of children. Jesus' attitude and af-firmations led to actions. He was interested and involved with children. He was an advocate for children. He prayed for children. Can we do any less? Will we do as much? If we really mean it when we say we love children, then let our affirmations and actions confirm our attitude.

Prayer: O God, creator and lover of children, help us to love children. May our love for children be evident in our attitudes, our actions, and our affirmations. And may the child in us come alive and come to You where we will be accepted, loved, and blessed. Amen.

Because the Kingdom of God Belongs to Such as These

Hymn of Commitment   Converse
     "What a Friend We Have in Jesus"

The Offertory Sentences
    God has befriended us and loved us. A tangible way of sharing God's love and friendship is by giving our tithes and offerings which will be used to communicate with others that God loves them and wants to be their friend. Let's bring our offerings with joy and great expectation of their use to share God's friendship with others.

The Offertory   "Jesus, Priceless Treasure"   Johann G. Walther
                   Variation 5

Receiving the Tithes and Offerings
*The Doxology

The Presentation of New Members
*The Benediction
The Organ Postlude

*Congregation Standing

Inviting children to share in the leadership of a service such as the one above demonstrates that the church wants the children to come to the church and be an integral part of the church. Many people learn better by doing. Children will learn a great deal about worship and worth by "doing" the worship service. Adults will gain greater appreciation for children as they participate in worship where children are sharing the leadership responsibilities. This is a great way to model the truth of Jesus' words, "Let the children come to me."

Notes

[1]Marian Wright Edelman, printed in *Lydia's Cloth*, 3:5 (September/October, 1993).

[2]Information by Shannon Daley, The Children's Defense Fund, reported in *Lydia's Cloth* (July/August, 1993) 3.

[3]Ina J. Hughs, *A Prayer for Children* (New York:William Morrow & Co., Inc., 1995)

Chapter 10

Teen Time at Church

I have been a teenager. I have been the father of three teenagers and the pastor of many teenagers in the congregations I have served. This I can tell you, "I would rather see than be one." While I have heard many people wish they could be someone or something they were not or wish they could relive a portion of their lives, I have never heard anyone say, "I wish I could be a teenager again." That does not mean there is nobody who would like to be a teenager again, but it does give a clue to the difficult stage of development of adolescence. However people go through that stage, most are glad to be through it, and few, if any, want to repeat it.

Congregations have had a passion for young people. Often they have sought an additional staff member, full-time or part-time, with specific responsibilities to work with youth. Congregations have recognized the difficult stage of development and transition of adolescence. Many of the members remember what an agonizing time it was for them and some of the crazy and risky things they did. They want someone on the church staff to work with the youth, anticipating and expecting that if young people are involved in church, they will be exempt from the struggles and pressures that others experience. Of course, that is not true.

The church can help with the emotional and spiritual development of teenagers by having people lead the youth who take seriously where they are in life and their needs. Congregations really have not done a very good job of assessing and evaluating where their young people are emotionally, developmentally, and spiritually. Many have not designed ministry that accept teenagers where they are and help them to get where they need to be.

The developmental issue that permeates the adolescent years is identity. Consciously and subconsciously teenagers are asking, "Who I am?" and "Who do I want to be?" The evidence of this struggle is seen the clothes they wear, their hairstyles, and how much time they spend looking into a mirror. They are trying to see who they are and what they will look like if they become who they think they are. Much of their struggle is wrapped up in developing an identity that is different from their parents. What is aggravating is discovering characteristics they have that are just like their parents.

Having various adult role models besides their parents is extremely helpful. Here, many congregations have done an excellent job. They have found people who really loved young people, enjoyed working with them, and wanted to be involved in their lives but respected the personal space of teenagers. This often works best when the adults do not have teenagers in the group themselves. Then, the youth feel freer to share, question, and wonder about things with these adults as trust and respect develop.

A congregation demonstrates its love and appreciation for young people as it involves them in the life of the congregation. One of the mistakes often made is for a congregation to provide things for the young people rather than involving young people in ministry in and through the congregation. In addition to a youth Sunday where young people accept leadership responsibilities for the day, having a young person serve as lay worship leader periodically conveys the acceptance of young people as important to the church and the expectation that they have responsibility as well. Involvement of young people in decision making about activities and events that affect them is crucial. Involving them in other leadership positions also is important. For example, in our congregation in the last three years, we have had three staff search committees, and at least one young person has been on each of those committees.

Observers of teenagers conclude the pressures are greater on youth now than in any previous generation. The resources available to them are greater than they have ever been, and teenagers seem to be brighter than previous generations. Does all of this say that it's a trade-off? I don't know.

I know cultures and different generations within cultures have found ways through the centuries to mark the transition from adolescence into adulthood. Erik Erikson's classical work *Childhood and Society* noted this in various cultures. Many people are aware of bar mitzvah and bat mitzvah services in Judaism. Various tribes of Native Americans had rituals that marked the movement into adulthood and responsibility. The Europeans who immigrated to the new world also had some rituals. One of those was primarily for boys. When a boy was about twelve years-old, he was taught how to use a gun, given a gun, and expected to do two things with it: help provide food for the table and protect the family from attack.

As the American culture became more mobile with the development and use of the automobile, the car key became more the symbol of expanded freedom and additional responsibility. Getting a driver's license and a key to the car became the symbols of a teenager come of age. To acknowledge this important time in the lives of teenagers, I developed a rite of passage service to include as part of worship once each year. On a Sunday in late May or early June, we recognize all young people who have celebrated their sixteenth birthday during the previous year. We call each youth by name in the worship service and give each one a key ring. Then we share responsively in a rite of passage reading which is included later in this chapter in the order of worship.

In the future there may be a more accurate symbol that portrays the transition that youth are making. The more attune the church is to the changes in young people's lives and the better it seeks to mark those changes, the greater contribution the church will have in their faith development. In return, the greater appreciation and involvement young people will have in the congregation.

The following worship service is an example of an attempt to acknowledge, accept, and affirm something of what life is like for adolescents. Teenagers are more like you and me than anything I know. They are human beings. Like other human beings, teenagers need and want to be cared for and heard. A worship service such as the one I am suggesting helps to do that. Depending on the abilities of the young people in a congregation, I encourage the involvement of as many youth as possible in presenting the various elements of the worship service.

Worshiping the God Who Loves All of Us
A Service of Christian Worship

The Chiming of the Hour

Teenagers Are Expected to Resolve More Issues

The Prelude	"Prelude in C Major"	J. S. Bach
The Choral Call to Worship		John Purifoy
	"Come Before His Presence Singing"	
	Youth Choir	

*The Invocation

*Hymn   "Rejoice, Ye Pure in Heart"   Marion

During Their Teen Years

The Welcome to the Worshipers
The Rite of Passage for Sixteen-Year-Olds
     (Participants in the congregation who have become sixteen during the past year are
called forward and given a key ring. After all have received their key rings, the following
litany is spoken.)

Pastor: We acknowledge that to become sixteen is a significant milestone in our culture.
People: We celebrate with these who have arrived at this threshold.
Pastor: To be sixteen is a key that unlocks many doors.
People: There is a mixture of freedom and responsibility behind those doors.
Pastor: We celebrate with you in this new freedom.
**People: And we call you to meet the challenge of being a responsible person with
            your life; what you do with it, what you take into your life, and what comes
            out of your life.**
Pastor: And we offer our prayers for you as the world opens before you.
**People: We offer our support to undergird you as you launch out into the
            exciting unknown.**
Pastor: May the love of God and our love bring you peace, encouragement, and support
            as you journey into a portion of life that has greater freedom and expanded
            responsibility.
People: Let it be so. Amen.

*Hymn   "Pass It On"
Old Testament Lesson   Genesis 37:1-11
The Solo   "God, Our Author and Creator"   Nall Avenue
New Testament Lesson   Luke 2:41-52
The Pastoral Prayer
The Choral Worship   "Stand Firm"   Don Schlosser

The Sermon   "Knowing Who You Are"

Have you considered all the issues that teenagers face and deal with between
thirteen and twenty? They are expected to come to terms with death and dying;
sexuality; getting an education; learn to relate to people of the same and opposite
sex; decide on a vocation; learn to drive; and become responsible for themselves,
self-reliant, and independent of their parents. These are a few of the weightier
issues, not to mention the physical growth and adjustment that are involved in
these years. Add to these issues some of the individual pressures that teenagers

face. Some have to deal with parents who divorce and remarry, and some experience serious personal injuries from automobile or sports accidents. There is the pressure of peers and the fear of loneliness. Frankly, I am amazed that as many as do come through the teen years in tact. Someone has said,

> Absorbed in his own minor tribulations of coin and conquest, the adult too often forgets that youth is a jarring time, full of excruciating first experiences and full-blown tragedies. It is a pimple on the cheek which everyone will see with distaste; it is the clothes which never seem to fit a gangly body; it is the ultimate disappointment, a broken promise, by a parent. It is a training ground for adulthood, a place and time to try for independence, a place and time to try and fail and succeed.[1]

During the teen years people are expected to come to terms with more issues than any other developmental stage in their lives. Maybe this is why I have never heard anyone say, "I wish I could be a teenager again." Most people are relieved to have survived the struggles and personal conflicts that occur during those years. It is not the most popular age to want to repeat. The church is a resource center for teenagers. A congregation can provide support and encouragement for teens as they grow toward adulthood. This worship service highlights youth and is but one way to say how important teenagers are in the life of a congregation. A congregation can continue to underscore importance of young people through emphasis and involvement of young people in the various components of the congregation.

I thought if we focused our attention for a few minutes on the teenage years of a well-known biblical character, we might discover some similarities in his life to what being a teenager is like today. We can learn from him some helpful and healthy ways to deal with the changes, fun, and struggles that occur in the lives of teenagers. Exploring Joseph's teenage experience will help teenagers identify with him, and it will help others of us have a better understanding of the dynamics involved in the teen years.

The experiences, fun, and struggles of any teenager must be understood in light of what his or her family situation is like. Joseph's family made some significant contributions to Joseph and some serious mistakes with him. Jacob and Rachel were his parents. Jacob came out of a family that had played favorites. His dad had favored his twin, Esau, and his mother had favored him. Jacob had some rough experiences as a result of the favoritism and his desire to be loved and accepted by his father. But Jacob did not seem to learn much from that experience because he repeated the mistake of his parents by playing favorites with his sons. As the father of twelve sons, Jacob liked Joseph best and gladly let it be known that he favored the older son of his favorite wife. He was either oblivious or did not care what this attitude said and did to his other sons or how it affected their relationship with Joseph.

Jacob's favoritism of Joseph was seen and felt by the other sons. The most blatant illustration was the gift of the coat with long sleeves. The King James Version translates the passage as a coat of many colors. But later scholarship has discovered that the meaning of the coat description is that it was a coat of extremities, covering the extremities, a long coat with sleeves. It was not the kind of coat that one wore to do any work. By giving the coat to Joseph, Jacob was saying, "You are so special. I don't want or expect you to do any work. You just enjoy being special." Can you feel the blood boil in Joseph's brothers?

Joseph did spend time in the fields with his brothers caring for the family flocks, but he reported to daddy that his brothers were being bad. Apparently, he was the family informant. He used his specialness to set himself apart from his brothers and by giving bad reports about them, kept the focus off himself. You can imagine how his brothers felt about this tattletale brother who wore his prim-a-donna coat out to the fields, doing no work but carrying negative messages about them back to their father. They would come in for dinner. Jacob would rake them over the coals for their activities, and Joseph would grin through the whole meal.

Joseph's parents gave him an enormous sense of delight. One of the vital gifts that parents can give their children is the sense of delight in their being alive. But there is a second and equally important gift that parents need to give children, and that is the comparable gift of the sense of purpose. Joseph's parents showed delight in him but gave him no sense of purpose. The result was that Joseph had an extremely inflated opinion of his own importance. This inflated view of himself is evident in his dreams about his family relationships.

Out of his special treatment and favored position in the family he dreamed that his brothers, his mother, and his father would bow down and worship him. Joseph was worshiping himself and concluded that all those in his family would worship him. He saw life revolving around himself. What he hoped to gain by telling these two dreams to his brothers is a mystery. Was Joseph so naive as to believe that his brothers would enjoy and agree with his dreams? Was Joseph so wrapped up in his own specialness and opinion of himself that he was oblivious to the tension in the relationship with his brothers and the animosity that wearing his coat and telling his dreams evoked?

Frederick Buechner points out that every person has three tasks in life: I have a person to become, I have people to love, and I have work to do. Joseph was clear that he had a person to become, but the tasks of people to love and work to do were lost on him as a teenager. The seeds for this emotional deformity were planted by his parents who gave him a tremendous sense of delight but no sense of purpose.

During adolescence one of the vital issues that must take place is the transfer of power from parents to the teenager. This is the movement from dependence to independence that later becomes more balanced as interdependence. This phased transfer of power occurs as the teenagers separate from their parents and as they assume responsibility for their own personhood. Teenagers separate from their parents voluntarily or involuntarily. They separate emotionally and geographically. The separation enables them to compare and contrast themselves to their parents as a means of determining their own identities. If this separation does not occur their growth and development are stunted, they remain too heavily dependent upon their parents, interdependence does not occur, and movement toward adulthood is averted. Some parents get emotional payoff by having a child remain dependent on them. They may complain about the child not growing up but continue to do things that urge and encourage dependency. The parents maintain a great deal of power over the person and stifle their child's growth.

Joseph's separation from his parents and family was involuntary. His brothers were going to kill him but were persuaded by Reuben to sell him to some traders who came by. We can only speculate what would have happened to Joseph and the person he would have become if he had not separated from his parents.

Separating from parents and assuming responsibility for oneself is a gradual process. There is not a magical time, day, or age for it to occur. We who are parents would do well to parent by objectives. We need to ask often, "What do we hope to accomplish as parents, how do we achieve these goals, and what are some target dates along the way?" Erma Bombeck said that she put a sign in the room of each of her children, "Check out time is eighteen years." That may sound a bit blunt; however, if that is a clear objective and parents and child are working supportively in that direction, the bluntness is softened considerably.

Tom Harper's son completed his college education and received his degree from the University of Georgia. After graduation he returned to his parents' home in Savannah, Georgia. Tom said to him, "It is time for you to be on your own. Your mother and I have provided for you while you were growing up. We made sure that you had the opportunity for a good education. Now it's time to move on. You've got two weeks to find a job to support yourself." What Tom did was to ask something of his son. He gave him a sense of delight and a sense of purpose.

In Joseph's story, he was forced to separate from his family. He wound up as a slave in Potiphar's house and actually became the manager of Potiphar's household. Potiphar was the first person to ask something of Joseph. It was Potiphar who gave Joseph a sense of purpose. Adolescence is a stage of growth and a process of development of letting go of the fantasies that everything will happen as we want, and we come home to the way the world is.

Teenagers are concerned with what they appear to be in the eyes of others as compared with what they feel they are, and with the question of how to connect the roles and skills cultivated earlier with the occupational prototypes of the day. As they search for a new sense of continuity and sameness, they usually refight many of the battles of earlier years. They may artificially appoint perfectly well-meaning people to play the roles of adversaries. Young people can be remarkably clannish, cruel in their exclusion of all those who are "different" in background, tastes, dress, and religious beliefs. This intolerance usually is a defense against a sense of identity confusion.

Each generation has a way of laying claim to its own experience. Teenagers of today readily tell about sexual matters and have a strong awareness of AIDS as a possible danger to hundreds of thousands of Americans. They note news stories about rising incidence of teenage pregnancy and of suicide pacts having been made and carried out. They are aware of the destructiveness of using drugs. They also have a tendency to respond like adults: none of these destructive things will happen to them. Although they are destructive things, they are convinced that they are things that happen only to other people.

The less input that teenagers have about decisions that affect their lives, the more resistant, resentful, and rebellious they will be. Preparing people to assume responsibility for their lives is a gradual process. They are greatly underprepared if someone makes all their decisions for them until they are seventeen of eighteen and then says, "Okay, you're on your own."

Teenagers get a lot of negative publicity these days. I guess every generation of teens gets more than its share of negative publicity. There are many reasons. Some teenagers do some terrible things. There are those who will stereotype all teenagers as the same. People who experience oppression and abuse eventually erupt. During a time of identity struggle is often when the eruption occurs. On the other hand, a lot of young people journey through the teen years with struggle, agony, stress, and pressure but manage very well. Nothing much is said about that. Perhaps it is because for every negative experience it takes three positive experiences, each equivalent to the negative one, to negate the negative one.

One of the mistakes often made is that decisions are made and opinions given about teenagers without ever hearing from teenagers. What do teenagers think about their lives and their needs? Listen to what some teenagers say about themselves and the perspective that others have of them. One sixteen year old said, "I think a lot of people who write about teenagers exaggerate. They make us sound like freaks, or they describe us as without morals. They say rock music is full of violence; and to listen to them, we're doing nothing but making love—morning, noon, and midnight."[2]

A seventeen-year-old young man questioned, "Did we invent war and crookedness and corruption? All this sleaze today—look where it's coming from. The ones who will tell you about those noisy teenagers and their music and their sex and their drugs, they're the ones you see in the papers, with all their lies and crimes being reported. [There are] a lot of hypocrites around"[3]

J. D. Salinger noted the marvelous capacity some young people have for righteous indignation—often directed at windbag politicians, professors, and preachers. Young people do have struggles and problems. Often what they see so clearly in others are the very issues and struggles that are going on within them. They resist looking at themselves just as many who have passed through the travail of adolescence resist looking at ourselves. One young man called for us to stop and look at people our own age. Robert Coles has remarked,

> A few kids take their lives, and everyone says teenagers are really in trouble—look at those suicide cases, they're an epidemic. But hundreds, maybe thousands of people take their lives every year. My dad is a doctor, and he says more doctors take their lives than do lots of other kinds of people; and doctors get into bad drug habits more than others. Why? Should we all be asking what is wrong with those doctors? Is it the music they listen to? Their sex lives? If one teenager commits suicide, you pick up the paper and read we're all in trouble, and we're all headed down the tubes because it's our terrible 'teenage culture,' they'll say and our wild sex habits, they'll add.[4]

All of us have room for improvement in our lives—adults, teenagers, children. It is easier, safer, and less painful to see what is wrong with others, what changes they need to make, to condemn them for their wrongs and mistakes than it is to examine ourselves. Jesus' instruction was that before we try to get the splinter out of another person's eye, we need to get the two-by-four out of our own. Michael Jackson expresses a similar idea in one of his songs,

> I'm startin' with the man in the mirror,
> I'm gonna make him change his ways.
> Through all emotion it doesn't fend any clearer,
> If you want to make the world a better place,
> Take a look at yourself and make that change,
> Startin' with the man in the mirror.

Joseph was not well prepared for life because the special, favored treatment he received caused him to see himself as one of exaggerated importance. When this perspective persists unchallenged, the person does not make commitments and feels the world owes him a living.

The fortunate teenagers in this world are those whose parents or other significant adults in their lives share their continuous affection and concern, their wish to uphold certain ethical principles and then live them, rather than merely mouthing them. These are the youth who are able to handle some of the non-sense and craziness the last part of the twentieth century offers us. Thomas Fry observed, "I have never talked with a young person who has not wished to be accepted and loved by his or her parents. They all need love and acceptance at home as much as in the group."[5]

Teenagers need emotional, moral support. They need the attentive, con-tinuing concern of others. They need a community of caring individuals who will make up for what they may have lacked growing up. The church can be a resource center for emotional, moral, and faith development. We want these teenagers and every teenager in our community to know that we know that being a teenager is both fun and frustrating. We desire to be their friends and to travel with them all the way through adolescence into adulthood because they are persons to become, they have people to love, and they have work to do.

Than During Any Other Stage in Their Lives

Hymn of Commitment	"Here Is My Life"	Mission 70
The Offertory Sentences		
The Offertory	"Amazing Grace"	Arr. Harold Waters
Receiving the Tithes and Offerings		
*The Doxology		
The Presentation of New Members		
*The Benediction		
The Organ Postlude	"Arise, O Youth of God"	Leavell
*Congregation Standing		

Although a service such as this focuses on one age group, in this case teenagers, it is intergenerational in application because it calls for all people who know teenagers to be sensitive, caring, and understanding of them. It calls for the church to nurture, nourish, and help people navigate the stormy waters of adolescence. Focusing on this through worship is one way of saying that the whole church of God is to be involved and help carry out this ministry.

Notes

[1]Lloyd Cory, *Quotable Quotations* (Wheaton IL: Victor Books, 1985) 455.
[2]Robert Coles, "Adolescence," *Sojourners* 17:4 (April 1988):17.
[3]Ibid.
[4]Ibid.
[5]Cory, *Quotable Quotations*, 387.

Chapter 11

Divorce Happens

One of the significant changes in relationships in the latter half of the twentieth century has been the significant increase in the number of people who divorce. The reasons people divorce are varied. The contributing factors are many. More women entering the work force away from home is often blamed. More to the point is that employment for women made it possible for them to provide much of their own financial security. No longer completely dependent on husbands for financial security, women in destructive relationships refused to stay in them.

Mobility enabled people to have geographical distance from their families of origin and from their extended families. For a husband and wife whose relationship was irreparably damaged, the pressure from family members for them to stay together for the kids sake or for the family's reputation or whatever the identified reason was lessened.

The civil rights movement brought a heightened awareness of the rights of all people. Many who were in oppressive and destructive marriages began to verbalize the wrongness of those situations and stand up for their rights to be treated with respect and dignity. If their spouses would not treat them with respect and dignity, the pain was intense enough for many persons that they were willing to end the relationship.

I have suggested only a few general reasons for the increased divorce rate. The point is that people make mistakes in choosing a person to marry. Some people get married for all kinds of wrong reasons: to get away from their parents, to feel more secure, pregnancy, or because of romantic fantasy, to name a few.

The decision to divorce is not made without difficulty, struggle, pain, and questions. Divorce represents a significant loss, a feeling of failure, and is a grief experience. Someone has noted that while death cuts with a clean, sharp knife, divorce cuts with a dull, rusty knife. And the cutting, the severing of a married relationship, is painful. The church can be compassionate toward people who are divorcing or who have divorced by the attitude the congregation conveys through a variety of ministries. For years many pastors and church staff ministers have worked individually or in small groups with people whose marriages were ending. This approach needs to continue.

Congregations need to address the needs of members in the context of worship as a way of helping members know and feel the support of the congregation—the whole church—in dealing with the feelings of failure and loss from divorce. Some ministers have prepared formal services for people who are divorcing to state publicly what they are doing as a way of bringing closure to the relationship. You may want to examine some of those materials. The United Methodist Church has some materials like this. Perhaps other denominations do as well.

The following is a worship service that deals with the issues of divorce and remarriage. The purpose of this service is to offer grace to those who find themselves divorced or divorcing and help members of the congregation to be caring and compassionate toward those who are dealing with this kind of loss. Those affected by the loss includes more than the couple involved. Also affected are the parents and extended family of the couple as well as the children, if they have children. While one service cannot do everything, a service like this one can communicate an attitude of understanding, acceptance, love, care, and grace that will help all involved to know that what happens to them matters deeply to the congregation of which they are a part.

On Hearing What Jesus Said
A Service of Christian Worship

We Gather To Worship

The Prelude
The Chiming of the Hour
The Silent Preparation for Worship

The Spoken Call to Worship
Pastor: Come, let us worship God who promises to journey with us through all our experiences.
People: We come to worship God and to celebrate our relationships with God and one another.
Pastor: Our relationships hold such promise when they begin.
People: Many of them fulfill their promise, but some do not.
Pastor: We need help and hope to cope when a relationship fails.

People: **That is why we are here. We are here to worship God, to celebrate our relationships that are enriching our lives, and to seek God's help in our relationships that have failed.**

Pastor: Come, then, let us worship God who promises to journey with us through all our experiences.

*Hymn   "God Himself Is with Us"   Arnsberg

*Invocation

Make your presence known to us, O God. Circle our lives with your love. Fill our relationships with your grace. Temper our speaking with your mercy. Guide our initiatives with your peace. Cover our dreams with your hope. Renew a right spirit in us and make your presence known to us, O God.

The Welcome to the Worshipers

We Hear What Jesus Said

The Old Testament Lesson   Deuteronomy 24:1-4
*Hymn   "O God, Who to a Loyal Home"   Xavier
The New Testament Lesson   Mark 10:1-12
The Prayers
    The Silent Prayer for Ourselves
    The Pastoral Prayer for Others
    The Lord's Prayer in Unison

We Wrestle with What We Hear

The Choral Worship   Mary Kay Beall/Jay Althouse
"Someone Is There"

The Sermon   "What Jesus Said about Divorce And Remarriage"

I do not know how many people have approached me through the years and read or quoted Jesus' words, "Whoever divorces his wife and marries another commits adultery against her; and if she divorces her husband and marries another, she commits adultery" (Mark 10:11-12). Most often the person is divorced or in the process of divorcing. Then comes the agonizing question, "What does this mean?" It's another way of saying, "I wish Jesus hadn't said that." The reason I wish Jesus hadn't said that is because the statement immediately creates tension for me. On the one hand, here are Jesus' words. On the other hand, here are people I know and care about who are divorced or divorcing. How can Jesus' words and their experience and needs be reconciled?

Reading the Bible reveals that marriage and divorce evolved over the many centuries the biblical material spans. In the early days of civilization, a woman was property. A trade agreement was worked out between her father and a man who wanted/needed a woman to mother his children, take care of his tent, and cook the food. Polygamy was an accepted practice in those days. Because a woman was property, she was protected and defended by her owner. If a woman failed to do what was expected of her, her husband might become less and less interested in her safety.

It was at such a juncture that a step forward was taken in marriage regulation. Moses required that a man who wished to be rid of one who was not fulfilling her responsibility as a wife must give the woman a bill of divorcement which freed the husband of responsibility and made it possible for the woman to find a more compatible relationship. However, the bill of divorcement could only be activated by a husband. A husband could divorce his wife if she burned his food, played the part of a fool, neglected the household, or belittled her husband. The only way a wife could get a divorce was to do one or all of these things so often that her husband would be glad to be rid of her.

It was against this background of such easy divorce and such depreciation of womanhood that Jesus spoke out in clear and certain terms. In Jesus' teachings there is neither sanction for divorce nor fanatic opposition to it. (Differences of view are expressed in Matt 5:17-32; Mark 10:2-12; Luke 16:16-18.) Jesus returned plain answers to plain questions but laid down no law. Rather, he acted on grace and forgiveness of which his relationship to the woman caught in adultery is a clear, specific example. Matthew records the grounds of divorce to be sexual immorality. Jesus said that those who divorce and remarry on flimsy pretenses are violating God's law. That is all that Jesus meant. Let's face it, there are many facets of marital immorality other than sexual intercourse.

Do you know what it is like to descend into the valley of marital defeat? Many of you do. All marriages face times of sorrow and pain, but sometimes intensity of the sorrow and pain are unbelievable and unbearable. In light of what Jesus said about divorce, what should people do who find themselves in the depths of a harmful and destructive marriage relationship?

This is an issue that often is hotly debated. It was hotly debated in Jesus' time. Divorce was common practice in the Jewish culture of the Old Testament. Moses set forth some guidelines in an effort to humanize divorce (Deut 24:1-4), but even those guidelines were debated. The school of rabbis, led by Rabbi Hillel, held that a man could divorce his wife for any reason. If she burned the eggs, spilled the coffee, or if he saw another woman that pleased him more—these were sufficient grounds for divorce. The group led by Rabbi

Shammai felt that marital unfaithfulness was the only allowable grounds for a man to divorce his wife. Notice that divorce was a male prerogative only, and women had no say in the matter.[1]

It was into this debate that the Pharisees tried to draw Jesus. They asked Jesus, "Is there any time when it is possible for a man to divorce his wife?" Which side would Jesus take? Would he side with the school of Hillel or the school of Shammai? It seems Jesus was always getting questions that tried to force his hand, attempted to make him choose either this or that. Jesus had an amazing ability to find a genuine, authentic alternative. The alternative Jesus chose in response to this question was to bring them back to God's intention from the beginning with the ancient "leave and cleave" theory of marriage.

For this reason a man shall leave his father and mother and be joined to his wife, and the two shall become one. So they are no longer two but one. What, therefore, God has joined together, let no man put asunder. (Matt 19:4-6)

"Well and good," the Pharisees said, "but what about Moses' commandment regarding a certificate of divorce?" Notice Jesus' response. He said it was because of their hardness of heart that Moses allowed them to divorce their wives. Jesus was talking to men, and he said the Moses' divorce order was to protect women from hard-hearted men! It was better for a man to divorce his wife than to bash her head against a wall. Jesus opposed the divorce practices of his day for the same reason Moses first instituted a bill of divorcement—to protect the woman, who was utterly defenseless and trapped by a destructive and evil practice. The word divorce means "to throw away," and women could be thrown away by a very simple procedure. No legal charges had to be brought; it was simply a matter of handing the woman a bill of divorcement that said she was divorced for certain reasons, and those reasons could be almost anything—from speaking out of turn to kicking the dog.[2]

Jesus elevated womanhood and taught the equality of men and women in relationship to God and to each other. He set forth the ideal that marriage is between a man and a woman to work for peace, harmony, and growth for the rest of their lives. What if the relationship becomes a battleground for insult and injury? Is adultery the only insult of the marriage relationship which is intolerable enough to warrant divorce? There is no point where Jesus has been represented as being more intolerant and unreasonable than on the subject of divorce.

Jesus held up the ideal as the pattern for us in human relationships. The ideal is that we tell the truth at all times. Have we? Certainly not! Are we to go through life with a sign around our necks, "I'm a liar. You can't believe anything I say because on August 25, 1949, I lied"? By no means! Forgiveness is offered.

We can receive forgiveness and resume our attempt to maintain the ideal of truthfulness. The ideal is that marriage is a commitment for a lifetime. The fact is that some people make wrong decisions in choosing a spouse.

I never met a person who was divorcing who wasn't hurting. Even those who years earlier divorced emotionally but remained legally married for the "sake of the children," or for a hundred other reasons, hurt at the time the divorce is finalized. But those who make every effort to get their marriage to work and those who seem to make no effort experience pain when divorce occurs. Many factors contribute to the pain.

Marriage may not be what the couple had hoped. Stanley Hauerwas has argued that we always marry the wrong person. That is, we never marry the one we thought we were marrying—because marriage changes us.[3] What happens is, one day you wake up only to realize that the person next to you is not the person you committed your life to seven years ago. Of course, you aren't the same person either. Nobody ever chose to marry a workaholic, or someone addicted to drugs, or someone who gets cancer. But sometimes people wake up in marriages to discover that is the person they've got.

Whenever divorce occurs, both spouses are injured, wounded, and wronged. No marriage dies suddenly. A marriage is not healthy today and dead tomorrow. A marriage does not suffer a heart attack or stroke that kills instantly. The awareness of the death of a marriage may come suddenly, but the death of the marriage has been occurring slowly, gradually over a long period of time.

Feelings run rampant through the couples' lives when their marriage dies. The feelings of anger, hatred, guilt, pain, humiliation, and confusion chase each other through the couples' lives. The persons affected by divorce will be shocked. At times the events will seem unreal.

Emotional and physical pain are real reactions to the death of a marriage. Death cuts with a sharp, clean knife. Divorce cuts with a rusty, jagged knife. The pain is real and intense. Helen Oppenheimer describes how painful divorce can be to those involved.

> A broken marriage is a broken marriage; something that stands out as an unnatural smashing of what was built to last, a blasphemy against the unity of Christ and his church, an amputation inflicted upon a living body. . . . The bond of marriage is indeed a real bond, affecting those who are joined in it forevermore. It can never be neatly untied, only harshly severed. When this injury has happened, the practical question is how the wound can best be healed, and the temptation is always either to cover it soothingly up at grave risk of festering, or to keep it open forever warning others.[4]

Some spouses have conflict that they are unable or unwilling to resolve. Divorce occurs. Emotional separation and divorce occur long before legal divorce. Although the marriage ended years earlier, there are couples who remain legally married until one of them dies. They have been divorced emotionally for years. When we fail in marriage, the forgiveness of God is available to heal our wounds and enable us to live life with meaning, purpose, and joy just as God's forgiveness is available to renew and restore us when any other destructive action has occurred in our lives.

Jesus opposed the evil practice of throwing women away. He said that for a man to divorce his wife made her an adulteress. What he was getting at was that a woman only had one of two ways to survive if she were thrown out into the street. She could either find another man who was willing to marry her or she could become a prostitute. That is one of the reasons prostitution was tolerated in the culture of the first century. Jesus was not trying to formulate a set of binding rules to determine when divorce was allowable. Jesus' statement in Matthew 5:32 may lend support to the view of adultery as grounds for divorce, but it does not mean this is the one and only allowable basis for divorce, or even that adultery should result in divorce in every case.[5]

Jesus was not establishing rules; Jesus was striking at the spirit in which people are to relate to each other in marriage. We must seek to get at the heart of Jesus' teachings on human relationships within the context of Jesus' ministry and seek to interpret those insights in the context of our world.

This is exactly what the apostle Paul did. The Corinthian Christians posed a serious issue to Paul. Many people in Corinth had become Christians, but their spouses had remained pagans. What was their marital status? Should they dissolve their marriages? If Paul had taken Jesus' statement legalistically, he would have had to tell them that they must remain married no matter what except for adultery. But that wasn't what Paul said. He told believers to remain married wherever possible. "But if the unbelieving partner desires to separate, let it be so; in such a case the brother or sister is not bound. For God has called us to peace" (1 Cor 7:15). Paul understood that the law of love was at the heart of Jesus' instruction on marriage and divorce.

We are not given a set of rules that tell us what to do in every instance. Nothing is said in Jesus' teachings or Paul's interpretation about emotional and physical abuse, an harassing relationship, marital rape, or incest. Since nothing is said about these horrible situations, are we to tell people they must stay married unless adultery has been committed or desertion has occurred? God forbid!

While it is God's intention for marriage to be permanent, mistakes are made in deciding who and when to marry. Divorce is not something we turn to because there is trouble in marriage. Frankly, few people turn to divorce quickly and easily as a solution to marital conflict and struggles. Charles Swindoll wisely notes, "Two processes ought never be entered into prematurely: embalming and divorce."[6] Within a marriage, one spouse grows and develops and the other does not. The changes that happen within them and between them become so drastic that even with their most concerted efforts they cannot resolve their differences, offer and receive forgiveness, and be reconciled to each other. To remain married will result in one or both of them being destroyed. God does not want us throwing life away!

If marriage involves a creative, courageous, demanding, and risky act, then it contains the possibility of failure. Marriage is made for people; people are not made for marriage. People are never to be sacrificed to preserve marriage. We must not bow down to the false god of marriage. Often we in the church take the position of enforcer and punisher. Someone has done wrong. S/he needs to be punished. We punish by ostracizing, informally excommunicating, or reminding the person periodically of the mistake that has been made. The past cannot be erased, only forgiven. Even the gravest wounds can be healed.

Perhaps nowhere is Jesus' response to failure so conditioned by grace as it is in his relationship to the woman caught in adultery. Jesus said, "He who is without sin cast the first stone." According to our belief about Jesus, by his own standard, Jesus had a right to stone the woman. But he released her from penalty with the word and act of forgiveness.

Everyone of us has been affected by divorce. The inner circle as well as the concentric circles of people affected by divorce need people who will accept them and listen to them without passing judgment and often even without making comment. They need another human being to bear their burden. We cannot face this kind of trauma alone, and we should not. We need a community of support.

A couple may have been unable to accomplish what they had dreamed and intended to achieve in marriage, and they feel a sense of failure. Each feels wronged in the relationship. Having tried everything they know to do, the couple chooses divorce. In spite of the relief of tension the divorce brings, there also is the fear, "Is there life after divorce?" Too often the church has said, "No." "No" has been stated collectively and individually. At times we have concluded there are certain jobs divorced people can't have and particular social functions they cannot attend. We have practiced more rejection than redemption in our responses to people who are divorcing and already divorced.

The church can do many things for those affected by divorce. We must work out our theology of divorce. Robert Elliot has said,

> Divorce is the only major life trauma for which the church has no ritual, no rite of passage to help a person transverse the dangerous passage from one stage of life to the next, to let go of the ties to the old.[7]

One of the most significant and life-changing things we can do for people who are divorcing is to pray for them. To pray for them means we embrace them, take their pain and hurt as our own, and communicate with God about their agony. We could pray something like this:

> God, after fourteen years of marriage, _____ and _____ are calling it quits. They're cashing in their marriage chips now. When and where did they go wrong? ____ said it began years ago when she started to feel intimidated by ____. Since he hit her, she has been frightened to disagree with him. ____ says the problems began when ____ went to work two years ago. All those women at work convinced ____ how great single life is, according to ____.
>
> This marriage has been in trouble a long time. So much damage has been done that neither ____ nor ____ is willing to risk the hurt to invest in rebuilding the relationship. O God, comfort them in their hurt and their lost dreams.
>
> God, help ____ and ____ admit their marriage has ended. Protect their self-esteem from erosion by guilt and self-pity. Cleanse them and make them whole. Guide them in redirecting and rebuilding their lives. Help them to be whole persons, wholly committed to you. Amen.[8]

People make mistakes in their lives. They make wrong choices and sin. Some become drug addicts. Later they change, and we have made religious heroes out of some of them. Others commit crimes. Later they see the foolishness of their ways, repent, and live life in another direction. We forgive them and accept them.

What about the people who make a mistake in marriage? Can they forgive each other? Will we forgive them? What about those who make a mistake in the persons they choose to marry? Can they get out of those relationships and be forgiven of the marriage decisions they made. What kind of person was Christ? Did he say that because mistakes were made people had to spend the rest of their lives paying for those mistakes?

How do you cope when a marriage dies? Find someone with whom you can talk out your feelings, your grief. This is best done with a professional counselor who will take seriously the various dimensions of your life. Whatever you do, don't go it alone. A counselor will help you make progress, keep you from only going in circles, and protect you from damaging other friendships by only using them to pour out your hurt, bitterness, venom, and humiliation.

When a marriage dies, the spouses can never be the same. They are affected by this major event in their lives. As painful as the death of a marriage is, it is not the death of the people who divorced. It is essential that a couple acknowledge that their marriage has died, but they as people are still very much alive.

Divorce is the end of a marriage, but it is not the end of life or the end of the world.

But there are times, when despite all efforts, a marriage dies. Every possible effort at healing has been tried, or at least everything that both spouses are willing to try. The marriage is immersed in destruction and bitterness. In such cases, the law of love dictates there should be a divorce. When it is clear that the continuation of the marriage is substantially more destructive than a divorce, then the marriage should end. When divorce is chosen, it must not be the cruel "throwing away" that Jesus condemned. Neither spouse should be left destitute.

What about remarriage? What about Jesus' statement that "whoever marries a divorced woman commits adultery" (Mark 10:11)? What was Jesus striking at by forbidding remarriage? In a day when a man could throw away a woman on a whim, Jesus was striking at such a destructive attitude of male domination. It is worth noting that in Jesus' interaction with the Samaritan woman at the well (John 4) there is no note of condemnation in Jesus' words to the woman. She had been thrown away five times. Jesus refused to victimize the victim.

Jesus did condemn the callousness by which a man might marry, divorce, and remarry with the same ease he might buy and sell sheep and goats. In Jesus' day a divorced woman often would be treated as a "second-hand" woman, a "used" woman. Jesus spoke of remarriage as adultery not because there was anything wrong with remarriage but because there was something terribly wrong with a contemptuous attitude that looked upon a woman as second-hand or used.

What we must not do is to turn these perceptive words of Jesus about remarriage into another set of soul-killing laws. We would not consider doing that with Jesus' other sayings. If we took his word as law about eyes and hands that offend us, we would all be blind and without hands. Jesus said not to invite friends and relatives and neighbors when we give a banquet (Luke 14:12), but we wouldn't think of making that a legalistic requirement. Haven't we all had parties and those were the very people we invited?

The ideal is that when two people marry, it is to be a lifetime commitment and they work throughout their lives for their marriage to have meaning and value. But there are situations, circumstances, decisions, and difficulties that make that impossible. When the people involved would be substantially better off and the kingdom of God more effectively advanced by divorce, then the law of love indicates divorce can and should occur. When the people involved would be substantially better off and the kingdom of God more effectively advanced by remarriage, then the law of love indicates remarriage can and should occur.

The healing process is long and involved. Experiencing acceptance and forgiveness is part of the healing process. As people are healed, they are ready to resume life with meaning, purpose, and joy. Some of them will choose to remarry, and some will choose to remain single. The complexities of life call for flexibility.

Right now someone is saying, "My marriage is dying. Where is the church?" What is your answer? You are the church. Your answer may very well make the difference for this person to experience, feel, and receive the grace, love, and care of God. You may be the only Christ that a person divorcing knows.

We Respond to What We Hear

The Invitation to Respond
*Hymn of Commitment   Maryton
          "O Master, Let Me Walk with Thee"

*The Offertory Sentences
The Offertory   "O Perfect Love"   arr. Kingsmore
Receiving the Tithes and Offerings
*The Doxology
The Presentation of New Members

*The Benediction
The Postlude

Notes

[1]Richard J. Foster, *Money, Sex, and Power* (San Francisco: Harper & Row, 1985) 141.

[2]Ibid., 142.

[3]William H. Willimon, "The People We're Stuck With," *The Christian Century*, vol. 107, no. 29 (17 October 1990): 925.

[4]Helen Oppenheimer, "Is the Marriage Bond An Indissoluble Vinculum?" *Theology Today* (May 1975): 242.

[5]Ibid., 143.

[6]Charles R. Swindoll, *Strike the Original Match: Rekindling & Preserving Your Marriage Fire* (Portland OR: Multnomah Press, 1980) 136.

[7]Sam R. Norman, "Ceremony for the Divorced," *Journal of Pastoral Care*, vol. 33 (March 1979): 61.

[8]Howard W. Roberts, *Learning to Pray* (Nashville: Broadman Press, 1984) 91-92.

Chapter 12

Searching for a Community of Faith

A major impact that mobility has in our society is a sense of rootlessness. As people relocate, they must pull up roots and transplant them in a new place. Relocation is not a simple, easy process for many people. Those for whom it is fairly easy perhaps have relocated several times yet no one is exempt from the feeling of rootlessness for a period of time during the relocation process. Finding silverware in a new home becomes an adventure for several days as you keep looking in the direction of where it would be in the former kitchen and as you try to remember which drawer it is in the new kitchen.

Part of the transplanting process for many people is putting down roots in a church, a community of faith. Of course, moving to a new community is not the only motivation people have in searching for a new church home. People search for a congregation to belong to during a crisis in their lives. Although there are exceptions, this is not a panic-driven, life-threatening crisis. A crisis is any event that alters the normal routine of a person or family's life.

The alteration of routine often causes people to reflect and examine their lives and determine there are unmet needs. Many persons search for a community of faith as a place and resource to help them with their unmet needs that may be related to relocation, a job change, the birth of a child, a child beginning school, the death of a family member or friend, or a sense of a void or emptiness in life. By no means is this an exhaustive list of experiences that may precipitate in people searching for a congregation of which to be a part.

Persons who search for a church these days have a different agenda than those who searched a generation ago. Those in the next generation who search will have a different agenda than the current generation. Here are some characteristics of people who are searching for a church today. First, there is no brand name loyalty. People are not denominationally oriented. If the congregation of their childhood was Presbyterian, they have been out of church for awhile, and they begin searching for a church, they will not look for a Presbyterian church only. If the church they find turns out to be Presbyterian, that is fine, but that is not a priority. The same is true of the family who is actively involved in a Baptist congregation and moves to a new community. While the family members probably will visit some of the Baptist churches in their new community, they will not limit their search to only Baptist congregations. Denominations and denomination loyalty is on the decline in the post-modern era and may completely pass from the scene.

Many people who seek a community of faith have a cafeteria mentality regarding church. They want to participate in a congregation that provides several options. They want to be able to pick and choose the activities and events in which they will participate. The time when even a core of church members participated in nearly every activity of the church is rapidly passing. Church leaders are less willing to agree to long-term commitments such as teaching a class for a year. However, there seems to be willingness and even eagerness in some circles where members are willing to accept leadership responsibilities for a short term. Courses or seminars of four to six weeks duration are popular in many congregations both for leaders and participants.

The risk of the cafeteria approach to church is that people will choose the events and activities of which they want to be a part. They will take what they want but will not give to the congregation of their resources, time, energy, insight, expertise, or money. The drain and strain on the congregation is extensive. Another risk is for a congregation to add new items to the menu but not remove anything. Eventually, the leaders of the congregation begins to feel they are doing more and more but accomplishing less and less. It is really difficult for most con-gregations to stop any program it has ever started, although the evidence is strong that some programs have outlived their value and effectiveness.

One of my unrealistic dreams as a pastor is to have everyone in the community where I live to be a part of the congregation where I am pas-tor. I hope my recognition of this as an unrealistic ambition is a healthy sign. While some congregations advertise that they have something for everybody, I think only a mega church of several thousand members can possibly ever have a chance of providing something for everybody. To do that requires one huge cafeteria. While the mega church has not passed from the scene, there seems to be growing interest in smaller congregations where people can be involved and feel they know a large percentage of the people.

People who are searching for a church have expectations of the church they join, and congregations have expectations of members. The expectations going both ways often are not identified or verbalized, however. The clearer a congregation is about its identity, the clearer it will be about its expectations of members, and the better this will be communicated to both members and potential members.

People expect a church to meet their spiritual needs. They do not always know what those needs are, and some of the needs they have they may not see as spiritual issues. Some people may be very specific about their needs and expectations. Others may know only that they have an emptiness and a longing and are hoping the church can give comfort and encouragement. People also come with some needs they may not have yet recognized or identified.

A common need of all who search for a church is relationships. These people are seeking to continue a relationship, to develop a relationship, or to renew a relationship with God. They also are seeking relationships with fellow believers. Part of the relationship need is for people to worship God. They benefit from joining their lives together with others in the public worship of God. People also need a place where they will be challenged to think, examine their lives, assess their growth, and find ways of ministering with others.

The church can provide worship services, learning experiences, and ministry opportunities that nurture and nourish people to develop generous spirits, kind hearts, open minds, cooperative attitudes, and to become servant leaders. When the church provides these opportunities of ministry, it becomes an inviting congregation. These acts of service are attitudinal signs of an inclusive church. Other signs include (1) a building that is easily accessible to all people, information that is easily obtained and understood; (2) signs throughout the church to guide people through the building; (3) facilities that are user friendly to the newcomer and the old timer; (4) many members who are hospitable and see their ministry as a ministry of hospitality; (5) openness to all people as expressed in words and demonstrated in actions; (6) uses inclusive language in worship services, classes, and communications materials; (7) involves worshipers in the worship service through leadership and liturgy; (8) encourages people to think and examine their lives; (9) celebrates diversity, works for unity, but resists uniformity; (10) celebrates when new members become a part of the congregation and seeks to assimilate new members into the life, ministry, and leadership of the congregation.

Celebrating the presence and participation of new members is done in a variety of ways. Some congregations recognize new members on an individual basis at the time they unite with a congregation. New member sponsors are vital in some congregations. A sponsor is assigned to each new member or to all persons from a household who join the congregation. This sponsor journeys with the new member through the life and ministry of the congregation for one year. The sponsor makes sure that the new member is informed about each activity of the congregation throughout the year and that the new member is invited to all activities that are appropriate for that person. The sponsor also assists the new member in knowing about policies of the church and how decisions are made. The sponsor discovers gifts and interests of the new member and seeks to involve the new member in ways and places that enhance the gifts and spark the interests of the new member.

Many congregations on a regular basis (monthly, quarterly, semi-annually, or annually) recognize all new members as part of a worship service. A litany of promise may be shared by the congregation and the new members as a tangible means of expressing commitment. The commitment is from the congregation to the new members and from the new members to the congregation in the context that both are committing themselves in service to God. The following service is an example of what might be done to welcome new members to the congregation.

Welcoming People to the Community of Faith
A Service of Christian Worship

The Chiming of the Hour

May We Be an Inclusive People

The Organ Prelude
The Silent Preparation
The Responsive Call to Worship
Pastor: Come, let us worship God with openness and integrity.
People: We gather as a community of faith joining our lives together in worshiping God.

Pastor: We have new members who have recently become a part of our faith community.

People: We welcome them and join our lives with theirs in worshiping and serving God.

Pastor: With the stability of the old and the excitement of the new, may joy and thanksgiving ring out as we worship God together.

All: May it be so! Amen.

*Hymn   "How Firm a Foundation"   Foundation
The Welcome

Inviting All Who Will

The Offertory Sentences

    We come at the beginning of worship to bring our tithes and offerings. All that we are and have are gifts from God. We bring our offerings representing bringing ourselves to God. We offer ourselves and this service to God. May our offerings and our lives glorify God in this hour and every hour. We offer all to God in thanksgiving.

The Offertory   "Because I Have Been Given Much"   (Solo)
Receiving the Tithes and Offerings
Doxology

The Prayers
    The Silent Prayers for Ourselves
    The Pastoral Prayer for Others
    The Lord's Prayer in Unison

*Hymn   "Stir Thy Church, O God, Our Father"   Madill

The Holy Scriptures   I Corinthians 12:12-26
The Choral Worship   "We Are Many Parts"   Marty Haugen

The Sermon   "Doing Your Part"

In the Hebrew language the psalmist describes the marvelous formation of the human body (Ps 139:15). The structure of this living masterpiece consists of more than 200 bones, each shaped and grooved with exquisite skill to perform an important function. To the bones are attached more than 500 muscles—some large, some minute, some obeying the human will, and others acting reflexively. Yet, all are arranged so that they never obstruct one another. Within this protective framework are the brain, heart, lungs, kidneys, and digestive organs—each a wonder in itself. And throughout the whole body runs a complex network of veins, arteries, nerves, and glands—each delicately interlaced.

Scientists tell us that the human brain consists of more than 10,000,000 nerve cells. Combined with the spinal cord, it forms an intricate electronic system infinitely more complicated than the largest computer ever designed. Our eyes have at lest 130,000,000 "rods" and 7,000,000 "cones," enabling us to see color and dimension. These tiny terminals of sight in turn are connected to the brain by an additional 300,000 separate nerve endings. Indeed, our bodies are wonderfully made.

Through the centuries people have marveled at the functioning of the human body. They have marveled at how it works, how it heals, how it compensates for deficiencies, and how it bounces back from serious abuse. In his amazement of the human body, the apostle Paul discovered an appropriate and helpful analogy of the church. Paul's analogy is mentioned in several of his letters, but the most detailed is in the text from 1 Corinthians. Paul emphasized how each body part must function as the part that it is in order for the body to function well as a whole.

I marvel at the human body and how it functions, and I marvel at the church, the body of Christ, and how it functions. The diversity, the opinions, the interests, the abilities, the attitudes of the people who make up the church are astonishing. Just consider those factors about our congregation which is a minute part, but a microcosm of the church. I often marvel that a congregation like us can function at all, much less carry out a significant ministry together in our community.

The only way it can happen is for each disciple of Christ, each member of the church, to function as the person he or she is in order for the church to function well as a whole. In other words, you must do your part, and so must you and you and you. What about it? What is your part? Are you doing your part?

We need to understand that each of us has different abilities and gifts. There are not better and worse gifts; neither are there greater and lesser abilities. All gifts and abilities contribute significantly to the growth and development of the church and to the nurture and growth of disciples of Christ. There are no superstars in the ministry of the church.

Roger Lovette, a friend of mine and a pastor, had this article in the church's newsletter several years ago.

> My son Matthew brought home the bulletin from the Maranatha Baptist Church, Highway 45 North, Plains, Georgia, the other day. The cover shows a typical Baptist church: four columns, large parking lot in front, predictable squatty steeple, one-story Sunday school rooms in the back. There are boxwoods out front, and it looks like the yard has been kept up. It is the kind

of church that you wouldn't look at twice as you drove by. There are thousands of churches just like it all over the country—and especially the South.

On the inside was the order of service, morning and evening. There were announcements, welcome to visitors, a plea to pay off their $12,000 sanctuary debt, an invitation to join the choir on Wednesday night and word that their Annie Armstrong goal of $500 had been surpassed by a little over a hundred dollars.

But it was the back page that I remember. This is the way that the schedule for April 14 went:

FRONT CLEAN-UP   Rosalynn and Sybil Carter
GROUNDS CLEAN-UP   Jimmy and Earl Carter

There were also names listed for back clean-up and who was in charge of the flowers and the nursery. But I loved seeing that the former first lady of the land was responsible for cleaning up part of the church on April 14, along with Bill Carter's widow. And I enjoyed reading where the former president of the United States will probably put on his blue jeans and join his cousin Earl in picking up the paper and the scattered beer cans, and get on the riding lawn mower that they hauled out from one of their houses and cut the grass and sweep off the walk up to the church. This is church. Everybody does his share. Everybody puts on an apron and sometimes blue jeans and gets their fingers dirty. And the church way is that we don't make a big to-do over anybody—not even the president of the United States. The ground at the foot of the cross is level. Everybody is the same. Everybody.

I felt good reading that mimeographed bulletin. It called me back to what church is really all about. People, all kinds of people, in love with a place called church who do whatever they can, for the glory of God, to make it work. No pecking order—no dignitaries or "important" Christians. Just plain folk. All equal and all with the same essential needs.[1]

When we develop and use our gifts, we are doing our part to build up the church, the body of Christ. All are equally important both in doing their part for the church and in receiving from the church. Sometimes we become distracted because our gifts and abilities aren't like another's. We may spend a great deal of time trying to develop a gift that another has only to become frustrated because that isn't our gift.

There is a popular story about a group of animals who decided that they needed to expand their gifts. They set up a curriculum for themselves that required everyone to master the activities of running, hopping, jumping, swimming, and flying. The experiment was a disaster. A rabbit, an expert at hopping, spent so much time in the areas in which he was deficient—swimming, climbing, and flying—that he nearly forgot how to hop. The eagle, who was a superb flier, got waterlogged and nearly drown in swimming class. The squirrel, a superior climber, only thought he could master flying—much to his chagrin. The turtle, an excellent swimmer, was a miserable failure in the jumping contest. The duck looked absurd trying to climb a tree. Soon it was evident that it was far more profitable for them to make use of the gifts they did have rather than to seek gifts that they did not have and really had no natural ability to develop.

As someone has said, "Never try to teach a pig to sing. It just wastes your time and annoys the pig." We all have different gifts. In order to be effective and to be the best servants of God we can be, we need to identify, nurture, and develop the gifts God has given us. What is your gift or gifts? How are you using your gifts to serve God and to communicate the love and grace of God to others? God has bestowed gifts and abilities on each of us. They are not just for show. They are to be used to express love for God and love for fellow human beings. How are you using your gifts? How are you doing your part to build up the church, to build up the part of the body of Christ that we call our congregation?

Here is one thing everyone of us can do this week. I want each of you to think of a member of our congregation who is able but is not coming regularly to worship. Take a moment right now and identify that person in your mind. Call them by name in your mind and get a visual image of the person's face. Now, make a commitment to talk with that person this week and encourage him or her to join you for worship next week. An important dimension of our ministry is reaching in to our congregation, encouraging and engaging each other.

Later in our service I will introduce new members of our congregation. We will have an opportunity to express our commitment to worship and serve God together. I hope you will also take responsibility to introduce yourself and to give your own personal word of welcome and encouragement to each of these who are now a part of this community of faith. All members of our congregation need to be here, to be encouraged and nurtured, and to examine how to be witnesses to others. We do that by encouraging well-established members to participate with us and by offering ourselves in support and friendship to new people as they place their lives with us.

Late in the book of Acts (27:27ff), Luke tells about the shipwreck experience of Paul. Paul's ship was caught in a storm that lasted for two weeks. In those days sailors did not have the benefit of either compass or sextant. All they could do was to ride out the storm. They could see neither sun nor moon nor stars, and they had no idea which direction to attempt to sail.

There are times in our lives when we don't know which direction to move. There are times when a congregation does not know which way to turn. But if we, as disciples of Christ and part of the body of Christ, will use our energy, abilities, and gifts to move toward the broken, the injured, the dispossessed, we can be confident we will be moving in the right direction.

The church has a struggle, and we in the church struggle because of our goal being conflicted, as Ed Dayton of World Vision has observed. One goal is to send people forth, and another is to care for them. People are always either getting on a stretcher or getting off. You've got this continual dynamic where relationships, not bottom-line numbers, are the key product. This makes the church perhaps the most complex of all human organizations.

All of us are needy, and we come seeking to have our needs met through the church. While we recognize our need to be ministered to, we often fail to see the need for us to be ministers to others. Our tendency often is to project our needs onto others and try to do to them or for them what we need. We fail to recognize that ministry is done with others, rather than to them or for them. All of this suggests there is more need for authentic church now than ever, but it is more complicated and complex to be the church now than ever.

What are your gifts? Are you a caring listener? Are you an excellent organizer? Do you establish and maintain relationships well? Maybe you are a person who can envision a new or modified ministry. Or perhaps you have the energy needed to get some new ministry underway. Maybe you have perseverance and can stay with a task until it is complete no matter how difficult the road becomes. Every one of us needs to assess our gifts and determine what they are.

Then each one of us needs to ask, "Am I doing my part in the body of Christ?" The church is a living organism because it is made up of living people. But the body of Christ is only as strong and viable as its weakest member. The church is weakened whenever a member, a body part, does not do his or her part. Are you doing your part?

Once you have identified your gifts and then seek to do your part by giving those gifts in ministry with others, new life is breathed into the body of Christ. Now, remember the person you thought of a moment ago. Be sure and contact that person this week. Start early in the week to get in touch with them, like this afternoon or tomorrow evening at the latest. This will help urge and encourage them to examine their gifts and to do their part. The more members of the body of Christ we have doing their part, the healthier the body is and the more wholesome the ministry that is carried out together. Come on people. Let's all do our part!

To Be Participants with Us in Worship and Service to God

The Invitation to Respond
*Hymn of Commitment   "Take My Life and Let It Be"   Yarbrough
The Introduction of New Members

The Litany of the Community of Faith

Pastor: What a beautiful sight! We welcome all of you to this community of faith. You bring such rich diversity, broad experience, and bountiful experiences to this faith community. Welcome.

New Members: **We are excited to be a part of this community. We want to be nurtured and nourished as disciples of Christ. We want to worship God here. We need friends, supporters, and encouragers.**

Pastor: You have heard the needs of these new members. What do you promise them?

Congregation: **We welcome them to this part of the body of Christ. They are family to us. Their needs will be ours. Their pain will be our pain. Their joy our joy. We will share our lives with them and together we will become united as members of the body of Christ.**

Pastor: You have heard the promise of the congregation to you. What do you promise to those who are already members of this community?

New Members: **We gladly place our lives alongside yours. We promise to do our part in ministering through this congregation. We promise to love God with all our lives and to love you as we love ourselves. We promise to be part of the body of Christ in this place with you.**

Pastor: What a beautiful experience to join together as a community of faith!

All: **May we worship and work together as one body with many parts. May we love, understand, support, and challenge each other to be the best human beings we can be, serving God as disciples of Christ. May we dream dreams and see visions together. May we truly be the body of Christ in this place. Amen.**

*Benediction
The Organ Postlude

(Luncheon for our new members and their sponsors in the fellowship hall immediately following the service.)

The first few months after people have been members of a congregation are crucial for them. The more sensitive a congregation can be to the crisis that energized their search for a community of faith, the better the congregation will minister and the better integrated into the congregation the new members will become. This worship service is one way for the congregation to act out their support and encouragement. It also is a way for the current members and new members to be formally joined as one faith community.

Notes

[1]Roger Lovette, "Acorns," *Cross Roads*, newsletter of Second Baptist Church, Memphis TN, 2:17 (24 April 1991) 2.

Part Four

Transitions

In a sense, everything in this book is about transitions. We are people on the move. The mobility of our society increases the number of transitions we experience. The biblical material has helpful guidance for us because for centuries the Hebrew people were nomads, moving from place to place. Jesus suggested that his followers would have a type of nomadic existence, living in perpetual transition, when he noted to a would-be follower that the Son of Man had nowhere to lay his head.

When people move from one community to another, they have a sense for awhile they are nomads. While they may have a place to lay their heads, several months of involvement and interaction are necessary before the new place becomes home. Having recently made a major move, I can testify about the feelings of uprooting life and transplanting it in a new place. Frankly, it just takes awhile for the events that transpire over a period of time before a person can sense that life has taken root in a new place.

A transition is a shift from one place to another in life. The changes that occur may involve physical, emotional, mental, and spiritual adjustment and adaptation. Some of these transitions are the natural movement through ages and stages of physical and emotional growth and faith development. The issues raised in section three come out of this type of transition. Some transitions are life-changing events. The chapters in section two reveal some of the rituals of the church that have developed around some of these experiences. Some events have such a powerful effect that their impact is pressed on people's lives forever. Dynamics identified in previous sections will be evident and applicable in this section as well, especially the grief process essential for the adjustment to death discussed in chapter six.

One of my objectives in writing this book has been to provide material that will help worship leaders and worshipers experience and express closure related to areas, people, and events in their lives. To experience closure is to have a sense of completion with regard to an issue or a person. In no way does this suggest that the issue or person is forgotten or erased from one's life. Rather, by experiencing closure, the issues and/or people are integrated into the lives of worshipers. Worshipers can then move and grow toward wholeness.

The chapters in the final section deal with the type of transitions that often involve physical, emotional, mental, and spiritual issues all in the same change. This is not to suggest that the events and changes discussed in previous sections did not involve all of these areas of life. It is to suggest that the events discussed in the final section more starkly portray transitions that radically affect all areas of life. In this section, let us explore the question of vocation, the issue of declining health, the issue of leaving home, the question of vocation, mid-life crisis, declining health, aging and retirement, and the expression of farewell when leaving a congregation.

The fourth section also deals with issues that are generally recognized and discussed by people as life-changing events. Marriage, discussed in chapter five, is a life-changing event but often is not seen in that light except in retrospect. Vocational choice is more likely viewed as a life-directional choice looking into the future. Dealing with a life-altering illness involves projection of what this illness means to the person and to the person's family and circle of friends. Leaving a community of faith is a fitting conclusion to my efforts to provide pastoral care through worship; the dynamics involved when it becomes necessary to leave a congregation are examined.

Chapter 13

Embarking on the Journey

Life is a journey or pilgrimage that begins at birth and ends at death. Relationships throughout the journey influence and affect the pilgrims throughout the trip. The early years are heavily influenced by the impact of primary caregivers in the lives of infants and children. In recent years we have become increasingly aware of many people who are left to fend for themselves at unbelievably young ages. Many of them develop a basic mistrust toward people with whom they relate because at the very outset of their lives they could not trust those in charge of them to care and provide for their basic needs. These people are desperately in need of relationships, but often they make it most difficult to relate to them simply because they cannot and will not trust anybody. We in the church have an enormous task in attempting to establish relationships with people who have had experiences such as these.

On the other end of the experience spectrum are those who grow up in a household with their parents, step-parents, or adopted parents present and involved to some degree with them in their growth experiences. While the journey began at birth, it began to take some sharpe curves during adolescence with lots of peaks and valleys. Then, sometime around the eighteenth birthday there is a major intersection to be negotiated. It is marked dramatically by the emotional task of leaving home. Often graduation from high school leads into this intersection.

Following completion of high school, many young people enter college. Some attend vocational schools. Others join the military, and still others find full-time jobs and begin functioning in the work place. At this point many people feel they are really embarking on life's journey, although they have been on it all along. What is different is they now are making the major decisions that affect their lives. They have no one with whom they must check each day about where they are going or when they will return. If they choose not to check with anyone, there is not necessarily anyone who will check on them. One young person in her first semester of college said, "College really is different than high school. At college they tell you one time about a deadline in class and that's it." Of course if a college student decides to skip a class, or never go to class that is an option. Eventually, there are consequences directly related to the chosen options, but no one is forcing the student to do differently.

People leave home gradually. They may leave physically but still be attached emotionally or financially or both. Currently, many young adults complete college and return to live with their parents for awhile. Other young adults may marry during their early twenties, but the marriage does not last. They return to their parents' homes for a season in an effort to establish themselves and be on their own. Still others finish high school or drop out of school and find employment. Their income makes it difficult for them to manage completely on their own. Many young adults in this group remain in their parents' homes until they feel they can "go it alone" financially and emotionally. In recent years, young adults in circumstances and characteristics such as these have been identified as the postponed generation.[1]

Leaving home physically symbolizes starkly what is happening in the life of the individual who is leaving. The leaving has an impact on all who are related emotionally to that person. The emotional upheaval, the pulling, tugging, and tearing that occurs as people leave home is a major issue in their lives. The upheaval affects every dimension of the life of the person who is leaving as well as those who are left. It is appropriate and helpful for a congregation to acknowledge this upheaval and to develop worship in a way that will address the issues involved and assist members in coping with the mixture of feelings that such an experience creates. The following worship service is one example of this approach.

Worshiping the God Who Guides Us on the Journey
A Service of Christian Worship

The Chiming of the Hour
The Prelude

We Are Invited to a Place

The Responsive Call to Worship
Pastor: Come, let us worship the God who guides us on our journey.
People: We come, eager to worship and to follow God who knows who we are and where we should go.

Pastor: Our journey leads over rough and smooth terrain, through recognizable and unknown passages, and brings us to major intersections where directional decisions have to be made.

People: One of those intersections is when a child grows up and arrives at the time to leave home.

Pastor: That's a tough intersection for those leaving and for those who are left.

People: We need help, guidance, strength, and encouragement to negotiate this intersection.

Pastor: We are here to worship God and to receive the help and hope we need to continue the journey.

People: We come to worship God and receive the guidance we need from God to continue the journey.

*Hymn	"How Firm a Foundation"	Foundation
*Invocation		

We Become Comfortable in that Place

The Welcome		
Holy Scripture		Genesis 12:1–9
*Hymn	"Guide Me, O Thou Great Jehovah"	CWM Rhondda
*Offertory Sentences		
The Offertory	"Higher Ground"	Higher Ground
Receiving the Tithes and Offerings		

And Through a Leap of Faith

Choral Worship	"To Everything There Is a Season"	Ed Harris
Sermon	"Leaving Home"	

Any trip we take has lots of intersections we must negotiate. Decisions must be made about which route to take. Of course, the route we choose is determined by where we want to go. In *The Wizard of Oz*, Dorothy asked the scarecrow for directions. The scarecrow asked Dorothy where she wanted to go. Dorothy replied, "I don't know," to which the scarecrow responded, "Then it doesn't matter which direction you go, does it?" Often we don't know where we are going or where we want to go. When this is true, it doesn't matter which direction we choose.

    Perhaps there have been times on a trip when you arrived at an intersection, chose a direction, and proceeded. Then, while traveling in that direction, you began wondering about the road you didn't take. You wondered where it led. You speculated about how your trip would have been different had you chosen that road instead of this one.

All of this trip-taking, direction-asking, intersection deciding, and reflecting on the road not chosen is a metaphor of our lives. Life has many major intersections: birth, leaving home, whether or not to marry, vocation, parenting, faith commitment, retirement, death. The safety principles for approaching intersections while driving apply to approaching the great intersections of life: stop, look, and listen.

Let's explore the major intersection of leaving home. When and how does a person leave home? What does it mean to leave home? Why would anyone leave one place and go to another? Considering these and other questions is helpful in negotiating the great intersection of leaving home, and the safety instructions to stop, look, and listen are helpful.

A few years ago my son and I were riding in the car when he popped the question, "Dad, why do some people, when they grow up, get an apartment and move away from home?" I responded with what I thought was a reasonable, logical explanation about the desire and value of people to be on their own, make their own decisions, and have a place of their own. Brandon thought about my comments briefly and then said, "I think I'll just stay with you and Mom." An appropriate response for a seven year-old, don't you think? But what about for a twenty-five-year-old or a forty-year-old? What is the meaning of leaving home? Is it necessary? If it is necessary, when is the right time? Does the Bible offer any help or suggestions?

The biblical material says Abram was seventy-five when he left home. Is there any help for us in what Abram did or when he did it? If we waited until we were seventy-five to leave home, only a handful of us would ever leave. However, according to the biblical material Abram lived to be 175. That means that seventy-five was roughly 43 percent of his life. Seventy-five in Abram's life is the equivalent of twenty-five to thirty in our lives, given our current age expectancy. Isn't this about the age when many people leave home today— emotionally and financially?

We are not told when and why Abram left his home. We don't know when or how or why he got the idea that God wanted him to leave his country, his relatives, and his dad's home and venture out into the unknown, toward a land, a place that God would give him. While Abram's ancestral roots were planted in Ur of the Chaldees in Babylonia, if the biblical account is in some semblance of chronological order, then Abram left his father's home in Haran in Canaan to move on to the place God would show him. Earlier, Abram had left Ur with his father, Terah, and they had settled in Haran. When Abram was seventy-five, he left his place in Haran in search of his new place, the place which God would show him.

Paul Tournier has suggested that each of us finds a place in life, becomes secure in that place, and then leaves that place for a new place. A leap of faith is required to leave one place for another and can be compared to the performance of a trapeze artist. The trapeze artist swings on a bar high above the ground and at the right moment leaves one bar and reaches for another, but for a moment is in-between bars. This is what Tournier identifies as the leap of faith.

Abram left the security of his father's home, the support of the relatives in his extended family, and the familiarity of many known quantities in his life. Abram left home and in leaving home he traded the familiar for the unfamiliar, the known for the unknown, the certain for the uncertain, and the comfortable for the uncomfortable.

Leaving home was a major intersection for Abram to negotiate. Leaving home for Abram had a physical dimension, but more significant than physically moving was the emotional/spiritual journey that Abram's leave-taking had on him. This same dynamic is at work in us. One person may leave home, move out of the house where she lived with her parents, and move in a house next door and be clearly described as having left home. Another person may move across the continent but the evidence is clear that person did not leave home.

Leaving home requires us to deal with what it means to us to be dependent on other people. We need to stop here and ask that question. There are some benefits of dependency. After all, someone else can be responsible for the decisions of life, receiving the blame or credit for those decisions. A major liability is that a dependent person never really develops a self, an identity that is clearly and uniquely one's own. We need to look around at life as we give serious thought to leave taking. We will have to give up some things like having others always take care of us. But we also will be able to take up some things like making decisions, being in charge of our lives, adventuring out into the unknown, and being thrilled by the challenge of sailing in uncharted water. Life for most of us began in homes where our every need was met. And that kind of dependency is appropriate for infants who cannot look out for themselves or take care of themselves. One of the major tasks of parents is to guide their children to grow out of dependence on them into dependence on God and interdependence with them and with others.

Have you heard how eaglets learn to fly? The mother eagle takes them on her back from the nest and flies away with them. Then, she drops out from under them and they struggle to learn to fly. She watches with her "eagle" eye to see how each is doing. As each has difficulty, she flies under it and catches it on her back, and then drops out from under it again. This process is repeated until her eaglets learn to fly. This is the way the mother eagle weans her young away from dependence on her for their survival. Parents are partners with God in guiding their children to learn how to be interdependent with other people and dependent on God. There are those who do not want to leave home and will not. Like the eaglets, they seem never willing to try their wings on their own. Although a difficult task, the healthy parents are those who can help their children leave home.

Professor Edward Wimberly has noted how things are a bit different for those entering young adulthood now and seeking to leave home. He comments,

> For socioeconomic and emotional reasons, many African-American and Caucasian young adults are postponing entrance into full participation in the major tasks of young adulthood. I have heard many comments by parents of young adults between the ages of eighteen and thirty, wondering when their children will finally leave home and establish their own lives. Although it is an expectation of American culture that young adults leave home and begin to make their own way in society, these expectations are being altered by the reality of what some ar now calling the "postponed generation." Many young adults feel ill-equipped emotionally to face the world. Many feel they do not yet have all the resources from the parental home needed to negotiate in the world.[2]

Usually there is a time of strong independence when a person is in resistance and/or rebellion to anything the parents have to say or suggest. Part of what has to happen in a person's life during this time is to decide what it means to leave home and what direction life is going to take. That is a difficult intersection to negotiate in life. The religious dimension often is seen starkly late in high school years or just after high school, especially if the family has been actively involved in the life of a congregation. The person physically leaves home, is still at home emotionally and financially. Participation in the life of the church takes a long vacation. Why?

The faith of the family, particularly the parents, is not the faith of the child. The one who is leaving home must decide on the faith issue for his or her own. By stopping and looking, the person leaving home is in a better condition to listen to the voice of God calling him or her to take the leap of faith and experience, as Abram did, that the promise of God is a relationship that begins then and there and develops and expands throughout life.

Having left home, people leave a lot behind that was part of home. Some of what they leave is healthy removal of baggage. Some of what they leave they discover later they would like to have, but it is hard to sort all that out. Our tendency is an either/or syndrome. Either take everything with us or leave everything behind, but the sorting and deciding and the choosing to take some things and leave some things is vital in the process of leaving home.

When someone leaves home, the person leaving is affected as well as those who are left. When the leaving is to go to something, the process is easier for the person leaving. When the leaving is to go from something, the process may be easier for those being left. But leaving takes its toll on all whose relationships feel the impact of the leaving.

Some people leave home and do not realize the impact or significance of what is happening. For some it is a gradual easing away. For others some event causes a sharp, distinct break. Physically and emotionally I left home when I entered college. I did not know that anything significant was happening until we had carried my things into the college dormitory and as my parents started to say good-bye, my mother began to cry. I was surprised. As it turned out I returned to my parents' home for Thanksgiving, Christmas, spring break, and the following summer. I bought a car that summer and drove myself to college in the fall. By the time I returned to college in the fall of my sophomore year, I had left home. I discovered a broad, expansive, unique world out there beyond home. The breadth, expansiveness, and uniqueness of the world has continued to intrigue me throughout my life since I left the home of my family of origin.

There are parallels and similarities between my leaving home during my eighteenth year and Abram leaving his home at seventy-five. Indeed, I had had a place in which I felt comfortable, safe, and content. Then, I moved to a different place that was uncomfortable, risky, and threatening.

Abram decided to leave his father's house and land in Haran and venture out into unknown territory heading toward what he understood from God to be the promised land. Now this was a man who lived among people that saw a god in every tree, gods behind every cloud, and a counsel of gods who met in the mountains to decided whether rain or drought would be the weather. How Abram received direction from one God who became the God of the patriarchs is a mystery.

Why Abram decided to go out into unknown territory following the leadership of this one God is a mystery. "Go from your country and your kindred and your father's house to the land that I will show you" was the instruction Abram heard. If one of us became convinced that such a voice was speaking to us with a bizarre invitation that would not go away—at times speaking just a faint whisper, at other times with alarming clarity—we would more than likely try to shake it off, ignore it . . . but following the voice would be hard. Wouldn't this have been even more difficult in Abram's day? To leave the house and land of his father, Terah, must have been an agonizing struggle because that was not twentieth-century mobile society where people were expected to grow up and leave their parents, starting new families in new places.

The how and why of Abram's decision remain mysterious to us. A summary statement of Abram's is: "Then he moved on from place to place, going toward the southern part of Canaan" (Gen 12:9). Abram and his family became nomads, tent dwellers, people who would put up their tents one day and take them down the next. After Abram started listening to God, he never again knew a settled life.

Have you ever had the notion that some day your life would be settled? I have, but I am finally permitting that illusive dream to die. When I was in high school, I was eager for college. That would be real life. In college I was eager to get on to seminary and make preparation for my vocation. I was eager to finish seminary so I could get on with real ministry. Having been a pastor for twenty-five years, I haven't found life to be settled by any means. There is always another sermon to prepare, one more hospital visit to make, a funeral, a wedding, or one more phone call to make or receive. Somewhere out there is the settled life, I fool myself into believing.

Maybe all of us are nomads, pitching our tents first here and then there. We camp out at a committee meeting, a worship service, at our jobs, at school, drop by the house for a bite of food and nap, and we're off again moving from place to place going toward the southern part of the promised land wherever and whatever that is.

I suspect there were times when Abram thought of his brother, Nahor, with envy. After all, Nahor was living a settled life in Haran, knowing he would die and be buried near their father. What a contrast Nahor and Abram were. One lived a settled life with many gods, and one became a nomad following the direction of one God. Nahor and Abram, two brothers, and which one is the household name?

Nahor's life was like an anchor. Abram's life, after he got involved with God, was like a sailboat on the open sea. Nahor's life was lived in one house on one piece of land. Abram was a tent dweller moving from place to place. I suspect many of us like Abram's rewards and Nahor's lifestyle. However, the rewards of God for Abram were not that clear at the time for him. The theme song for Abram and his family must have been "On the Road Again." Neither Abram nor his descendants considered the wandering a blessing. They didn't like the struggles and the changes and living in a state of having-not-yet-arrived any more than we do.

But what if the blessing weren't the land at all? Maybe we've been missing the point all these years. What if the land were a metaphor for something more important than being able to call a piece of land your own and to build a house on it and keep a family there from generation to generation? What if the blessing were not the land but the covenant itself? The moment Abram walked out of the house in Haran he began a journey that put him into a covenant-relationship with God. Centuries later when Moses died on the east side of the Jordan looking over into Canaan, no bitterness or remorse is evident in his life. Maybe that was because the blessing was the relationship with God and not the land.

Relationships are for a lifetime. They change because life is constantly changing. Abram's worldview changed because his covenant-relationship with God caused him to redefine his world. Abram's life from the time he left Haran was much harder and much better than he ever imagined possible. Hasn't this been true of your relationship with God? Ever since you got involved with God hasn't your life been unsettled, moving from place to place, emotionally if not also geographically? The blessing is the covenant relationship, and it contains both threat and promise. The threat is that we will be changed. The promise is that we will be changed. Ever since you got involved with God and left home, hasn't your life gotten harder and better at the same time? As we journey in covenant-relationship with God, it becomes clearer that to live our lives on God's terms is a nomadic existence, moving from place to place. The only thing settled in our lives in covenant-relationship with God is how unsettled our lives are. Covenant has to do with the way we live our lives with God and with each other. The blessing from God is not the settled place but the relationship.

God said to the old man Abram with no children, "I'm going to give you a dream so big it'll bust your seams. You'll never believe it. Come on, you craggy-faced old fellow, I'm going to give you a dream big enough, exciting enough, and challenging enough for a boy with peach fuzz on his face. You don't believe it? Well, just leave home and follow me." And to everyone's surprise, maybe more to Abraham's surprise than anyone's, he went.

There is no way that you and I can comprehend what that journey meant to a man or a woman in the time of Abraham. When God said, get up from where you are, leave the land you know, leave your clan and kin—as important as they were in that day—and go away to some place called Canaan and live in tents instead of this fine walled city—one of the most modern of ancient time—and go to some vague place, with some vague promise to a man his age of children to come, it was incredible that Abraham went. "Leave your old gods on the other side of the river," God said, "and all of the icons you've touched all your life; put your hand in my invisible hand, and I'm going to give you and all the world a wonderful dream."

Would it seem a little extravagant to you if I should say that God has the same sort of dream for you? If I should say that God has called you also to leave the conventional wisdom of your generation, to believe there is more than just "making it big" for yourself or even your family? To leave behind some of the things you've been taught by a culture that does not know where it's going and has become confused between dreams and nightmares? To walk toward a promise, reaching your hand out towards something you have not seen and may not see in your lifetime? And to believe that God will not only bless you and your family by doing so but, believe it or not, that through you all the families of the earth may touch a blessing.

I never thought about all of this when I left home. Probably you didn't either. But the value of reflection is the discovery of some of the possibilities and probabilities that lie before us when we take the leap of faith to leave one place, home, and move to a new place that will become home for awhile. Indeed, leaving home is one of life's great intersections. The way we negotiate this major intersection has tremendous implications about the manner in which we will negotiate many of the future intersections of our lives.

We Move to a New Place

*Hymn of Discipleship   Landas
            "My Faith Has Found a Resting Place"

*Presentation of New Members
*Benediction
*Choral Response   "Blessing"   John Harman
The Organ Postlude

Regardless of what form leaving home takes, and regardless of whether it is an immediate event or one that occurs gradually, this leave-taking creates upheaval. There is physical, emotional, financial, and spiritual upheaval for all involved. For the one leaving, the process of uprooting—being transplanted—and growing in a new place is not easy and simple even when it is exactly what the person wants to do. For the ones who are left, there is a void, an emptiness with which to deal. When the leaving ones take their things, a physical emptiness remains in the house that represents the emotional change and loss that is experienced. While the adjustment to this type of change and loss varies with people, acknowledgement and support from a congregtion, a family of faith, will be strengthening and hopeful for those on this trail of the journey.

Notes

[1]Edward Wimberly is credited with this identificaiton.
[2]Edward P. Wimberly, *African American Pastoral Care* (Nashville: Abingdon Press, 1991) 57.

Chapter 14

Vocational Choices in Life

We spend an exorbitant amount of time working. The motivation for working varies with people. We work to earn money to provide for the basic necessities of our lives and those who live with us. We work to earn money to spend to buy things we want, like, or desire. We earn money to have power. We accumulate possessions to give us security. We collect possessions because they represent status and station in life. We often live our lives in the comparative mood and use the inventory list of all that we own to compare our achievements and accomplishments with others, hoping the comparison puts us ahead of those with whom we compare ourselves. We may work to avoid issues and relationships that are troubling or threatening to us. If we can just bury ourselves in our work, we think we can avoid those painful situations that frighten us.

If the previous paragraph is an accurate description of our understanding of work, then about all we are attempting to do is making a living. I do not think what is described makes much of a life. We easily become distracted in life and begin to confuse the ends of life with the means of life. When this happens we follow this flow for awhile, but then realize how dissatisfied we are. We are unhappy but often do not identify the source or basis of our unhappiness.

We go through the routine of our jobs, but routine is what it is. Few of us can work very long at a job before we begin asking the question, "What does this mean?" What is the meaning of our work? Why do we do what we do? We do what we do out of love, but the question is who are we loving. Are we working for ourselves or for someone else?

This chapter wrestles with the issue of vocation. The struggle involves determining the difference between a profession and a vocation. The word vocation means calling. Applying this word to describe the work we do indicates that the motivation for our work has a spiritual quality that expresses a dimension of our relationship with God. According to Jesus, basic to meaning and value in life is loving God with all our hearts, minds, and souls, and loving our neighbors as ourselves. Whatever work we do, therefore, must be motivated by this love or it will begin to lead to discontentedness and unhappiness caused by a lack of integrity.

Bernard of Clairveaux suggested that the motivation for our work is love. He indicated that people move stages of development in examining and expressing meaning and motivation behind their work. The first stage is loving yourself for your sake. If pressed much at all, this motivation is purely selfish and has a very small circle of interests. The second stage is loving the world for your sake. This is a slight improvement over the first stage. The third stage is loving the world for the world's sake. The ultimate stage is to love the world for God's sake. This is what we are invited to do as children of God and disciples of Christ.

Vocation means calling. We are called beyond ourselves to apply our lives and gifts in ways that benefit the world. Indeed, we could conclude that every child of God and disciple of Christ has the same vocation: to love the world for God's sake. The following worship service has been designed with this calling in mind. Each element of the service is intended to accentuate the calling of all Christians to use their gifts and abilities in their employment, through their hobbies, and as volunteers to love the world for God's sake. May a worship service like this help all who worship God to respond to God's invitation to commit their lives to love the world for God's sake.

Worshiping God and Loving the World
A Service of Christian Worship

When Our Vocation

The Chiming of the Hour
The Silent Preparation for Worship
The Prelude
The Choral Call to Worship   Price
          "Stir Thy Church, O God, Our Father"

The Invocation
      God, create an attitude of love in our lives. Remind us of the gifts you have given us. Inspire us to use these gifts to love you and to love one another. Draw us close to you that we might sense your deep love for the world. Then, fill our lives with your desire that we might love the world for your sake. Amen.

Is Loving the World for God's Sake

| *Hymn | "We Praise Thee with Our Minds, O Lord" | Clenmel |

Welcome to the Worshipers
The Holy Scriptures   Philippians 3:12-21
The Pastoral Prayer and Lord's Prayer
*Hymn   "O Lord, Who Came to Earth to Show"   Forest Green

*Offertory Statement
*Offertory   "Lord, Who Dost Give to Thy Church"   Seventh and
                                                              James

Receiving the Tithes and Offerings

Then Our Work

The Choral Worship   "For All the Saints"   Sine Nomine

The Sermon   "The Highest Calling in Life"

The kingdom of God is made up of people from all nations of the world. Christians, regardless of nationality, are citizens of the kingdom of God. As disciples of Christ we need to be aware everyday that we are citizens of the kingdom of God. While we have different gifts, abilities, and interests, as citizens of the kingdom of God we all have the same calling. We are called to love the world for God's sake.

Children often are asked at young ages, "What are you going to be when you grow up?" An appropriate response would be, "An adult." College students are often asked, "What is your major?" An appropriate response might be, "Life." People in the work force often are asked, "What do you do?" Wouldn't we be surprised if someone said, "Well, I'm using my gifts and abilities to build a sense of community with the people I encounter in my daily routine."

Regardless of our age or station in life, we often are asked what we do. What is it that occupies much of our time and energy? What is the attitude and motivation underneath the actions we take? What is your calling in life? What is your reason for being? The highest calling in life, according to the letter to the Philippians, is the call to discipleship. The highest aim in life is to do the will of God, which is to love God with all our hearts, minds, and souls and to love our fellow human beings as we love ourselves. Therefore, all of us have the same vocation but different professions, the same calling but different responses, the same destination but different routes to travel.

There are times when we try to go many directions at once. We juggle several things simultaneously, not really giving ourselves to any of them. When we go at life this way, we get bogged down and are immobilized. We spin our wheels, stuck in the cross ruts of multi-directions. We are without purpose because we have not answered a basic question, "To whom or to what will we give our lives?"

Ken Chafin, a retired pastor, told about going to the Grand Old Opry and hearing someone sing. While the audience was applauding, he pronounced to the friend with him that that song would never make it. The master of ceremonies came out and thanked the singer for the song that had just sold a million copies. Chafin repeated the same mistake several times throughout the evening. The next day, while telling another friend about the experience, he said he could not understand how those people could be so successful. His friend said, "That shouldn't surprise you. Anybody with average intelligence or less can be successful. These country-western singers have one idea. They start out with family and friends, whoever will listen to them. Then they sing at dances and honky tonks all in the hopes of going to Nashville. They have one idea, and they give their whole life to it." Is there one idea to which you will devote your entire life?

Vocation means calling. It is a concept suggesting that a person is led or drawn into one's life work because of the essence and importance of the task. The person also has the conviction that s/he has the skills and interest to contribute significantly to the betterment of human beings through the calling. This combines giving attention to one's gifts and inclinations with a careful listening to the Christian story and vision. Vocation, then, is not so much found as it is negotiated.[1] Paul suggested in writing to the Romans that "we are to use our different gifts in accordance with the grace that God has given us" (Rom 12:6).

Vocation is the response a person makes with his or her total self to the address of God and to the calling to partnership. The shaping of vocation as total response of oneself to the address of God involves the orchestration of our leisure, our relationships, our work, our private life, our public life, of the resources we steward, so as to put it all at the disposal of God's purposes in the services of God and neighbor.[2] Vocation is calling by God to love the world.

The perceptions we have about our vocations are related to our views about work. Is there meaning in the work that we do? If there is, what is the source of the meaning? And if our work is meaningless, why is that? To identify the work we do as a vocation is to give a spiritual and religious dimension to our jobs. A question that all people need to ask in deciding on the kind of work they will do and that each person needs to ask periodically in reexamining and evaluating job choices is, "In what type of work can I best use my gifts as a human being to love God and to love my fellow human beings?" All people have gifts and all people are responsible and accountable as stewards of the gifts that they have. How we can best utilize our gifts is a probing journey.

Often we need the assistance of another person to help call out our gifts and to focus them in a specific direction. When my great-uncle was graduating from high school, his family's doctor asked him to come by his office one afternoon after school. Uncle Mack went by, and Dr. O. M. Carter gave him a fountain pen as a gift for high school graduation. Then, Dr. Carter asked Uncle Mack if he had given any thought to becoming a doctor, and my uncle had not. Dr. Carter encouraged him to consider it. He told my uncle that he would experience a great deal of joy in bringing calmness and hope to people who were sick and in despair. Eventually, my uncle decided on medicine as his life's work. He began considering the calling to that work which Dr. O. M. Carter extended. Through the years my uncle has offered to assist young people with loans for college education who would consider being doctors, nurses, and pharmacists.

Perhaps you are in your particular type of work because a teacher seemed to take some special interest in you and asked if you had considered your particular vocation. It was this approach by Edwina Hunter that caused me to decide to major in public speaking in college.

One of the best known Baptist pastors was George W. Truett, but Truett did not start out to be a minister. Actually he studied law. At a church business meeting in the church where Truett was a member, one of the men got the floor and made a motion that the church license Truett to preach. A second to the motion came immediately. When Truett protested, the man who made the motion said that many of the members had discussed it, and they were convinced that Truett had the gifts needed to be a minister. Thus was born the ministerial vocation of George W. Truett. Of course, Truett did not have to become a minister as a result of this action. However, the action caused him to pause and give serious thought to the ministry and to examine his gifts in light of what the congregation was saying.

Usually when someone or a group of people says something positively surprising about us and our abilities, we react with a certain amount of introspection. We need to go aside at such a place to explore what meaning this has. This seems to have been the concept of calling that Jesus had with regard to his disciples. He invited people to follow him in the sense of joining with him and learning from him. He gave no indication what form their discipleship would take. While many of us have an image in our minds of the disciples becoming preachers, very few of them did. Jesus had 120 disciples, most of whom we do not know their names. Of the few names we have, Peter became the best known preacher. James and John may also have preached, as did Philip. What professions the others had, we don't know. Some remained fishermen. Matthew,

Mark, and John became writers much later, but writing was not the way they earned a livelihood.

Cotton Mather, one of the leading Puritans in New England, suggested there are two callings for a Christian, a general calling to discipleship and a particular or personal calling of employment. The Puritan culture encouraged people to make connections between their faith and their work. We must seek to do this continually. There must be continuity between what occurs on Sunday in the worship place and what happens on Monday in the work place. Our work may be the biggest bore of our lives, or it can be the highest form of prayer and praise to God. Work is a form of prayer and praise when we see it as an act of service to God and to our neighbors. In this sense our work takes on meaning, value, and purpose. This approach and attitude help make the distinction between work being a job, a profession, or a vocation.

When work is a job only, we are interested in making a living. When work is a vocation, an act of service to God, then work is an integral part of making a life. As you go about doing your job, whatever it is—teacher, coach, police officer, street repairer, mail carrier, fire fighter, minister, childcare provider—are you making a living or making a life? There is a direct correlation between your internal motivation and your external behavior. Attitude and action are inescapably intertwined. Whether you are making a living or making a life is determined by what attitude motivates your action.

In a vocation, the primary concern is the use of one's abilities in serving God for the benefit of other people. Jesus is our model for this. He was clear about the beginning and destination of his life when he said, "I know where I came from and where I am going" (John 8:14). This kind of clarity gives the journey authenticity.

Philippians 3:13-14 speaks to the issue of vocation and to the related matters of commitment and single-mindedness. Paul summarized well the one way we are to live our lives when he wrote, "This one thing I do, forgetting what lies behind, and straining forward to what lies ahead, I press on toward the goal of the upward calling of God in Christ Jesus."

What a sense of priority this sentence states, "This one thing I do!" Isn't it amazing what can result from a person being committed to one thing to keep life focused? Martin Luther King, Jr. summarized one woman's actions by saying, "When Rosa Parks sat down, the world stood up." She said she was tired, tired of moving and giving up her seat to white folks. The one thing she did was to sit and stay seated on a Montgomery bus.

What is the one thing that you do? What one thing permeates your purpose and reason for being in life? The one thing we are to do is the will of God, but what is that? Oh, I think it is fairly easy to determine what the will of God is. We often want to make it so difficult to know. We cloak the will of God in all types of struggle and mask it in mystery, but the will of God for all of creation stands out clearly in scripture. The will of God for our lives is to love God and love our fellow human beings as much as we love ourselves. How we best fulfill and carry out this mandate in our lives is up to us to determine. Here is where we are to use the freedom and creativity that God has given us to determine how we will go about communicating our love for God and our love for all of God's creation. The avenues available to us in fulfilling God's call to the world are limitless.

There are those who suggest that God has a specific and definite design for each person's life and that each person must determine what that design is. Implied in this suggestion is that God is an architect who has drawn a set of blueprints for each of us. If we can just find our sets of blueprints, then all of life will be mapped out for us. At least two traps are in this line of thinking. First, it is contrary to the nature of freedom with which God created the universe and the freedom that God gave human beings to think and to make decisions. Second, this attitude turns life into a game of guessing what is in the mind of God. It suggests that if you guess right, life will go smoothly. This is a contradiction to what has happened in the lives of people through the centuries who have sought to follow God. Many of those who seemed to have followed God most closely have had the greatest problems and difficulties in their lives. No one served God any better than Jesus did; and no one had any greater difficulties, disappointments, and mistreatment than did Jesus.

Paul's reference to the "upward calling of God" has been interpreted to mean that the ministry is the highest vocation or calling one can receive. Ministers are the ones who have given this interpretation! But the calling to which Paul referred is the invitation to be a disciple of Christ. Often we have suggested that the ministry is a full-time Christian vocation and implied that all other vocations are either unchristian or only part-time Christian vocations. Nothing in the New Testament makes such a distinction or division regarding vocation. Was Paul in a Christian vocation when he spoke in the synagogues and helped form churches in the Gentile world, but in an unchristian vocation as a tentmaker because that was not a position in the church? He did not understand it that way.

Through the years a class system has developed in Christianity suggesting that those who are ministers are in the highest calling and are in full-time Christian service. Such an attitude suggests that all other Christians are second-class citizens and in a lower or lowest calling. The highest calling is to be a disciple of Christ. The ways that you find to live out the life of being a disciple is just as important as how anyone else does it. I have yet to meet a full-time Christian. Part of the time is about all the time any of us are interested or willing to be Christians. All we need to confirm such an accusation is to review our actions and activities during the past week. None of us could conclude from such a review that we have been full-time Christians for the past week.

Sometimes the suggestion is made that certain jobs or professions are off-limits to Christians, and even that some "Christian" professions are off-limits to certain Christians—like women being pastors. We are continually narrowing the realm of possibilities while God is continually expanding the realm of possibilities for options of God calling us to the world. Our sense of calling, our understanding of vocation, gives us the motivation and insight to commit ourselves to travel one way. The motive for service determines whether what we do is a ministry. Elton Trueblood has given us insight into the meaning and motive of calling by writing, "In the basic Christian pattern there may be a division of labor, and there may be a conductor, but all play, all are performers rather than auditors or observers."[3]

In the setting of Christianity, vocation is a calling or invitation that causes a person to be motivated internally to meet external needs that benefit people. The types of work and jobs that this involves are numerous and varied. We each need to find the ways in which to use our gifts for the best benefit of sharing the good news. Our decision on a profession does not mean there can be no alteration of the course or changing of direction. We may find ourselves changing directions often and even being accused at times of having left the ministry. But we haven't left the ministry. We have stopped ministering through the channels we once ministered and found other ways to use our gifts in sharing love for God and for fellow human beings. Our jobs are affected by our attitudes, our actions, our availability to God, and our accountability for the gifts that have been entrusted to us.

The New Testament is clear about vocation. Disciples of Christ are called to develop their lives, every aspect of their lives, in the church and through the church to help build up the church, the body of Christ. Just as the human body has numerous and various parts and it takes all of them to make the body a whole, living organism, so it is with the church. The church is made up of numerous, various people. There is tremendous diversity in the church, which contributes to the life and aliveness of the church.

At least twenty gifts are mentioned in various places in the New Testament. The list is by no means exhaustive, nor are these twenty the only gifts that are available for development in our lives. The fact that there are twenty clearly indicates the variety of gifts the members of the early church identified. They saw the importance of each member of the body of Christ developing and using those gifts to build up the church. Building up the church, the body of Christ, took place then and is to take place now both in the worship place and in the work place. The highest calling in life according to the letter to the Philippians is the call to discipleship. The highest aim in life is to do the will of God, which is to love God with all our hearts, minds, and soul and to love our fellow human beings as we love ourselves. Therefore, all of us have the same vocation but different professions, the same calling but different responses, the same destination but different routes to travel. All of us have the same vocation. Our vocation, our calling in life is to love the world for God's sake. Some will love the world for God's sake as childcare providers, some as musicians, some as artists, some as ambulance drivers, some as care providers for people with AIDS, some as firefighters, some as ministers, some as teachers, some as carpenters, some as clerks, some as physicians. What about you? How are you going to love the world for God's sake?

Is a Prayer

The Invitation to Respond
*Hymn of Commitment   Webb
              "To Worship, Work, and Witness"

The Presentation of New Members
*Benediction
The Organ Postlude

Our lives are fragmented and segregated. We have responsibilities and expectations at home, work, community, and church. How can we live integrated lives? The worship service in this chapter is designed to address that question. By helping members of the congregation see their calling as loving the world for God's sake, with God's help they may begin to weave all the components of their lives into one living tapestry that is offered as a loving gift to God. Such an approach can enrich both the individual and the congregation to love the world for God's sake. Then, worship has informed and nourished people to care for the world for God's sake which is the vocation for all of us.

Notes

[1]James Fowler, *Being Adult, Being Christian* (San Francisco: Harper & Row, 1984) 126.
[2]Ibid., 95.
[3]David Elton Trueblood, *Your Other Vocation* (New York: Harper Bros., 1952) 51.

Chapter 15

Negotiating the Midpoint

A number of people have identified the age between thirty-five and forty-five as the Deadline Decade. Usually during this span of life, people admit they will not live forever or accomplish all of the ideal goals they had been holding in their minds. In a sense, during the season, people are confronted with the downside of life. The movie *City Slickers* was a popular presentation of this dimension of life. The biggest question people ask during the deadline decade is, "How can I be over the hill when I haven't seen the top yet?"

The years between thirty-seven and forty-two are peak years of anxiety for nearly everyone. Elliot Jaques, a psychoanalyst, has postulated that a critical transition begins around thirty-five, not only in creative geniuses; it manifests itself in some form in everyone. Jaques called it the "Mid-Life Crisis." He noted that the process of transition runs on for several years, and the exact period will vary among individuals.[1]

Although much has been written and spoken about mid-life crisis in recent years, it is not a new phenomenon. What is new is that we are more conscious of it and people interested in human development are studying it. People have journeyed through mid-life crises for centuries.

Dante wrote about this stage and struggle in his life in the opening stanzas of *Divine Comedy*. Those words express the psychological impact of this period:

> In the middle of the journey of our life, I came to myself within a dark wood where the straight way was lost. Ah, how hard it is to tell of that wood, savage and harsh and dense, the thought of which renews my fear. So bitter is it that death is hardly more.

Dante wrote those words in his forty-second year. He had been experiencing the struggle in his own life since the age of thirty-seven. Dante's mid-life crisis was at the beginning of the fourteenth century.

Gail Sheehy, author of *Passages*, has formulated in words what this crisis is like. She says it all starts with a vague feeling:

I have reached some sort of meridian in my life. I had better take a survey, reexamine where I have been, and reevaluate how I am going to spend my resources from now on. Why am I doing all this? What do I really believe in? Underneath this vague feeling is the fact, as yet unacknowledged, that there is a down side to life, a back of the mountain, and that I have only so much time before the dark to find my own truth.[2]

F. Scott Fitzgerald wrote in *The Crack-Up*:

I began to realize that for two years of my life I had been drawing on resources that I did not possess, that I had been mortgaging myself physically and spiritually up to the hilt.[3]

The spiritual crisis that surfaces during the Deadline Decade is a matter of purpose and meaning. To what or for what am I giving my life? When my life is over, what will it matter that I have lived? The solution many persons have found is to launch second careers. In and through those they give themselves authentically and know that what they are doing and who they are being has meaning and purpose. Others reevaluate their original careers, sharpening the focus of their work and commitment.

Many people appear to wing it past this midstation without pause. They deny the down side. They play more tennis and run more laps, give bigger parties, seek better hair transplants and higher face lifts, find younger partners to take to bed. That is not to suggest that jogging is not worthwhile or that having parties cannot help revitalize relationships, but people who rely on only these outlets may be losing in the bargain even more than a critical chance for personal development. To disallow the momentous changes underneath forces a skimming of all experiences. The eventual price is superficiality.[4]

The only way, finally, to make fear of the down side go away is to allow it entry. The sooner we allow the truths of this period to fill our container, the sooner they can be integrated with our youthful optimism and reground us with true strength. The most important words in middle life are "let go." Let it happen to you. Let it happen to your partner. Let the feelings happen. Acknowledge their presence. Let the changes happen.

The creative crisis may express itself in three different forms. The creative capacity may emerge and present itself for the first time. A person may burn out creatively or literally die. The person's work will undergo a decisive change.

New studies shed light on mental health at mid-life, according to Douglas LaBier, a psychoanalytic psychotherapist in Washington, D.C.

> Two widely held myths are that we pretty much cease to change after adolescence, and that mid-life is primarily a time of loss and decline. New research tells us that mid-life is more a time of expansion, a period of greater self-direction, creativity and passion.[5]

> Healthy development through mid-life is a byproduct of how we actually live. Restoration of an open vision results from altering how we live in practice. Therapy helps when it focuses on the core mid-life need: to restore, expand, and integrate powers of choice, moral vision, and disciplined action.[6]

What seems to be occurring at mid-life is that we are becoming better authors of our stories. We write the song, as Barry Manilow would say. In some ways we have been doing research on the story all along, and at mid-life we begin to write. We would be wise to see our lives as an ongoing novel that we are writing and in which we construct the plot as we go along. It means cultivating aspects of ourselves by practicing them. What is occurring is referred to as mid-life crisis because it is a dangerous opportunity in which a person is up against reality. Seeing reality as it is, rather than what we want it to be, is cleansing. It enables us to let go of self-centered needs while pursuing clear goals with passion: to embrace the paradox of trying everything—but expecting nothing.[7]

The needs of mid-life to develop lives of expansion include equality in intimate relations, purpose, and enhanced creativity. Specific changes occur in three areas: (1) Redefining Success: This is an outgrowth of viewing one's life as an ongoing project, similar to the way a person in business would plan and carry out an entrepreneurial venture. (2) Being Conscious at the Crossroads: This means a heightened sense of urgency about life as it exists within the present moment, a sharper awareness of when we are at a new crossroads, a new turning point. (3) Life as a Practice: A healthy mid-life involves changes in our life practice that reduce the gap between our inner values and vision and who we are in reality, both in career and in relationships. All of this is needed for us to write our stories with clarity and understanding.

Douglas LaBier explains the needed changes in the process:

> The preparation for self-authorship at mid-life sounds ironic: We need enough
> experience with failure and setback in our lives, and need to go down enough
> blind alleys of self-delusion to accrue the critical mass of experience necessary
> for the perspective, discipline and focus that support adult maturity. This is part
> of the reason why one cannot fully grow up before entering mid-life.[8]

Much of what has been said and thought about mid-life crisis by the average person has been negative and derogatory. Irresponsible behavior has been excused as "having a mid-life crisis." Many people have suggested that only those who didn't have their lives together have had crises at mid-life. While these attitudes are descriptive of some persons at the midpoint of life, they are not descriptive of all. What is descriptive of all is that somewhere between age thirty-five and forty-five, we enter a developmental stage where we reexamine the purpose and meaning of our lives. The conclusions we draw about purpose and meaning have a significant impact on our identity. The identity impact causes some people to redirect their lives, and for others it is a reaffirmation of the direction they were traveling.

At any given time several members of a congregation will be wrestling with the issues that negotiating the midpoint of life raises. It is appropriate and valuable for the congregation to recognize this need and find ways through worship to care for people as they navigate the churning waters of mid-life.

The following is a worship service seeks to address the stage of mid-life and identify some of the issues that are bubbling in people's lives. By acknowledging this stage of life and identifying some of the issues with which people struggle, members of the congregation can know they are heard, understood, and not alone in the middle of life.

Worshiping the God Who Helps Us Renegotiate Life
A Service of Christian Worship

The Chiming of the Hour

When We Arrive
The Prelude

The Call to Worship

Pastor: We are all on a journey and need guidance along the way.

People: We are at different points on the way, and our needs vary with where we are.

Pastor: Some are just beginning the journey. Some are about to finish. Still others are about to crest the hill at mid-life.

People: That is where many of us are, and it is a tough spot to be.

Pastor: Come, then, let us worship the God who is at the beginning and the ending and the middle of life. God will help navigate the difficult places in our lives.

People: We come to worship, eager to find help and hope for our journey.

Pastor: Come, let us worship God together.

*Hymn   "Guide Me, O Thou Great Jehovah"   CWM Rhondda

*The Invocation

O God, we lift up our lives to you. We know our help and our hope come from you. Instruct us in the paths we need to take. Guide us in the decisions we make as we write the stories of our lives. Open us to your creativity and renew a creative spirit within us. Calm our anxieties and raise our consciousness of your presence and grace available in our lives. Amen.

The Welcome

The Holy Scriptures   Genesis 32:22-32

At Halftime in Our Lives

The Pastoral Prayer

*Hymn   "If You Will Only Let God Guide You"   Neumark

The Offertory Prayer

The Offertory

The Receiving of the Tithes and Offerings

The Choral Worship   "The Race Set Before Us"   Anna Laura Page

The Sermon   "Forty-Something"

I find myself returning often to the story of Jacob as an illustration of how many of us approach life. There are clues in Jacob's story for our stories. If we will examine the points where Jacob's story and our stories intersect, we will learn a great deal about Jacob and even more about ourselves. The passage of scripture that is our text describes in some detail Jacob's mid-life crisis.

You may recall Jacob's late adolescent, young adulthood years when he swindled his brother and deceived his father to receive the coveted blessing of the firstborn. With the aid of his mother, Jacob left home to save his neck. Esau was ready to kill him! Isn't it strange how Jacob's actions fulfilled the meaning of his name, trickster?

Eventually, Jacob's day of reckoning with Esau had to come. Although Jacob had run away from home, settled with his Uncle Laban, gotten married twice, been swindled by his uncle turned father-in-law, he could have avoided Esau for the rest of his life, physically that is. But emotionally and spiritually Jacob had to come to terms with himself and his brother. Bubbling and brewing deep in his being, in his unconscious, was an incongruence for Jacob. The dichotomy that Jacob had caused had to be rectified. The biblical material gives no hint that any of this is a struggle for Jacob. Apparently, what Jacob did with the feelings he had about the way he had treated and tricked Esau was to deny those feelings, keep them suppressed, never ever let them come to the surface. Jacob kept the lid on those feelings by keeping busy and spending huge amounts of energy out-swindling his father-in-law.

For some reason when Jacob was on the run from the wrath of his father-in-law, he decided to meet up with his brother. Regardless of what kind of a trickster Jacob was, he had to know that there was an unsettled score between them. He probably pushed that aside as much as he could, but the first part of Genesis 32 tells of the elaborate preparation that Jacob made to meet Esau. The night before Jacob was to meet Esau, he sent his family and his crew across the Jabbok River toward Esau, but Jacob remained on the other side of the Jabbok. He slept there that night and dreamed of being in a wrestling match. Whom was he fighting? He was fighting Esau whom he had cheated. He was fighting with his father Isaac to whom he had lied. He was fighting God who was calling him to accountability for his actions. He was fighting the dark side of himself whom he was afraid to see in the light of day.

The dream Jacob had was a reality check. Dreams come up out of the unconscious and play out the themes a person is wrestling with in life. At least since adolescence, Jacob had carried around a fantasy of what he was like and what he would accomplish in life. But that night when he went to sleep by the Jabbok River, the reality of being forty-something, of there being unresolved conflict in his life, of him not liking who Jacob had become was held in bold relief for him in his dream. It was such a strong reality check for Jacob that he called the place Peniel, which means the face of God. He had seen what God was like and lived to tell about it. The event caused him to reexamine his life and consider how he might live the remainder of his life with meaning and purpose. This was a struggling event for Jacob. It was tough for him to let go. He had spent so much time and energy manipulating, maneuvering, and controlling circumstances to get all he could for himself with no thought or consideration of anyone else. His dream was a scary, frightening, invigorating, liberating experience as he wrestled with God, Esau, Isaac, and himself all at the same time. No wonder all he could do was limp away after the dream was over! If you want to know what a mid-life crisis will do to you, read Jacob's story. While you're reading, will you dare think about what your mid-life crisis did or is doing to you?

All of us go through a crisis at mid-life just as all of us go through the developmental process of adolescence. Our teenage wrestling and struggle has many common qualities with what others experienced. However, certain aspects of adolescence were more troublesome and more euphoric for us than for some of our peers at the time. And so it is with mid-life crisis. Having a mid-life crisis is a natural event to happen in our growth and development. As with adolescence, so with mid-life; there are better and worse ways to cope with the crisis.

A helpful way to look at mid-life is to consider it halftime in life. In team sports like basketball and football, the teams that do the best are the ones that are able to make adjustments at halftime related to the way they played in the first half and related to the game plan the opponent is attempting to execute. The mid-life crisis is a dangerous opportunity where we can make adjustments in our lives related to what life has been like in the first half and what we need, want, and hope life will be like in the second half of our lives. What adjustments do you want and need to make as you move into the second half of your life?

A minister lived through the experience of a tornado striking his town, and he learned a lesson from it that was valuable. The only things that managed to survive had two qualities: roots and flexibility. If there were no secure grounding or connection with the earth, the structure blew away. By the same token, if there was no give, that is, if something were utterly rigid, that was fatal also in a high wind. He went on to say that the same qualities are essential for both the people and the institutions who are called on to live amid the high winds of change.

Repeated in the lives of many biblical characters are features revealing the presence of roots and flexibility. These characters survived their own mid-life crises and lived to tell about them. Our awareness of how they negotiated those crises can be helpful to us in our journeys. While Jacob may provide the most insight for us. We also can learn from Samuel, Moses, and Joseph—just to name three additional guides for those of us negotiating the passage from the first half of our lives into the second half.

Samuel, an Old Testament prophet, is one who had firm rootage in the past, but he was flexible as well. Both qualities are needed if you and I are going to survive the kind of world in which we live. If people are going to survive the Deadline Decade of mid-life, neither absolute conservatism or total radicalism is likely to work. Roots and flexibility are crucial qualities for all of us.

Mid-life crisis struck Moses on the backside of the desert when he looked at a burning bush. The way Moses had thought about life when he lived in Egypt and the way he had been thinking about life as he tended sheep collided. How he thought life was earlier collided with the way life really was. This dangerous opportunity confronted Moses with a decision. The opportunity for Moses was an invitation for him to live his life from that time forward with clear meaning and purpose. The danger was that Moses would recede into nothing by having no meaning or purpose for which he would live. Moses had to decide whether to relinquish fantasy for reality or reality for fantasy. He chose to relinquish fantasy for reality.

At this point, perhaps the traditions of family lore helped Moses to grow as he did. Being alone in the desert, Moses may have remembered how one of his ancestors, a man named Joseph, had handled a similar experience. He, too, had begun the pilgrimage of personhood with a grandiose image of himself and God and, by acting impatiently and arrogantly as Moses had, he had gotten himself rejected by his kinspeople and become a lonely refugee far from home. Their situations were remarkably alike, and Moses remembered how Joseph did not give up in the face of adversity. What he did do was stop dreaming all those grandiose things about himself and his destiny, and he went to work paying attention to the things that were at hand, the day-by-day realities which one can handle with integrity and creativity or not.

This was the crucial breakthrough for Joseph—becoming attentive and faithful with the realities in reach, and it was there as collaborator in day-to-day struggles that Joseph discovered God to be at work. God is not just the Lord of the spectacular; God is to be found in the little things as well, and this is how God worked in the life of Joseph. Joseph did not become the grand vizer of Egypt in one miraculous swoop. That goal was reached more subtly, by Joseph's patient and faithful handling of little details—first as a slave, then as a prisoner. The ways of God were neither quick nor immediate nor obvious in Joseph's life. The "mill of God" ground slowly and through much struggle in this one's life, and I am guessing such a memory was of enormous help to Moses as "fresh out of prep school" and ready to conquer the world, he found himself a total failure, wandering the wastelands of the Sinai Desert.

But like Joseph before him, Moses did not give up or collapse. His vision of God as a wonder-worker gave way to a vision of a God who collaborates with us in the day-by-day struggle with little things. Thus, he settled down, not just to make the best, but the most of the opportunities that were at hand. He became a shepherd in that desert region, and proceeded to learn the terrain of a country that he would one day need to know in leading a whole people. More importantly, he learned to be patient with a God "whose ways are not as our ways and whose thoughts are not as our thoughts," one who is always good but never obvious. And it was this attentiveness to detail, this willingness to let God be what God was and do what God would do, that led up to Moses' call years later.

This is how the great work of liberation got started, a still small voice articulating God's purpose.

The tension we experience at forty-something during the deadline decade is caused by our struggle with whether to be superficial or real. It really is a matter of integrity. Will I be authentic or just pretend? I like the answer given in the children's book, *The Velveteen Rabbit*. One day the young rabbit asks the Skin Horse, who has been around the nursery quite some time, what is real? And does real hurt?

> "Sometimes," said the Skin Horse, for he was always truthful. "When you are REAL you don't mind being hurt."
>
> "Does it happen all at once, like being wound up," he asked, "or bit by bit?"
>
> "It doesn't happen all at once," said the Skin Horse. "You become. It takes a long time. That's why it doesn't often happen to people who break easily, or have sharp edges, or who have to be carefully kept. Generally, by the time you are REAL, most of your hair has been loved off, and your eyes drop out and you get loose in the joints and very shabby. But these things don't matter at all, because once you are REAL you can't be ugly, except to people who don't understand."[9]

It is well documented that each of us has or will have a mid-life crisis when we are forty-something. Usually the crisis begins with a vague questioning of why I am doing this and do I really believe in this sometime in our late thirties. But the crisis is full blown and resolved in some way when we are forty-something.

Each person who has survived a mid-life crisis can point to a time, an event, a circumstance that marked their moving out of the crisis and forward into the second half of life with a clearer view of reality, a stronger sense of identity, and a more congruent sense of inner values and vision and reality. When or what was yours? For Moses, it was the burning bush. For Joseph, it was the agony of imprisonment caused by his actions and his brothers' reactions. For Jacob, it was his anticipation of meeting Esau symbolized in the crossing of the Jabbok River.

In all of Jacob's wandering and swindling days in Laban's land, he must have often heard footsteps and looked over his shoulder convinced that he heard and saw Esau coming after him. The watershed event in Jacob's life was the night before he crossed the Jabbok River to meet Esau. Jacob developed a different perspective and outlook on life after his restless wrestling dream at Peniel on the other side of the Jabbok River. His perspective on life was so different after the dream that his name, his identity, was changed from Jacob to Israel.

To Jacob's credit, after his wrestling dream, he was willing to face his worst fear: Esau who had wanted to kill him. Even though Jacob met Esau and their reunion went better than anyone imagined or expected Jacob, now known as Israel, never was comfortable in Esau's presence. Jacob's life practice underwent a decisive change. He is no longer known as the grand swindler. But everything about him did not change as a result of his struggle and his new perspective. He showed favoritism toward his younger sons, first Joseph and later Benjamin. Favoritism had been at the root of problems in Jacob's biological family. Even with his new insight and his new identity, Jacob repeated the favoritism mistake. God really does have a tough job getting people like Jacob and me to permit God's grace to flow to every part of our lives and change us totally for the better.

Some of you have already passed forty-something. For you, what was your Jabbok River? Some of you are approaching forty-something. I hope you will be on the lookout for your Jabbok River. It is coming. It is right that it should because it is a vital part of your development as a child of God. Some of us are in the midst of forty-something. Perhaps identifying our Jabbok River is most difficult for us because we are in the midst of the dangerous opportunity that forty-something provides. But whether we are approaching the river, find ourselves in midstream, or are safely on the other side, may we be confident that God has, is, and will collaborate with us to make a safe journey through forty-something and across the Jabbok River.

Is an Appropriate Time to Make Adjustments for the Second Half

The Invitation to Commitment
*Hymn of Commitment   St. Catherine
            "Our Hope Is in the Living God"
*The Benediction
The Organ Postlude

The purpose of this worship service is to help people recognize and identify that the struggle at mid-life is a natural, important age and stage of development as are our childhood and adolescence. Addressing this stage of life through worship helps people to recognize that God and the people of God are with them in their journey. They discover available resources to help them negotiate the transition from the first half of life to the second. Among the available resources are the stories of biblical characters. When we see where our lives intersect with the lives of biblical characters, we discover a wealth of help and hope to provide the roots and flexibility we need to grow to be people with meaning and purpose in our living.

Notes

[1]Elliot Jaques, "Death and the Mid-Life Crisis," quoted by Gail Sheehy, *Passages: Predictable Crises of Adult Life (New* York: E. P. Dutton & Co., 1977) 369.

[2]Sheehy, 350.

[3]Quoted by Sheehy in *Passages*, 371.

[4]Sheehy, 363.

[5]Douglas LaBier, "Our Mid-life Expectancy," *The Washington Post*, 30 April 1991, C5.

[6]Ibid.

[7]Ibid.

[8]Ibid.

[9]Margery Williams, *The Velveteen Rabbit* (New York: Doubleday, 1958).

Chapter 16

More Limits, Less Energy

In my third pastorate I met a husband and wife who were amazingly devoted to each other. They were about fifty years of age. Nearly fourteen years earlier the woman had been diagnosed with multiple sclerosis. The disease had progressed to the point that her speech was impaired and she was unable to move her limbs. A wheelchair was her method of mobility, provided someone placed her in it and pushed it for her. After a night's sleep she had to remain in bed until someone lifted her from the bed into a chair. Her sense of humor was delightful, and her views about life were insightful. Her husband's eyes still sparkled with devotion. When they married, I doubt they thought about the ramifications of the statement in their vows "in sickness and in health." This couple lived daily with the limitations caused by long-term illness. They experienced at a relatively young age what more and more people are experiencing as life expectancy increases. As we live longer, we also experience greater limitations.

How often have you heard someone who has faced difficult times say with resignation, "Well, at least I still have my health"? Basically, what people mean by such a statement is that they are still independent, able to look after their own affairs, and do not have a crippling, debilitating disease. They may not see or hear as well as they once did, but they remain able to take care of themselves.

Of course, many people contract diseases or have accidents that greatly limit their abilities and activities at young ages. Although they manage to cope, they would benefit from more interaction and involvement with people. Often we treat people with limitations as if they have a contagious disease. When we meet someone with a physical or mental limitation, we are made aware of our own frailty and mortality. We avoid someone with limitations at times because they remind us of what could happen to us. Becoming wrapped up in ourselves, we fail to care for and minister to those who would benefit from interacting and relating with us.

On the day I wrote these paragraphs, I visited a ninety-four-year-old woman who resides in a nursing home. She was so appreciative of my visit and commented during our conversation, "You know not many people come in here to see us." During that same afternoon in the nursing home, I was being guided by a nurse to visit another resident. As we walked along the corridors, I was impressed with the nurse who spoke to each person we met or passed in the hallway and called each one by name. Visits with people in nursing homes or who are confined to their homes will be tremendously meaningful to them. We may be amazed what the visits do does for us as well.

There are several ways a congregation can help members cope and deal with the issues related to long-term illnesses and disabilities. Seminars led by health care professionals, caregivers, family members, and ministers provide an excellent forum for people to raise questions and begin identifying some of their needs and struggles with these issues. Church school classes may adopt residents at long-term care facilities and nursing homes. These adoptions can lead to visits and involvement with the residents. A congregation also can approach the needs these issues and situations raise through worship. What a congregation does in and through worship guides people in forming and shaping their theology and vision of ministry. If the church never says anything through worship about segments of the population, by its silence it says it has nothing to say on the subject or that it should say nothing about the issue.

The following worship service was designed to heighten awareness of the needs of people who experience long-term illness or disability and to help members of the congregation begin to grapple with the issues that long-term illness and disability raise for all of us.

Worshiping the God of Hope
A Service of Christian Worship

The Chiming of the Hour

Let Us Lift Up Our Eyes

The Silent Preparation for Worship
The Organ Prelude

The Responsive Call to Worship
Pastor: Well, here we are gathered to worship. Why have you come?
People: We have come to worship God because we need help and hope.
Pastor: Why are these needs so paramount?

People: Some days we are willing to recognize and admit our limitations.

Pastor: How are we limited?

People: We cannot do things as quickly as we used to. We cannot drive at night. We have family members who have major health constraints. We are becoming more dependent on others to assist us. This is the frustrating way life is for many of us.

Pastor: As we gather to worship, we bring our frustrations with us.

People: Yes, we do because we need help and hope to cope with life. God has been our help in ages past and is our hope for years to come.

Pastor: Then, come, let us worship the God of hope who will help us with all our limitations.

People: We come eager and ready to worship.

From Where Does Our Help Come?

*Hymn	"O God, Our Help in Ages Past"	St. Anne
Welcome		
The Old Testament Lesson		Psalm 130
Solo	"O Rest in the Lord"	Mendelssohn
The New Testament Lesson		Romans 5:1-5
*Hymn	"Search Me, O God"	Ortonville

The Prayers
    The Silent Prayers for Ourselves
    The Pastoral Prayer for Others
    The Lord's Prayer in Unison

Our Help Comes from the Lord

The Choral Worship	Mendelssohn
"He That Shall Endure to the End"	

Sermon   "Coping and Hoping"

A new phenomenon began occurring in the last quarter of our century. Many people now have the opportunity to live what has been identified as the "third age." Numerous people are discovering that they have twenty-five to thirty years of life after they retire. This gift of an additional age results from a combination of factors. The advances of medical science contribute to longer life spans. People are more health conscious and active. Many people adhere to healthier diets and exercise more than did previous generations. Interests in activities other than work are being developed by people throughout their lives. When they arrive at retirement, they have the opportunity to pursue one or more of those activities or interests with concerted energy and effort. I hope the church is contributing to the development of the "third age" with a healthy emphasis on stewardship. As children of God we are called upon to manage the lives we have been given, and this includes taking good care of our lives through exercise, nutrition, physical examinations, and spiritual inventories.

The downside of living longer is there is more opportunity for disabling accidents, debilitating diseases, and long-term illnesses. There has developed a group of people known as the sandwich generation. These are the people who have children who are in late adolescence and early adulthood and who have aging parents who require some attention and/or assistance in managing their lives.

During the next few minutes I want us to explore the dynamics and issues involved in a debilitating disease or a long-term illness. I also want us to consider how the church can respond to the needs of these people, their families, and friends. Indeed, one of the things the church can do is to be a deliverer of help and hope in the context of worship for people as they grapple with these tough, difficult, painful issues in their lives. There is a strengthening that is available to people through the church as the church takes seriously their needs and struggles. There is help and hope for people as they are pointed beyond themselves and as the church points beyond itself to God as the source and author of hope for all of our lives regardless of the circumstances, limitations, and difficulties we experience.

The scripture passages that are the basis for this service each direct us to the source of our help and hope. Psalm 130 has become one of the great penitential psalms in the Christian tradition. It is often used during the Lenten season as worship leaders urge congregants to be reflective and examine their lives in relationship to God. This psalm also has application in other ways as well. The realization of personal need may be easy for many of us to identify and express in some way. To assume responsibility for that need is a bit more difficult. However, to express an unquestioned trust in God to do something about the need is rarer still. Psalm 130 has an unabashed proclamation of such trust in God and the benefits that result. This Psalm has excellent application for us in our long-term struggles with illness and disabilities.

In writing to the Christians at Rome, Paul spoke of the great trinity of gifts that meet our needs: faith, hope, and love. These gifts enrich our lives all along the journey, but nowhere do we need them more nor do we benefit in a more powerful way from them than during those difficult, agonizing experiences that go on and on, seemingly lasting forever.

The assurances and promises that are expressed through these two passages of scripture provide a basis of support and encouragement for us as we face debilitating diseases, long-term illnesses, or disabilities. All of us are faced with these if not for ourselves, with family members, and if not with family members, with friends and/or acquaintances. The calling of the church is to be with people in these kinds of circumstances. That means that all of us who are a part of the church are to have a part in being with people in their struggles and adjustments that these types of circumstances bring. Let's consider what some of the issues and needs are that surface as a result of long-term illnesses. Then, let's explore how the church can respond to these issues and needs in ways that will minister to and care for those who have these experiences as well as their families and friends who journey with them through the illness or disability.

A disclaimer is appropriate at the outset. Let us never say, suggest, or imply to anyone that their disease or disability is the will of God. Nothing is further from the truth, and nothing is more blasphemous. Blasphemy is attributing evil to God. To suggest that God causes disease or disability is to say that God causes destruction, and that which destroys is evil. Paul's word to the Romans was, "We know that trouble produces endurance, endurance brings character, and character creates hope" (Rom 5:4). One who had experienced chronic illness that has lasted years will probably respond, "I really didn't need this much character." Lord Reith said, "I do not like crises, but I do like the opportunities they provide." Once we can work through the question that verbalizes our anger, "Why did this happen to me?" then we can ask the helpful question, "What can I do now that this has happened to me?"

When anyone experiences something that debilitates, there are stages the person goes through in coping with the illness or the disability. Grief is experienced, and the stages in the process are similar to the stages of grief experienced in coping with death. The first reaction is shock expressed as, "This is not me. This isn't happening to me." Then, there is the expectancy of recovery as the person says, "I'm sick, but I'll get well." As the process drags on and wellness or return to the way things were before the incident delays, the person goes into mourning feeling, "All is lost." Next, the person seeks to muster strength by developing a defense often expressed, "I'll go on in spite of this." Eventually, the person who copes best with this change expresses adjustment by saying, "It's different but not bad."

The issue that permeates the experience of being disabled or coping with long-term illness is meaning in life. The person affected directly is continually confronted with the question that is raised from deep within, "What is the meaning of my life? What purpose does my life have?" Dealing with the situation caused by illness or disability requires that the person have strong reasons to want to struggle. In other words, life must have meaning and value in order for a person to have the energy, the courage, the fortitude, the stamina to continue living with intention and meaning.

With any disease or disability, it is important to recognize that no one is ever totally disabled. However, the terminology used by insurance companies, the federal government, and others often does identify a person as totally disabled. My father suffered many injuries as a result of being hit by shrapnel from an artillery shell in World War II. Many years later, additional problems developed with one of his knees and he had to have the joint replaced. Until then, he had been categorized as 90 percent disabled. After that surgery, he was listed as totally disabled. Although my dad is limited as to how rapidly he may move and his mobility is affected, he can walk anywhere he wants and drives a car. After he was classified totally disabled, he continued his work as a rural letter carrier. After retiring from the postal department, he was elected mayor of his hometown and served in that position with distinction. For people who are disabled, there are things they can do well and things they cannot do well or at all. That is true of all of us, isn't it?

Beatrice A. Wright has helpfully distinguished between the terms "disability" and "handicap." Here is her distinction:

> A disability is a condition of impairment, physical or mental, having an objective aspect that can usually be described by a physician. . . . A handicap is the cumulative result of the obstacles which disability interposes between the individual and his maximum functional level.[1]

In ministering to people who are disabled or who find themselves dealing with an illness over an extended period of time, our purpose is to help these people bring into focus a meaning, calling, and hope out of boredom, purpose-lessness, despair, and sin of human existence. We want them to establish durable, meaningful relationships so they and we are challenged to discover the calling in life to participate in a true and mature fellowship with God and with people.

One of the tasks of the church is to help people, including those who are disabled and those coping with long-term illnesses, become conscious of their own unique, God-given capacities and values and to discover meaning in life. The greatest danger for people suffering from long-term illness is the possibility of losing awareness of their own worth and dignity as human beings.

The focus of ministry for the church in its effort to care for those who struggle with a life-altering illness is to help them discover their calling in life, to participate in a true and mature fellowship with God and fellow human beings, and to discover for themselves meaning in life. Franklin C. Shontz pointed out several years ago that the primary need for people with life-altering illness is meaning in life.

It is not hard to justify the argument that the patient himself, particularly the patient with severe chronic illness, is not primarily concerned with physical health, home, job, except as these hold for him the prospect of furthering his deeper human wants. From his difficult position, the patient seeks for what might best be called a "meaning in life."[2]

Religion plays a major part in helping people discover meaning in their lives. Religion is an expression of a person's desire for the ultimate meaning in life. Victor Frankl has pointed out through his experience of surviving Nazi concentration camps and working with others who did that the central longing of people is a will to meaning. Meaning is found through the attitudes adopted toward unavoidable circumstances or the limiting factors of one's life. Life, therefore, has meaning to the last breath.[3] Religion is a clear affirmation of attitudinal values. It is an expression of our desire to conserve all values that can provide a sense of the Eternal within our transitory living.

Franklin Duncan has identified three trends of religious ideation by people. These are descriptive of what appears to be the overarching pattern of the religious ideas and values of disabled people with whom Duncan worked. The trends are religion of works, religion of pleasure, and religion of faith. A person who tends toward a religion of works focuses on the functional goals of living. This person's ultimate concern is with physical or vocational activity as necessary and essential for a satisfactory life. The person who tends toward a religion of pleasure ultimately is concerned with what life can give without having to encounter any unpleasant experiences. The person with a religion of works has a perverted sense of responsibility, and the one with a religion of pleasure has an avoidance of responsibility. The person who tends toward a religion of faith has meaning and purpose of life as the ultimate concern. This person seeks those religious values which are unconditional and give consistency to life. This attitude is characterized as a spirit of openness to life and the spirit of God, a willingness to stand firm in one's encounter with the anxieties and sufferings of life, and a patient waiting for the grace and creative spirit of God.[4]

Suffering is a significant dimension of life. Suffering is especially present in the lives of people experiencing life-altering illnesses or disabling events. The suffering may be physical pain and that is agonizing, but more intense and more agonizing is the emotional and mental anguish that occurs as people seek to adjust to what has happened in their lives. Suffering is not something that is sought or desired. Neither is it avoided or denied. Suffering in a religion of faith is seen as that aspect of life which must be accepted and turned to constructive use in service of others and the kingdom of God. Suffering can be a pathway to a richer, more mature relationship to life and to God. With this understanding, then, meaning in life is not dependent on the length of life. Any length of time is viewed as an expression of God's grace and mercy and the opportunity to affirm one's uniqueness before God.

There are three forms of care and ministry that we in the church can offer to people who are dealing with a life-altering illness or a disabling event. We can provide comfort, catalysis, and challenge. While these are distinct, they also are interrelated. We comfort a person through our genuine acceptance of who the person is. We make clear to the person the right to grieve, feel bitter, want to give up, to hold unrealistic goals, and to be angry. The primary goals of comfort are the person's consciousness of freedom and the possibility of a meaningful life. We can provide comfort through suggestions and through catharsis. The presence of a minister or member of the congregation or the person being in a worship service suggests and reminds the person of God's acceptance and unconditional love and meaning which remain to assure the possibility of a new way of life. One person who was in a rehabilitation program said to the chaplain, "I like to see you down here, because you help me to remember that there is a purpose in what I am doing."[5] We provide comfort through the power of suggestion.

We also provide comfort through catharsis. Our willingness to empathize with people in their fears, confusion, suffering, despair, love, and courage strengthens and encourages them. Empathy helps people tell their hidden doubts and fears, and then they are able to do something about them. Empathy also provides people with the possibilities of help that is necessary for the creation of hope. Comforting people through suggestion and catharsis communicates love for them, God's love and ours.

We may also serve as a catalysis for a person. Through the relationship we have with a person and through their participation in worship, people may be urged to think about who they are and who they are to become. A worship service may serve as a catalysis that focuses on God's unconditional affirmation of people and who they are created to become. Hymns, scripture, prayers, and sermons often raise questions that provoke people to discover meaning in life. To encourage people to ask reflective "as if" questions, they are moved to think about possible future positive goals and values. The catalysis is an outside fulcrum of help that offers people hope. Their hope is grounded in God who is the source of all hope.

The person who has experienced a life-altering illness also needs to be challenged. The person is challenged to a commitment by furnishing temporary motivation through positive, healthy relationship. Provoking questions can be raised in individual conversations and through worship that provoke the person to take action. And then, the congregation in various ways can support the person's successes such as welcoming them to worship, relating warmly with them, and offering prayers that express the person's needs, dreams, and gratitude.

Through challenge faith is implemented as people are encouraged to develop commitment. In other words, we as a congregation minister to people coping with life-altering illnesses and disabilities and provide pastoral care through worship by implementing love, hope, and faith as Paul suggested in Romans 5:1-5.

Constantly present for all of us is the shadow of death. Periodically, each of us is reminded of how temporary and fragile life is. The reminder may be a near accident or the death of a friend. The reminder may be an illness or the surgery a family member faces. The ominous shadow of death is a constant reminder to the person dealing with a disability or a life-altering illness. I am reminded of the best known passage of scripture, the twenty-third Psalm, and the promise it offers. "Yea, though I go through the valley of the shadow of death, I will not be afraid" (Ps 23:5). The reason for no fear is the assurance of God's presence. The promise is not that some terrible disease or accident will not happen to us. None of us are exempt from that possibility. If we live long enough—and the chances are increasing that we will live a long time—all of us are going to be affected by life-altering illnesses or accidents, if not directly ourselves, then indirectly through family members or close friends. The word of assurance the Psalmist experienced and that is offered to us is we do not need to be afraid because God is a constant companion journeying with us as a friend, helper, and supporter in all that we face.

All of us are faced with the same dilemma. All of us are terminal. We cannot get out of this life alive. Death shadows our every move. Those who are having to cope with life altering illnesses challenge all of us to recognize our limitations, disabilities, and mortality. By coming to terms with these issues, we learn how to die. When we learn how to die, we really learn how to live. We learn how to live by discovering meaning in life and in the midst of that discovery we experience hope, God's gift to us. An archaic usage of the word hope was that it designated arable land that was surrounded by swamp. Isn't that a graphic image of God's presence in our lives. Our lives are surrounded by the swamp filled with hurt, disease, agony, and frustration. But right in the middle of it all is God giving us love, faith, and hope. When we have these gifts, even the ominous shadow of death cannot make us afraid.

The Elephant Man is a powerful play based on the life of John Merrick. He lived in London during the latter half of the nineteenth century. Merrick was horribly deformed and was a freak attraction in traveling side shows. As a young man he was abandoned and left helpless until he was admitted to Whitechapel, a prestigious London hospital. The most striking feature about Merrick was his enormous head. From the brow there projected a huge bony mass like a loaf, while from the back of his head hung a bag of spongy fungous-looking skin, the surface of which was comparable to brown cauliflower. The bony mass nearly covered one eye. A mass of bone projected from the upper jaw that turned his upper lip inside out and making his mouth a wide slobbering aperture. The nose was a lump of flesh, only recognizable as a nose from its position. The deformities rendered the face utterly incapable of the expression of any emotion whatsoever. The right arm was of enormous size and shapeless. The right hand was large and clumsy. No distinction existed between the palm and back, the thumb was like a radish, the fingers like thick tuberous roots. As a limb it was useless. The other arm was remarkable by contrast. It was not only normal, but was moreover a delicately shaped limb covered with a fine skin and provided with a beautiful hand which any woman would have envied. Eventually Merrick was thrown out of the side shows and was admitted to Whitechapel, a prestigious London hospital. Under the care of a physician, Merrick was educated and introduced to London society. He changed from being an object of pity to being urbane and witty. His deformity remained, including his one deformed and useless arm. Throughout his stay at Whitechapel, Merrick used his one good hand and arm to build a beautiful wooden replica of Saint Peter's Church of London.

None of us is perfect. All of us have limitations, disabilities, and deformities. Some are not as obvious as others. But with our limitations—those that have always been a part of us or have come to us lately because of some accident or debilitating disease—we are called to build the church, the body of Christ. May the gifts of faith, hope, and love give our lives meaning. With lives that have meaning, may we be found coping and hoping.

The Maker of Heaven and Earth

The Invitation to Respond
*Hymn   "Day by Day"   Blott en Dag
*Offertory Sentences
Offertory
Receiving of Tithes and Offerings
The Doxology
The Presentation of New Members
*Benediction
The Organ Postlude

Notes

[1]Beatrice A. Wright, *Physical Disability—A Psychological Approach* (New York: Harper & Row, 1960) 9.

[2]Franklin C. Shontz, "Severe Chronic Illness," in *Psychological Practices with the Physically Disabled,* James F. Garrett and Edna S. Levine, eds. (New York: Columbia University Press, 1962) 422.

[3]Victor E. Frankl, *The Doctor and the Soul* (New York: Alfred A. Knopf, Inc., 1965) 49-50.

[4]Franklin Duncan, "Pastoral Care of Disabled Persons," in *Pastoral Care in Crucial Human Situations,* Wayne E. Oates and Andrew D. Lester, eds. (Valley Forge: Judson Press, 1969) 154.

[5]Ibid., 160.

Chapter 17

Aging and Retirement

Retirement and aging intersect in our lives. While more in this chapter will deal with retirement, it cannot be addressed without at least some attention to concerns about aging. Retirement is one of the major transitions in life. People navigate this transition with varying ease and levels of comfort. There is a correlation between how people have coped with other transitions in their lives and how they cope with retirement. Persons who have used work as a way to avoid relationships, as an escape from some difficult circumstance, or as a way to deny some problems in life often experience retirement as a nightmare. Those who have dealt with life in a rather straightforward manner, maintained healthy relationships, been open to change, and adaptable to circumstances discover retirement to be a kind of dream come true.

A lot more is said and done about retirement now than in any previous time and with good reason. It is fairly common for a person to retire and live another twenty to thirty years. The slowest growing age group is eighteen year-olds, and the fastest growing one is people over eighty. What a shift! Notice that I had barely begun talking about retirement before I was also talking about aging. Retirement, aging, and death are related. To talk of one implies the other two. No doubt one of the reasons many people do not talk about or make plans for retirement is because it reminds them of aging and death. Anxiety and fear about aging and death also get focused on retirement as well. Retirement, aging, and death are bound together. Paul Tournier said,

> In the last analysis, all anxiety is reduced to anxiety about death. Proof of this is the large number of stories in which a [person] freed from the fear of death is seen to be freed from all other fears: he [or she] has no more fear of anything or anyone; no one can overcome him [or her] even by killing him [or her].[1]

Another reason for more awareness of and planning for retirement is that we live in an age of specialization. Indeed, we know more and more about less and less. Two generations ago—in an agrarian culture, where an extended family lived together—as persons of the older generation reached a time when they were not able to work as hard or as much as others, they remained, a part of the household and participated in the less demanding chores. Thus, they continued to contribute to the well being of the family. I recall my great-grandfather Rhodes Rose Roberts in his eighties helping to feed the livestock on the farm, and I remember him riding his sorrel mare five miles into town in the mid fifties. It was the same sorrel mare he saddled for me and let me ride around in the barnyard. My great-grandfather lived in the big house with Uncle Harry and his family. They continued to operate the farm. No one ever referred to my great-grandfather as having retired. In those days retirement was a city word, and only people who worked in the cities ever retired.

Rhodes Roberts' son, Mack, continued the tradition of not officially retiring. Mack was a physician who began practicing medicine in Monticello, Kentucky, in 1932. He continued his medical practice until his ninetieth birthday. Beginning around age seventy-five, however, he lightened up on the chores. He stopped delivering babies or admitting patients to the hospital. He continued to see patients in his office and at his home when they came by after hours, and he made house calls until he was ninety.

What these two relatives of mine have done is what all of us need to do during retirement. We need to do things that have meaning and worth to us. For some of us, these activities may be a modified continuation of how we had earned a living. Others may develop a hobby or avocation into a full blown, nearly full-time activity. Many retirees are able to continue with their employment or with one in a similar field on a part-time basis. Many retirees enjoy the benefits of retirement while continuing to use their experience and expertise. Retirement is a significant change in life, but it can be met with eager enthusiasm. The motto of the Golden Club in Rio Piedras, Puerto Rico, is, "Retired from work but not from life." That is a healthy motto for all of us to adopt as we approach and move through the major intersection of retirement.

The retirement intersection has several hazards that must be negotiated. Is the person retiring from one job, but intending to move into another one? Or is the person retiring from active employment? A major hazard that must be negotiated is financial. Will the person be able to live and do the things he or she wants to do on the limited, fixed income that accompanies retirement? One of the jolts retirees feel is the actual reduction in pay from their last pay period while actively employed and their first retirement check. Anxiety also rises as the retiree awaits the first retirement check. When will it arrive? Why isn't it here yet? Has there been a mistake or mix up in my retirement? Is the company going to come through on its promise? Has the government lost my file?

For persons who are retired and married, there must be consideration of the spouse and the spouse's feelings. Is the spouse working away from home? What will it be like for the retiree to remain at home while the spouse leaves for work? What about the retiree remaining in bed when the spouse gets up to go to work? What does this couple do with the additional availability to each other?

The person who is retiring is shifting gears and changing direction. Having gone to work every day for years and then suddenly to end that routine is a physical and emotional jolt. It is not unusual for new retirees to have work withdrawal symptoms. Manyof them struggle with feelings of guilt because they are not going to work. Others are euphoric with the freedom they have and the variety of activities they schedule. The euphoria usually lasts only about six months; retirees realize they have pretty much done all the things they had on the list, or they have spent all the available money and will have to save awhile before they can continue down the list.

Of course, this is only a partial list of the hazards that must be negotiated as a person approaches and travels through the intersection of retirement. All of these hazards do point in one direction, toward one issue. The retiree wrestles with the question, "What will I do with my life in the rocking chair years that will have meaning and worth for me and for others?" Answering this question to one's satisfaction will result in delightful growth for the retiree during what is referred to by some as the "third age" of life.

Several years ago a group of retired people at the Central Baptist Church of Wayne, Pennsylvania, developed the Senior Service Corps. Members of this group are professionals who have retired. According to one of them, Paul Madsen, "We feel we still have gifts to give and that, though [we're] retired, God still has a place for us."[2] Members of this group give of their time and abilities to assist people in the areas in which they earned their living as professionals. Some of them go to Jamaica each year to provide dental care for people who would never have it otherwise.

Paul Tournier has suggested there are two great turning points in life. The first is from childhood to adulthood and the second is from

adulthood to old age.[3] Although I think there are several other major intersections in life, certainly the one from adulthood into retirement and
aging is a major one that calls for preparation, planning, and skill to
negotiate.

People best prepare for retirement and aging by taking a positive
attitude throughout life, living each stage fully. Developing an attitude of
gratitude makes a major contribution. To have an attitude of gratitude
about life is the result of seeing life as a gift, accepting the gift, giving
thanks for the gift, and giving the gift away. When asked if they have
accepted retirement and aging, some people respond, "You've got to."
But that attitude is fatalism rather than acceptance. Acceptance is directly
related to being in harmony with oneself. Acceptance is tied to our ability
to evolve. The more difficulty we have evolving the more neurotic we
are. The writers in Genesis said that the patriarchs died in peace because
they had lived their "full span of years" (Gen 25:8). They accepted their
lives as gifts and were able to evolve into in harmony with themselves.
When people are in harmony with themselves, they move into the future
with hope and affirmation. Here are two examples I read about recently.

Bishop Herbert Welch of the Methodist Church lived to be 103 years
old. Mark Trotter, pastor of the First Methodist Church of San Diego,
said that on Bishop Welch's ninetieth birthday someone asked if he
thought he would live to be a hundred. Bishop Welch said, "Of course;
statistics show that very few people die at the age of ninety-nine."

Arturo Toscanini, one of the greatest conductors of this century, had
the same kind of spirit. At the age of eighty-eight Toscanini was invited
to conduct the British Broadcasting Company orchestra at Royal Albert
Hall in London. It was a spectacular performance. After its conclusion
the trustees of the BBC invited him to become the regular conductor of
the orchestra and offered him a two-year contract. Toscanini said, "I'm
disappointed. I was hoping the contract would be for ten years." Both of
these men, in spite of their ages, maybe because of their ages, were filled
with hope and affirmed the future.

In tandem with the gratitude attitude to prepare for retirement and
aging we need to develop interests beyond our specialization. When we
retire, we reverse our development in a sense. During the technological
and informational ages in which we live, we have gone at life as if we
were looking through the wrong end of a telescope. We have moved
from a broad general view and approach to an ever smaller and smaller

specialization. In retirement the movement is away from specialization toward a more open and wider horizon. It is rare for the person who had only one or two interests during the employment years of his or her life to take up new interests in retirement. On the other hand, persons who had multiple interests during employment years find the most contentment and meaning in life during retirement because they find many useful things in which to invest their lives.

Paul Tournier said, "So long as we talk only of the use of leisure, we seem to be suggesting that all that matters is to find the means of killing time without getting too bored."[4] We must be converted from earning a living to cultural activity. To acquire culture is to develop oneself, contribute to human progress, and find meaning in life that survives the end of professional activity. There is a close relationship between health and fulfillment of life, and between sickness and death and non-fulfillment of life. Life is felt to be a task to be performed, and a feeling of fulfillment is a necessary condition of health and life. We want and need something worthwhile to which to give ourselves. Jean-Marie Domenach noted, "Leisure in our society must always have something sacred about it."[5]

C. G. Jung observed,

> In our time the man of mature years is likely to experience a pressing need for a somewhat deeper individual culture, since he has been trained in an exclusively collective culture in childhood and later at the university, so that his whole mentality is a collective one.[6]

Jung differentiated between two forms of culture. The first is oriented toward production, the second is more meditative.[7]

Erik Erikson produced the classic work on the stages of development. He noted that the issue of struggle for people approaching and moving into retirement age is the struggle of integrity versus despair in their lives. Those persons who come out of the struggle on the side of despair feel that life is meaningless and useless. They will give themselves to nothing Despair, as Kirkegaard pointed out, is a sickness unto death. Those who arrive at an awareness of integrity, wholeness—that life makes sense and fits together—develop the characteristic of wisdom. Therefore, we often are willing to listen to the observations and insights of aging adults.

We perceive to be wise because their lives are integrated. They have been on the journey a long time and drawn from it insight and understanding. Albert Lacy observed, "We refer to older persons as being 'over the hill.' But it is precisely because they have covered life's hills that they are ready to serve—and to do so better than ever."[8] Part of the wisdom gleaned from aging is the value of staying connected to life and with life. As Richard Morgan noted, "As long as we keep our hopes and dreams alive, as long as we stay involved in life, our spirits will be renewed. There should be no wrinkles on the soul."[9]

Aging Gracefully

As the baby boomers have had an impact on each stage of life, the area of senior adults will be no exception. The first of the baby boomers will be fifty in the middle of this decade. One writer encourages us to imagine that it is the year 2020. Virtually every consumer product is designed with the comfort of the aged in mind—from clothing with Velcro fasteners instead of zippers to cars with swivel seats to ease getting in and out. There are no senior discounts, however; there are far too many seniors. Everywhere are the signs of an elderculture—books on "making the most of your golden years" and "the joys of elder sex." Large numbers of old people are found hanging out in shopping malls, and a blossoming of the spirit will mark a return to the culture and life-styles of the 1960s.[10]

As Golda Meir, fourth prime minister of Israel, noted, "Old age is like a plane flying through a storm. Once you're aboard, there's nothing you can do." Since we are on board this plane of aging that is flying through the storms of living, what can we do to insure ourselves that we can be evaluated as having been pretty good at what we did? How can we grow older gracefully?

The church can be a tremendous resource of support and encouragement to people as they face and journey through the transition of retirement. By celebrating with people when they retire, by affirming senior adults and their gifts, by helping senior adults deal with the spiritual issues of aging, and by encouraging senior adults to be actively involved in ministry, the church can nurture and nourish people during their "third age" of life.

Many congregations have events and activities for senior adults on a regular basis. Most congregations have a Senior Adult Day at least annually. Inviting senior adults to share in the worship leadership on such a day and emphasizing some of the needs, concerns, and gifts of senior adults through the worship experience is an effective way for a congregation to provide pastoral care for senior adults through worship. An example follows.

Worshiping the God of All Ages
A Service of Christian Worship

The Prelude
Maturity Is Not a Station in Life

The Chiming of the Hour
The Choral Call to Worship   Camacha
"Teach Me Thy Way, O Lord"

The Invocation
The Welcome
Hymn   "O God, Our Help in Ages Past"   St. Anne

The Holy Scriptures   Psalm 71:1-24
The Pastoral Prayer
The Lord's Prayer

Hymn   "Day By Day"   Blott en Dag
The Offertory Sentences
The Offertory   "Let Others See Jesus in You"   Coleman
The Receiving of the Tithes and Offerings

But a Direction

The Choral Worship   "It Is Well With My Soul"   Beck

The Sermon   "Retirement"

The time has come. Today I am announcing my retirement, effective December 31, 2006. It's a bit premature, isn't it? Why would anyone announce his retirement more than a decade in advance? The evidence clearly shows that the people who have most enjoyed and benefited from retirement and who have continued to make contributions to life during retirement are the people who anticipated and planned for retirement. Of course, just to announce my retirement does not prepare me for the changes involved and certainly doesn't guarantee that I will continue to make life contributions during retirement. However, having a target date for retirement does help a person focus on retirement and begin planning for the event and the season of life that has become known in some circles as "the third age."

As soon as the subject of retirement comes up, the issue of aging is underneath the discussion. That is understandable and appropriate. Generally, it is people who arrive at senior adult status who retire. The exact age of being a senior adult varies. The American Association of Retired People put people on their mailing list when they arrive at the big **5-0**. Some businesses give discounts to people who are fifty-five and over. Some companies and organizations have mandatory retirement at age seventy. Others offer early retirement incentives related to reorganization and restructuring of their businesses.

My father-in-law married later in life than many in his generation. He retired early. The result was that during his marriage, my father-in-law was retired more years than he was working full-time for his employer. Given the current life expectancy in the United States, it is fair to say that many people who do retire will live twenty to thirty years retired. This is why retirement is referred to by some as the "third age." The aging process often enables people to recognize a sense of accomplishment and meaning in their lives. Retirement and aging may also bring pain and despair into focus. Aging provides the opportunity for new life to be born. Let's explore these three things that come into focus in people's lives during the "third age."

First, we can recognize that aging often brings a sense of accomplishment and a feeling that life has been meaningful. We need to get rid of the stereotypes we have of older people.

> Older people are as likely to play tennis as checkers. Many are more likely to travel than to sit in a rocking chair. With more retirement years, they have found new interests and explored new opportunities. 'Our society is getting older but the old are getting younger,' said Robert B. Maxwell, while he was vice-president of the American Association of Retired Persons.[11]

When we allow ourselves to believe stereotypes, we fail to develop relationships. Our minds are made up about what people are like. If we already know what people are like, there is no room for surprise, no opportunity for encounter, no chance to learn from one another because we already know it all. Senior adults know they don't know it all, and they are willing to admit it. We who are younger would be wise to learn from them.

Some understanding of the character and characteristics of senior adults will help them and us recognize their accomplishments and achievements. The older generation in this country are known as the pre-boomers. They also are referred to as the Strivers and Survivors, the Suppies (Senior, urban, professionals), Opals (Older people with active lifestyles), and Rappies (Retired, affluent professionals). Their formative years were in the 1920s, 30s, and 40s. Their formative events were rural lifestyle, radio, automobile, depression, low tech, Pearl Harbor, World War II, Korea, big bands, family, school, and church. Their characteristics include high birth rate, high view of marriage, low divorce rate, early marriage, strong family, traditional roles, low education, respect authority, save money, private, save everything, complete tasks.

A woman from Berkeley Springs, West Virginia, noted that people born before 1945 are survivors. Then she lists changes that these survivors have witnessed:

We were born before television, before penicillin, before polio shots, frozen foods, xerox, plastic, contact lenses, frisbees, and the Pill.

We were before credit cards, radar, split atoms, laser beams, and ballpoint pens; before panty hose, dishwashers, clothes dryers, electric blankets, air conditioners, drip-dry clothes—and before man walked on the moon.

For us, time-sharing meant togetherness, not computers or condominiums; a "chip" meant a piece of wood; hardware meant hardware; and software wasn't even a word.

In our day, cigarette smoking was fashionable, grass was mowed, coke was a drink, and pot was something you cooked in. Rock music was a grandma's lullaby and aids were helpers in the principal's office.

No wonder we are so confused and there is such a generation gap! But we survived! What better reason to celebrate?

As people get older, often there are events or points of transition in their lives that put them in a reflective mood. Some of these transition points include the arrival at middle age, when children leave home, moving to a new place, death of a spouse, and retirement. These events are so significant and powerful in our lives that they often result in an assessment and evaluation of how life has been lived to that point. Often the evaluation is summarized, "So far, so good." Such an assessment may suggest that the person is glad to have survived, but she doesn't feel like she has thrived.

One of the things I urge senior adults to do is to reflect and evaluate their lives. What have you done with your life? What have been the joys and accomplishments of your life? Take some time alone and reflect on your life. Take a pencil and paper and write down the things you have done in your life that you enjoyed. List your achievements and accomplishments. Don't forget the time you spent helping the P.T.A. or being a classroom parent. Remember the charity organization that you worked for to help raise funds. Call to mind the special relationship you developed with a neighbor or a co-worker. Remember how significant each of you became to the other. Think about the class you taught or the time you enjoyed being in the choir. Don't forget the idea you offered at work which was accepted that improved the working conditions or the production of fellow workers.

What has brought meaning to your life? You have a sense of fulfillment and accomplishment. Why? Why have you done what you have done with your life? Aging does provide the opportunity to reflect and evaluate life, remembering and acknowledging accomplishments and achievements and perhaps discovering some that had not been thought of previously.

In evaluating life, John Wooden, former basketball coach at UCLA known as the Wizard of Westwood, advised, "Don't measure yourself by what you have accomplished, but by what you should have accomplished with your ability." He also encouraged people to "Be more concerned with your character than with your reputation. Your character is what you really are, while your reputation is merely what others think you are."

If you have been concerned with your character and are able at any point in your life to be pretty well satisfied with your character, I suspect it could be said that you were pretty good at what you did. Aging often brings a sense of accomplishment and a feeling that life has been meaningful.

Second, aging through life does not come without pain and despair. Someone has said you know you're getting old when you take a stroll down memory lane and you get lost. Haven't we all done that? While we are on memory lane, we are reminded of some of the pain and despair we have experienced in our lives. Almost inevitably as we age we lose something—home, spouse, friends, and the physical ability to do things we've been capable of doing. These and other loses cause pain for us.

The losses often cause people to collect things as part of their assurance of security. Tony Kornheiser expressed this in his column in *The Washington Post* as he wrote about his dad.

> My father attributes his eccentricities to growing up in the Depression. He explains this is why he is reluctant to throw anything away—because he remembers when he didn't have anything. So he reuses things. Unfortunately, one of the things he reuses is Saran Wrap. He calls this "recycling."
>
> He has no china anymore, just plastic plates he steals from the airlines. He is obsessed with the supermarket styrofoam they wrap the meat in. He has them stacked up in his closet. He must have 400 of them. He tells me he saves them because he can cut them down and use them to store individual portions of meat in the freezer. He says you never know when you'll need one. I ask, "But when will you need 400? Who are you having over for dinner, 'Up with People'?" I point out he doesn't have to save them, because every single cut of meat in America comes with its own styrofoam tray. It is an endless supply. I tell him he should throw out all the styrofoam trays he has collected—if only to make room for his glass jar collection.[12]

All of us are aging. Many of us struggle with that issue. I suspect most of us want to receive the benefits of aging but not the limitations and liabilities. Some of the benefits of aging include wisdom, efficiency, establishment of lasting relationships, discernment and clarity in decision making. Liabilities include loss of quickness, feeling the effects of fatigue quicker, taking longer to recuperate from strenuous activity or an energy draining experience. Those who play sports professionally or for exercise and recreation often deny that they are getting older and their aging is having an adverse effect on their playing ability. Our minds know what we want to do, but our bodies simply will not—cannot—respond as quickly as they did when we were younger.

Our culture denies aging and its impact on us. Commercials are geared to the young, vigorous, and attractive implying that vitality and attractiveness are directly related to the products being advertised. Just one example is the product being marketed with the one liner, "You aren't getting older. You're just getting better." At best that is a half truth. Many people do get better at many things as they age, but they also are getting older. It is possible to get older and not get better, but it is impossible to get better and not get older.

It is helpful to keep in mind that it is not a number that makes us old but rather a sense that life has dealt us all the cards we are ever going to have. Often there is an episode or situation that happens in a person's life that is seen as the turning point. It was from that event onward that she sensed her life changed, slowed, a sense that she has been dealt all the cards she has left. When my father-in-law was eighty-seven, he began struggling with some health problems and said that he did not begin to feel old until he was eighty-two. He sensed in those five years from eighty-two to eighty-seven that his mind and body did not respond and rebound as rapidly and easily as they once did, and he pointed to the time during his eighty-second year when he began to feel and notice the change in his life.

Close your eyes. Go away from this time by forty years—forty years forward or forty years backward. Some of you will project yourselves into the future; others will remember and reminisce. Touch your skin. What would it feel like? What would it feel like to walk or run? What kind of activity would you be doing? Can you bend over to tie your shoe? What do you look like? What does your voice sound like? How is life in this imaginary world different from real life for you? What feelings do you have? You may feel sadness, anticipating some of the limitations you may experience or some of the people who will be gone from you life. You may feel sad remembering what you once could do, recalling people who once were a part of your life.

More and more of us have the opportunity to relate to aging parents. It is becoming increasingly common for people to reach retirement and have at least one parent still living. Having not had much experience with this, we do not relate too well. Part of the reason may be we didn't anticipate dealing with aging parents during retirement. Another reason is we have not maintained the relationship very well through the years, and so we seem to be on very different wave links when it comes to communicating with each other. The tendency is for both to do some things out of duty rather than genuine interest. What results is embarrassing. Again Tony Kornheiser of *The Washington Post* shares his observation about his parents and himself.

> These are the facts of life between grown-ups and their aging parents: You invite them to stay with you because you think it is the right thing to do—even though you don't really want them, because they've become wildly eccentric and do things like invite the mailman in for a cup of Metamucil. They come because they think it's the right thing to do—even though they'd rather stay in their own home where no one will consider it strange when they walk around the living room in a mink stole and swim fins.

Aging through life does not come without pain and despair, but the pain and despair are not the end of it all. With a healthy assessment of accomplishments and acknowledgement of the pain and despair that have been a realistic part of life, then, new life can be born even in the midst of old age.

Third, new life can and often does come with aging. There is some truth to this bottom line on aging: If you don't care how old you are, you're young. If you lie about how old your are, you're middle age. And if you brag about how old you are, you're old. But the sense of bragging about one's age often expresses both an appreciation for the accomplishments of life and a perspective on life that has a vitality, a newness, and a freshness that invigorates the person who is aging.

With aging comes laughter, humor, surprise, and a unique sense of fulfillment. Abraham and Sarah are biblical models for us. The most obvious symbol of life is birth—something is being created and will continue. There's a new you waiting inside to be born—no matter how old you are. One elderly woman observed, "Age puzzles me. I thought it was a quiet time. My seventies were interesting and fairly serene, but my eighties are passionate. I grow more intense with age."

Senior adults usually do not take themselves too seriously and add a dash of humor to life. My father-in-law said that he no longer bought green bananas. He might not live long enough for them to ripen. Senior adults must become stewards of freedom like they have never known before. Many people who retire will have twenty to thirty years of life to manage after retirement. What promise! What possibilities!

Of course, there are fears that are part of aging. Intensified are the fears of dependency, illness, disability, and loss of quality of life. Here is one woman's observation of what some of these issues look like in the flesh of a family member.

> Edward's passing is due, or so my soul says; its whispers augmented by medical authority, and his present existence just short of life support, institutions, and a vegetative brain. I know now what I didn't know three years ago, when Edward first gave evidence of these hallucinations. I know that none of us were prepared for our father to age as rapidly and as sadly as he did. We were not ready for him to change from a man who was writing a novel and managing the house to one rapidly unable to make his bed in the mornings. . . . Together, we trekked from specialist to specialist, each trip, each test increasing our fear. In the final analysis, he was found to have an unusual and progressively degenerative neurological disorder seen only in aging populations.[13]

Senior adults need friends and need continually to develop new friends. The experience of many senior adults is their circle of lifelong friends begins slowly to dwindle, and then suddenly the dwindling accelerates. It is imperative that senior adults establish new relationships. As they get older senior adults also must negotiate becoming less mobile, more dependent, and the need to have some assistance to maintain their lifestyles.

The mystery and myth of aging is best captured in an old legend:

It is said that once upon a time the people of a remote mountain village used to sacrifice their old people. A day came when there was not a single old man left, and the traditions were lost. They wanted to build a great house for the meetings of the village assembly, but when they came to look at the tree trunks that had been cut for that purpose, no one could tell the top from the bottom; if the timbers were placed the wrong way up, it would set off a series of disasters. A young man said that if they promised not to sacrifice their old people anymore, he would find a solution. They promised. He brought out his grandfather, whom he had hidden safely away; and the old man taught the community to tell top from bottom.[14]

God encouraged Sarah to share herself and her gifts. God called Sarah not to give up but to have hope. God encouraged Nicodemus to believe that being old did not mean giving up on experiencing new life. God called the psalmists to cry out with their feelings of sadness and of joy. God called Job to claim his faith in the midst of his suffering. God bears the same messages to us and calls us to bear these messages to others. These calls are not dependent on age. Throughout our lives, we are called to share ourselves with others and develop our gifts. At any age, we are called to laugh and cry. At no age does faith become unimportant.[15]

What better assessment of your life could there be than to be told that you were pretty good at what you did? To be pretty good at what you do is a helpful goal that will help us grow older gracefully. To all senior adults, congratulations on the accomplishments and achievements in your lives. Be assured of the church's continued love and care for you as you deal with the pain and despair that is a part of your life. And like so many of the biblical models such as Abraham, Sarah, Job, and Nicodemus, may aging bring you new life. As new life comes to you, may you share your wisdom, your humor, your love, your devotion, and your faith with us.

To Be Moving

The Invitation to Decision
The Hymn of Commitment   Slane
                    "Be Thou My Vision"
The Presentation of New Members

*The Benediction
    Go now surrounded by the presence of God. May the hope of God go before you. May the peace of God be beneath you. May the joy of God hover over you. May the love of God dwell in you. May the grace of God follow you. May you go today and all of your days surrounded by the presence of God. Amen.

The Organ Postlude

This worship service is designed to celebrate with senior adults that they have more life to live. A service such as this also provides the opportunity for a congregation to affirm the gifts of senior adults and to affirm that senior adults continue to grow, to be shaped and formed as children of God and disciples of Christ throughout their lives including their experiences in the "third age."

Notes

[1]Paul Tournier, *Learn to Grow Old* (New York: Harper & Row, 1972) 216.

[2]Laura Alden, "God Still Has a Place for Us," *The American Baptist*, 189:7 (September 1991): 25.

[3]Tournier, 9.

[4]Ibid., 5.

[5]Quoted by Tournier, 23.

[6]C. G. Jung, *Structure and Dynamics of the Psyche* (London: Routledge, 1960).

[7]Tournier, 11.

[8]Quoted in *The American Baptist*, 189:7 (September 1991): 15.

[9]Ibid.

[10]Wade Clark Roof, "The Spirit of the Elderculture," *The Christian Century*, 107:17 (16–23 May 1990): 529.

[11]Ibid., 530.

[12]Tony Kornheiser, "Well, Your Daddy Don't Rock 'n' Roll," *The Washington Post*, 19 (January 1992) F1, F4.

[13]Mary Weidman, "Edward's Aging" (Unpublished essay shared with me in 1990) 1.

[14]Simone de Beauvoir, *The Coming of Age* (New York: Putnam, 1972). 77.

[15]Mary Kendrick Moore, "Portraits of Aging," *Pulpit Digest*, LXXI:503 (May/June 1990): 26.

Chapter 18

Exiting a Congregation

Most churches with which I have had any association are intentional in their efforts to welcome new people. Some effort is made to follow up with those who visit the congregation. New members are recruited. When people join a congregation, some type of recognition and/ or celebration occurs. At some point new members are introduced to the congregation. This may be at the end of the worship service when they indicate their desire to affiliate with the congregation if an invitation is part of the service. The process may involve an inquirer's class through which people explore membership and then indicate their intentions, or the process may be a conversation with a minister and the request to join is made. Whatever the joining process, some means of formal recognition and celebration of the presence of new members is made.

What about when people leave a congregation? What happens then? Is anything said or done? That may be determined by the manner and reasons for which they are leaving. If they are angry with the congregation and/or an individual in the congregation, they may drop out or join another congregation in the community. Some people leave a congregation because they are moving from the area. They know in advance the last Sunday they will be with the congregation.

Traditionally the church has had the responsibility of dealing with termination. The church has taken this responsibility or had it thrust upon it. The majority of families seek a minister to assist them with the funeral for a family member who has died. There are many death-like experiences in our lives. With our mobile society, the ending of relationships is one that happens frequently because people move from one community to another. Often the move is a great distance. While people intend to keep in touch with their old friends and do so, the relationships are not the same at long distance as they were when they were in the same community.

As I learn of members in the congregation thinking about leaving the church, I contact them to discuss with them their decision. If they are leaving the congregation because this congregation does not meet their needs, is no longer the church for them, or because they are hurt, angry, or upset with someone or some group, I seek to be of help to them in processing those feelings. When they have made up their minds to leave the congregation, I share their decision with the deacons along with the reasons they have given me for their decision. My purpose is to help the people leaving and the congregation to have closure on the relationship. It is also a way to help people sift fact from fiction in what is said and heard about why someone is leaving. In most cases, people who are leaving under these circumstances do not want any kind of public acknowledgement of their departure in which they participate.

Of course, people leave congregations because they are relocating. Their experience with the congregation has been healthy and helpful. One of the pains of moving is that they are leaving a community of faith that has contributed to their lives and to which they have contributed. Several people in circumstances this have responded positively to a suggestion of some formal way of saying good-bye to the congregation and the congregation saying good-bye to them. Often this occurs in small groups as friends and close associates gather to bid them farewell, but seldom does the church at large provide a way of formally saying good-bye.

What follows is a worship service designed to help participants cope and deal with their feelings when relationships end. Grief is a process through which we journey when any relationship ends. The intensity of the grief is in proportion to the intensity of the relationship as well as the circumstances of the ending of the relationship. If the circumstance is death, the intensity is greater. If the relationship is a spouse or a child, the intensity is greater than if it is a business acquaintance. I have included the final sermon I delivered as pastor of the Broadview Baptist Church.

At the conclusion of the service is a litany of departure that can be used as part of a regular worship service when recognition is made of someone who is leaving the congregation. Many times when people are leaving and some formal expression is to be made, the entire service will not revolve around this. The litany can be used as part of those services as well as part of a specifically designed service of bidding farewell. This litany could be used in other settings by the church. A farewell luncheon may be held, and a litany such as this one could be used as a formal expression. The purpose is to provide the opportunity for those persons leaving and those left to express their support and encouragement to each other. This helps all congregants involved to bring closure to their relationship. Then, they are better prepared and better equipped to move on to other places and other relationships.

Worshiping God as We Say Goodbye
A Service of Christian Worship

The Chiming of the Hour
The Silent Preparation
The Organ Prelude

The God Who Brought Us Together

The Choral Call to Worship   Nun Danbet
      "Now Thank We All Our God"
The Invocation
*Hymn   "Joyful, Joyful, We Adore Thee"   Beethoven
The Welcome
The Scripture Reading   Philippians 1:3-11
The Pastoral Prayer

And Has Journeyed with Us Through the Years

*Hymn   "Jesus Lives and Jesus Leads"   Varndean
Offertory Sentences
Offertory   "Guide Me, O Thou Great Jehovah"   CWM Rhondda
Receiving Tithes and Offerings

Now Is with Us in Our Parting

The Choral Worship "A Mighty Fortress Is Our God"   Ein' Feste Burg

Sermon   "Snapshots of Our Trip"

Well, this is it! This is the last sermon I will deliver as your pastor. I hope we can respond to our journey together as Dag Hammarjold responded to life many years ago when he said, "For all that has been, thanks. For all that is to be, yes." Indeed, we are in the midst of transition in our lives. We are caught between has been and not yet. We are experiencing the ending of a relationship. As with most endings; there also are beginnings that occur simultaneously with the endings, but I will dwell this morning on the ending of our relationship as pastor and congregation by highlighting some of the moments we have shared over the last fifteen years.

As I look into your faces this morning, I am reminded of the variety of personal encounters I have had with you. I brought my mental photo album with me. I want to share with you some mental snapshots of our journey together. I suspect you have collected some snapshots of your own, and I hope you will share them with me. I have attempted to arrange my snapshots in sequential order, but I have discovered the difficulty of remembering the exact day or year when some of these events occurred. I have heard that as a person gets older the memory is the first thing to go.

The first snapshot I will describe for you is before any of you met me. The setting is the beautiful campus of Southeastern Baptist Theological Seminary with its gorgeous magnolia trees, plush grass, and Georgian-styled buildings located in Wake Forest, North Carolina. There I am in the picture, fifteen years younger and twenty-five pounds heavier. I am standing next to a brick building talking on a pay telephone. I am pastor of Memorial Baptist Church in Savannah, Georgia, and enrolled in my final course for the doctor of ministry degree at Southeastern Seminary. The date of this snapshot is June 16, 1977, my thirtieth birthday. I have a message to return a telephone call to someone named Sandra Gardner. She is the chairperson of the pastor search committee for Broadview Baptist Church. She had called to invite me to come to Temple Hills, Maryland, for an interview with the search committee. The caption for this photograph reads, "Temple Hills, where?"

Snapshot number two was taken on Monday evening, June 22, 1977. It is a group picture in the living room of Joan Lowell on Andrews Air Force Base. The people in the picture from left to right are Joan Lowell, Jean Hammer, Miles Hudson, Bob Smoak, Sandra Gardner, Rick Sampson, Carolyn Hedges, Jim Sutton, Bob Rowland, Eileen Lister, and yours truly. The caption reads: "Have we got a job for you!"

It is a hot July evening when the next picture was taken. Approximately 175 people are gathered in this sanctuary. I am standing down front. The congregation has been without a pastor for eleven months. This is the first time that most of us have seen each other. A lively discussion is in progress. This sharing time revealed many of the complexities of the congregation and the struggle that relationships often are. The caption for this picture comes from one of my references who encouraged the search committee: "Judge him on his track record rather than on his press conference."

Snapshot number four was taken about 5 P.M. on a crisp October afternoon. Partially empty boxes are evident in several rooms in our house. Coming through the front door are fifteen women. One is carrying a pumpkin. Others have dishes of food. These are members of the Joy Sunday School Class bringing us dinner.

The caption reads: "Welcome, pastor and family."

Snapshot number five captures an exchange in our home on a Saturday afternoon. Leonard Lane, who had accepted extra responsibilities during the fourteen-month interim period, is handing me a key ring. The captions says: "You don't know how glad I am to give you this set of keys to the church."

Snapshot number six is of Steny Hoyer and me talking at the door after worship service. Steny said to me, "I take voting seriously, and votes are important to me. Because I could not be here the Sunday of your trial sermon, I want you to know that on Judy's advice I voted for you, and I'm glad I did." I was able to return the favor when Steny was a candidate for lieutenant governor. The caption reads: "Politics in and out of the church."

Snapshot number seven was taken in the fellowship hall in May of 1978. Following an evening worship service you surprised me with a gift and a cake decorated with a cap and gown celebrating my receiving the doctor of ministry degree. As we were preparing to attend the graduation services, we explained to Melanie and Danita that I would be receiving a doctorate and that many people would refer to me as Dr. Roberts. Melanie's response is the caption for this picture: "But Dad, you won't be a real doctor, will you?"

The next photograph was taken in July 1978. Pictured are Jerry Cauley leading the congregational singing and Susan Cauley playing the organ. While talking with the pastor search committee, I asked, "What are the first three things I should do as your pastor?" The response given was, "Move to Temple Hills and get staff." There was no third suggestion. The caption for this picture reads: "Jerry and Susan Cauley join the Broadview staff."

Picture number nine is taken in the fellowship hall. It is September 1978. Ninety-nine people are sharing a meal. The caption: "Wednesday evening fellowship dinners begin at Broadview." What began in 1978 has continued as a regular weekly activity now in its fifteenth year.

On the Sunday following Thanksgiving in 1978, worshipers entered the sanctuary to see crismon trees decorated and an Advent wreath on the communion Table, and they received a booklet with the orders of worship for the Advent season. Caption: "Broadview begins Advent celebration."

It was Easter 1979 when this next picture was taken. Banners are displayed across the front of the sanctuary. Under the theme "abundant living" we had just completed our first Lenten season of worship. Caption: "Lent Is spring training for Christians."

Snapshot number twelve was taken early in the morning on September 18, 1979, at the University of Maryland Hospital in Baltimore when Brandon was born. A child has been born to us in each of the places where we have lived. That makes me a bit nervous about moving to a new place. I thank God for the love, support, encouragement, and friendship you have given to each of our children. The caption for this picture: "Brandon Thomas Roberts born to Howard and Peggy Roberts."

An ordination service is in progress in the next snapshot. Mariel Fails is being ordained as a deacon. Out of 36,000 Southern Baptist congregations, Broadview became one of 300 to ordain women as deacons and join that line of Baptist heritage and tradition that can be traced to John Smyth in 1609. Caption: "First woman ordained by Broadview."

One year later the following picture was taken. It is a photograph of Jerry Cauley and Susan Cauley being ordained to the ministry. They are two of the six people Broadview has ordained to the ministry. Jerry and Susan were one of a select few couples that had been ordained by a Southern Baptist congregation. With Susan's ordination, Broadview became one of approximately 100 Southern Baptist congregations to ordain women as ministers. The caption reads: "Broadview ordains couple to the Ministry."

The congregation is involved in an October business meeting in the fifteenth picture. The budget is the major item of discussion, and several members are nervous about the proposed budget. With little awareness of the impact of the action, several motions were passed that affected the day-to-day operation of the church. The cost in staff time as a result of this approach far exceeded the amount of the budget reduction. Caption: "Proposed budget slashed."

Snapshot number sixteen was taken at the annual meeting of the District of Columbia Baptist Convention in November 1981. Broadview was welcomed into the District of Columbia Baptist Convention resulting in the congregation being members of one Baptist association, two state Baptist conventions, and two national Baptist conventions, SBC and ABC, USA.

This next snapshot shows me walking down the hall toward my office after making a hospital visit early in the afternoon. It is October 1982. In the hallway is a table with streamers, balloons, refreshments, and a sign that reads, "Congratulations Author." I had received a contract to write my first book. Caption: "Howard signs contract with Broadman Press to write *Learning to Pray*."

The fellowship hall is the scene for snapshot eighteen. It is the last Sunday in October 1982. A reception is in progress celebrating my fifth anniversary as your pastor. One person came through the receiving line and made this comment to me: "I didn't think you would make it five years in the ministry much less five years as pastor of this congregation." Caption: "Most people satisfied with the pastoral leadership."

Snapshot number nineteen was taken in April 1983 in the sanctuary where more than 150 members had gathered to participate in a business meeting. The issue for discussion and action was whether to change the constitution to accept as full members people who had received believer's baptism by sprinkling or pouring. After much discussion, the vote was seventy-five to change the constitution, seventy-four to keep it the same, and two abstained. A two-thirds vote was required to change. Caption: "The mode of Baptism is an emotional issue for many Baptists."

Novasibirsk, Siberia, is the scene of the next photo. I am speaking during a Tuesday evening worship service at the Novasibirsk Baptist Church as a member of the first Baptist Peace and Friendship Tour of the Soviet Union. I gave greetings to them from you. Caption: "Broadview pastor sent to Siberia."

This snapshot was taken on September 8, 1985. The sanctuary is packed. We are celebrating the twenty-fifth anniversary of Broadview Baptist Church. Caption: "Quarter of a century of ministry."

September 10, 1985, is the date of the next photo. I am on my way to Boston to begin a sabbatical semester of study as a Merrill Fellow at Harvard Divinity School. What a rich learning experience! I thank God for your generosity in affording me this opportunity. Caption: "Howard has a seminary degree and a Harvard education."

This snapshot is dated October 1986. It is picture of Meredith Moore at Hunington Ridge in Winchester, Virginia, with several senior adults. She had coordinated Broadview's first senior adult retreat. Caption: "October 16, 1985, Meredith Moore became associate minister for Christian education."

Snapshot number twenty-four was taken in January 1986 as I presented a copy of *The Lasting Words of Jesus* to the congregation. Caption: "Howard's second book dedicated to the members of Broadview."

The next snapshot was taken in June 1986. It is a picture of a small choir. If you look closely, you will recognize three members of the group, Nancy Ricker, Peggy Roberts, and me. We are singing during a week night worship service in a Baptist congregation in Riga, Latvia, in the Soviet Union. Caption: "Three Broadviewers worship with Lativian Baptists."

My twenty-sixth snapshot is of a joint service between Broadview and Shaare Tikvah congregations in September 1986. The two congregations co-adopted prisoners of conscience, Yuli Edleshtein and Vladimir Filipov. Yuli has been released and will immigrate to Israel in the next few weeks. Caption: "Baptists and Jews united."

This photo is of an autograph party in January 1987 sponsored by the media center following the release of my third book *Redemptive Responses of Jesus*. Caption: "Write on."

Snapshot number twenty-eight is of me standing at the Wailing or Western Wall of the Temple in Jerusalem. Caption: "What a complex, complicated world this is."

The next picture is of me presenting a copy of the book *Doc*, the biography of my great-uncle, to the congregation. Caption: "Doc influences ministry at Broadview."

My thirtieth snapshot was taken in July, 1987. I am standing in front of the congregation while we are singing the hymn of commitment. To my surprise who should come walking forward committing herself to be a Christian and desiring to be baptized but Melanie, bone of my bone and flesh of my flesh. Caption: "Pastor cries in front of congregation."

My thirty-first snapshot is a snapshot of a snapshot being taken of Nell O'Rear and me at the door to the sanctuary. Later that picture showed up on the front of 30,000 brochures we developed and mailed to people in our community. Incidentally, our brochure has been used at conferences to give other congregations an idea of what can be done and done well through mass mailing to invite people from the community to church. The caption on the brochure says, "We're close to you."

My thirty-second snapshot was taken in the early spring of 1989. I am holding a letter that tells me I have won honorable mention in the best sermon contest sponsored by Harper and Row Publishing. My sermon, "God and the 'L' word," was one of eighteen selected from over 2,000 international entries. The prize was $250 worth of books of my choosing from HarperCollins Publishing Company.

The next snapshot is dated July 17, 1990. We are welcoming Ramonia Lee and Hank and Janice Hinnant to our congregation. This was their first Sunday as members of our staff. What an exciting day it was for us to welcome three gifted, committed ministers to our staff and congregation. They quickly became important people in our ministry and our lives.

My thirty-fourth snapshot is of Danita singing her first solo in worship service. I am impressed, proud, and my eyes are filled with tears.

My thirty-fifth snapshot is of a worship service in 1991. The picture is of Hank Hinnant being ordained to the ministry. The caption reads: "Broadview ordains sixth minister in its thirty-year history."

The next to last snapshot is dated October 18, 1992. Bob Kessler requested permission to speak to the congregation at that end of the worship service. He then proceeded to say some very warm, expressive, appreciative words about my family and me. He expressed gratitude on behalf of the congregation for the fifteen years I have served as your pastor and gave me a generous love gift from the congregation. The caption of this picture reads: "Pastor appreciates being appreciated."

The last picture on my roll of mental snapshots was taken this morning at 11:00 as I walked into the sanctuary to lead you in worship for the final time as your pastor. Many of you have invited me to be an intimate part of your lives. I recall conversations in my office as you shared personal struggles, often not so much wanting or expecting me to say or do anything but needing someone who would listen and hear out what was happening in your life. I celebrated with many of you in your weddings. I rejoiced with some of you in the birth of your children. Many of us have cried together in the face of the death of important people in your lives. I have journeyed with many of you through the anxious wilderness of preparing for and waiting for surgery and test results. We have planned and shared a variety of ministries. We have agreed on many things and disagreed on a few. I am grateful for the ministry we have shared together. I am thankful to you for the love, support, care, and friendship you have given to my family and me during the past fifteen years.

Part of what makes this such a difficult day emotionally for us is that for many of us, this is the last time we will see each other. We don't like to say it so bluntly, but part of the reason we feel such strong emotions is that deep inside us we recognize the truth that for many of us this is the last time we will see each other. Ending a relationship comes loaded with emotions. On occasions like this our minds astound us because of what they remember. Suddenly there are snapshots flashing before our eyes of past events we shared together. I've shared some of mine. I hope they have helped call to mind significant snapshots for you.

I have not tried to summarize or evaluate fifteen years of ministry in this sermon. That is both inappropriate and impossible in the context of this worship service. I have attempted to capture some of the events, experiences, and emotions we have shared together. Being your pastor has been the best job I have ever had. Being your pastor has been the hardest job I have ever had. It also has been the longest job I have ever had. No doubt there is some correlation between this being the best, the hardest, and the longest job I have ever had. Just over fifteen years ago I walked into my office here and began my work as your pastor. Frankly, I have difficulty realizing that we have worked together and related to each other for fifteen years.

The scriptural text from Philippians is especially pertinent as the basis of our worship today, certainly from my perspective. Clearly, the apostle Paul's letters reveal that he had his greatest appreciation for the congregation at Philippi. They were the only congregation that Paul visited who provided completely for his welfare, freeing Paul to use all of his time and energy working with the congregation rather than having to make tents to earn a living as was the case in other towns. Joy flows throughout the Philippian letter as Paul expresses his gratitude to and for the Christians in Philippi.

Paul's words to the Philippians express well my feelings for you.

I thank my God for you every time I think of you; and every time I pray for you, I pray with joy because of the way in which you have helped me in the work of the gospel from the very first day until now (Phil 1:3-5).

You have been a tremendous support to me. You have provided well for my physical, emotional, mental, and spiritual well-being. I thank God every time I think of you. We have been co-workers together in receiving and sharing the good news, and I am grateful for the love and care we have shown to each other during our fifteen years together.

Well, it all comes down to this. "For all that has been, thanks. For all that will be, yes." Good-bye. I love you. I'll pray for you. "May the road rise to meet you. May the wind be always at your back. May you be held in the palm of God's loving hand." May the hope of God guide you. May the peace of God comfort you. May the love of God dwell in you. May the grace of God sustain you. May the joy of God surround you.

The Invitation to Respond
*Hymn of Commitment   "The Bond of Love"   Skilling

And Will Be with Us Wherever We Are

The Litany of Departure

Minister:	We are relational creatures by nature and by need. God comes to us through the lives of others. We enjoy our relationships with one another and we grieve when one of those relationships ends. These sojourners who stand before us are leaving our congregation this week What do you want them to know?
Congregation:	**We love you. You have been fellow strugglers with us in the faith. You have invested your lives with us, and we are richer because of you.**
Minister:	What do you, sojourners, want us to know?
Sojourners:	**We, too, are richer because of you. We love you. We want you to remember us. We want to continue to be a part of your prayers and shared concerns.**
Congregation:	**We will remember you with joy. Our thoughts and prayers go with you as you leave us. You are family to us, and we shall never forget you.**
Sojourners:	**We shall never forget you. Our memories of you will inspire us to deepen our faith, and we will continue to be supportive of this community of faith.**
All:	**Now, may the God who called us from separate places to this place, and who has journeyed with us as we have traveled the same path, go with us on our separate paths. We are grateful to God for our years together, for mutual support and mutual forgiveness. We say good-bye and pray that our memories of each other will be vivid and joyful. We depart assured of God's help and hope. Amen.**

*Benediction
*The Choral Response   Turner
          "May the Road Rise to Meet You"
The Organ Postlude

Thanks for reading to the end, or thanks for turning to the last page to see what I had to say at the end. I trust what I have written will help you and the congregation of which you are a part to provide pastoral care through worship. In all of your endeavors to care and minister to people my prayer is: "May the road rise to meet you. May the wind be always at your back. May the sun shine warmly on your face. And may you be held in the palm of God's hand. Amen."

Afterword

I hope you have found this book helpful. There are additional needs in people's lives that can be addressed through worship. I trust that what I have shared will stimulate you to explore and offer pastoral care through worship in additional areas that affect people's lives and their worship of God.

May you find innovative ways to address pastoral need and concern though worship. May the church continue to be a place where people celebrate and mourn, address God and are addressed by God. May the service of worship be a place where the afflicted are comforted and the comfortable are challenged to grow in wisdom and in favor with both God and people.